DG

DG

The Memoirs of a British Broadcaster

ALASDAIR MILNE

Hodder & Stoughton
LONDON SYDNEY AUCKLAND TORONTO

British Library Cataloguing in Publication Data
Milne, Alasdair.
  DG : memoirs of a British Broadcaster.
  1. Great Britain. Broadcasting services.
  British Broadcasting Corporation. Milne,
  Alasdair
  I. Title
  384.54′092′4

  ISBN 0 340 42772 8

Hodder and Stoughton Editorial Office: 47 Bedford Square, London WC1B 3DP.

FOR SHEILA –
AND RUAIRIDH, SEUMAS AND KIRSTY

ACKNOWLEDGMENTS

I have a vast army to thank, not so much for the writing of this book for which I alone am responsible; but for the shared experience of more than thirty years in broadcasting, most of it in the BBC. The professional excitements have been intense, the friendships rich and enduring.

I wish, though, to thank my old friend Aubrey Singer for access to his electronic bunker and thus to his word processor; and Judith Murrell who has toiled through the many drafts I have produced. My thanks are due, too, to Deirdre Lyndon for the use of material about *Tonight* which she collected for a book that was never published. Tony Jay has been an indefatigable reader and adviser throughout the book's production; and my wife and daughter have given me valuable advice over the past months. And I thank the BBC and others for permission to reproduce the photographs used in the book.

Above all, I thank my family who lived with me through most of these experiences but were not always able to enjoy the fruits of being at the very centre of things during the developing years of British television.

CONTENTS

ILLUSTRATIONS

Acknowledgments
[1] From the author's private collection
[2] By courtesy of the BBC Enterprises Picture Library
[3] By courtesy of the BBC Hulton Picture Library
[4] By courtesy of *The Evening Standard*, London
[5] By courtesy of R. L. Nicholson and the BBC

PRELUDE

I don't remember ever being as nervous as I was on the morning of 10th December, 1981. This was the day of the appointment board for the job of Director General. Although I had been interviewed five years earlier when Ian Trethowan was appointed, that had been more of a canter round the course than a serious race. Ian had clearly been groomed for the top. But, this time, for me it was real. As Managing Director of BBC Television and Deputy Director General, I was assumed to be the front-runner, but front-runners often fall. I knew that if I fell, I could not stay in the BBC. The job had been advertised outside, as it had when Ian got it. I knew what the competition was. The BBC applicants – Bill Cotton, Aubrey Singer, Dick Francis – I had personally urged to have a go. I was aware of the outsiders – Tony Smith, now Director of the British Film Institute and a man from the Cambridge University Press – because I happened to have seen a list in large type poorly concealed in George Howard's outer office a couple of days earlier. I was due on first at 9.15 a.m.

I have a bad habit of being too early for things, a trait I think I inherited from my grandfather who always had us down at the Caledonian Station in Edinburgh at least an hour and a half before our holiday train was due to leave. This morning, I was at Broadcasting House at 8.30 a.m. and bumped into George Howard, the Chairman, on the front doorstep. Both of us were a touch embarrassed. We bid each other good morning and went our separate ways. I had been told to present myself at his office at 9.10 a.m. but I could not possibly sit there for forty minutes like a schoolboy waiting for a dressing-down from the headmaster. Where to lurk in the meantime? All potentially friendly offices were firmly locked. I settled, feeling hunted, for the lavatory on the second floor where I paced up and down until discovered by a friendly face and forced to flee. Somehow, I filled in the intervening time. Once in the Board Room, with all Governors present, the interview followed a pattern I did not expect. George, the soul of affability, invited me to sit next to him, where the Director General normally sits, and chatted away amiably to me for twenty minutes or so, while the other Governors

1

looked mystified and uncomfortable. Eventually, he threw the ball to them. William Rees-Mogg, the Vice-Chairman, asked about the advancement of women in the BBC – a theme which he was to favour in his time on the Board. Stuart Young, an accountant who was soon to succeed George as Chairman, wondered whether my programme background implied that I would ignore the disciplines of finance. I replied, I hope not too tartly, that I knew quite a lot about finance having been responsible for five years for handling three-quarters of the BBC's budget. They were very friendly. But I was, I confess, happy to escape when the moment came. I then went home to await the outcome.

It was a long day. It was 7.20 p.m. before George rang to say I had been appointed DG. My elation was complete. I had made it! I went cheerfully to have supper with the Governors at Broadcasting House and returned even more cheerfully to celebrate with my family.

When the alarm clock went off early next morning, the streets were inches deep in snow. We skidded to Broadcasting House to do the *Today* programme; crawled to Marylebone High Street to appear on Radio London; slithered to the Television Centre to hold the main press conference. As all this went on, it struck me that I faced a difficult problem.

Weeks earlier, George Howard had invited Sheila and me to stay at Castle Howard, his famous Yorkshire home, for a weekend's shooting. This was the appointed weekend, though it might certainly have turned out an odd one if I had failed to get the job of DG! Clearly we couldn't drive – the radio reported that the roads in the Midlands were impassable. The news was that the trains, too, were badly disrupted. I was going to be up to my neck in interviews and press briefings all day; I felt we must get out of the weekend at Castle Howard. I asked my secretary to ring the Chairman's office and make our apologies: 'Tell him,' I said, 'that Sheila isn't very well.' George was too fly to be put off that easily. He rang Sheila at home, told her the roads were clear north of Leicester; 'I'm game,' he said, 'and I shall be very put out if you don't come.' That was the message I got. So, after a hectic day of interviews and press conferences, we found ourselves at King's Cross for the 5.00 p.m. train to York, in a great queue – we laden, of course, with guns and cartridges and clothes and boots.

Somehow we found seats, had several stiff Scotches and a good dinner. The train, it was announced, was expected to be very late. In fact, we reached York around 8.30 p.m. to be met at the very train door by a kindly soul who directed us to a veteran Daimler, in which we were whisked over roads only lightly covered with snow to a magically lit Castle Howard. There Simon, one of George's sons,

2

came down the steps to meet us looking as if he had just come off the set of *Brideshead Revisited*. The family were all eating dinner and we could hardly face another one, but there was a roaring fire in the Abbot's Room and bed seemed a wonderful prospect.

The next morning was frosty and brilliantly clear. But George was grumpy. His health was not good and the doctors had ordered him, a chain smoker, to stop smoking. We prepared for the shoot. He took Sheila with him in the car and, his temper being unusually short, did not address a word to her for two hours. By teatime, though, he was in better spirits and we were bidden to appear at 8.00 p.m. in dinner jackets in the Great Hall. There were a good many guests round the huge fireplace but, at first, no sign of George. Eventually, he entered wearing a magnificent silver kaftan (he rather fancied kaftans) with a great red bird embroidered across his chest. 'Good heavens, George,' I said, 'you must have got that from the wardrobe of the *Borgias*!' (One of our recent and most expensive drama disasters.)

And with that (which he did not greatly relish) we began a partnership as Chairman and Director General.

1 THE AGE OF INNOCENCE

I joined the BBC in September 1954 almost by chance. Sheila and I completed our Finals, she in English and I in Modern Languages, and immediately got married on Midsummer's Day in New College Chapel at Oxford – in total silence. When I asked the Warden's permission to marry in the chapel, he was in a state of high dudgeon because one of the 'Founder's Kin' (the Founder was William of Wykeham, Chancellor to Edward III) had recently got married and the attendant choirs, swelling organ music and peals of bells had apparently disturbed some of the Fellows. 'So you see, Milne,' said Warden Smith, 'there can be no music, you see, nor any noise, you see.' For us no choirs, no music: impressive silence.

Then I set about trying to find a job. A number of applications failed to come off: at Tootal's Ties they did not find me promising material because I could not put a bicycle pump together and so failed the aptitude test; at Yardley's in Stratford East I was told how many millions of Hungarian rose petals went into making an ounce of perfume, but they didn't seem to want me. Others were equally unwelcoming. At the time, it was fashionable for undergraduates to fancy a career in advertising, rather as, until very recently anyway, they seemed all to batter at the doors of the City. So I applied to Mather and Crowther, a well-known advertising agency and, for a while, prospects there looked brighter.

In the meantime, Sheila noticed that the BBC was advertising for something called a General Trainee – the first time they seemed to have extended a traineeship beyond news or engineering. I knew next to nothing about broadcasting. Like everybody else in the country during the war, the radio had been a daily necessity for my family; when I was at school at Winchester and busy learning, my father used with great diligence to take down and type out the weekly *Into Battle* series on the Home Service to keep me abreast of war events. Again, like a good many people in the country, my parents acquired a television set to see the Coronation in 1953; there my interest in broadcasting ended. For want of anything better, but without much enthusiasm, I applied for the General Traineeship at the BBC. After what seemed endless interviews, and within a day or two of being rejected finally by the advertising agency, the BBC offered me a General Traineeship.

In 1954 the BBC was just over thirty years old and obviously a very different place from what it is now. Its worldwide reputation, greatly enhanced by its performance during the war, had given it supreme self-confidence. Above all, it still enjoyed what Reith called 'the brute force of monopoly' even though Selwyn Lloyd's minority contribution to the Beveridge Report had stirred the Conservative Party to indicate their intention to break it. ITV was now due to come on the air in the following year. The BBC, when I joined it, was in the last days of being the sole arbiter of taste over the air in drama, in music (where its impact over the thirty years of its existence had been revolutionary), in news and current affairs. It was already a great institution of state.

Some eleven hundred, we were told, had applied for these new jobs as General Trainees. By some mystery, two of us – Patrick Dromgoole, now with Harlech Television, was the other – came through to be appointed. The plan was that we should spend two years in a variety of BBC departments; at the end of that time, if we had not found a permanent job, we would part company without regret. We began with a spell in Bristol where Frank Gillard, the famous wartime correspondent, was Head of Programmes and guided our first steps as broadcasters. Then I moved to the Overseas Service to help produce a daily ten-minute commentary on the world news; and did a turn in the Home Talks Department where the rigidity of the departmental bureaucratic machine meant it took me all of three months to get some simple reminiscences of a First World War flyer on the air. I found myself one day sitting on the floor at a Talks Department meeting (there were so many producers present that there wasn't a seat left) grumbling to an equally impatient Robin Day about the intolerable torpor of the production process. Robin was lucky, I thought – he was just leaving to join the new ITN. But I also enjoyed some very lively weeks on a daily radio programme called *Going Places, Meeting People* where one of the first people I met was Alan Whicker. Alan, a household television name now, was then an unknown reporter; but his moustache was as trim, his manner as cocky, as they have been ever since.

Beyond the walls of Broadcasting House, there was a fizz in the broadcasting air. Commercial television was just about to start and though most BBC people regarded the newcomer with disdain, things were clearly going to change. I was working in the Publicity Department the night ITV started – the very night the BBC killed off Grace Archer, dashing into a blazing stable to save a horse, as a spoiling tactic. Then, as the next part of my training, I was despatched to the Television Service and Lime Grove, the home of BBC Television's current affairs department – Television Talks, as it was then called. At Lime Grove, close to Shepherd's Bush in West London, I was told to report to Mrs Grace Wyndham Goldie.

Casting one's mind back thirty-odd years, what was BBC Television like as 'the competitor' arrived? I contracted a painful attack of shingles almost at the same time as we bought our first television set; and for two weeks, shifting uneasily in bed, I watched television from the children's period (the gap between 6.00 and 7.00 p.m., the 'Toddlers' Truce', was still there) until closedown. I remember it vividly. There were quiz shows like *What's My Line* and *Animal, Vegetable and Mineral*, hypnotic to the popular press. Will Gilbert Harding be rude again tonight? Will Sir Mortimer Wheeler pull off another astounding description of some hitherto unidentified Etruscan pot? The press was obsessed, too, with the presenters who did the linking between programmes – the clothes and deportment of Mary Malcolm and Sylvia Peters, the smooth good looks of McDonald Hobley. There were bold dramatic ventures – the marvellous adaptation of George Orwell's *1984*, the first *Quatermass* series from Nigel Kneale. But there was a great deal of dross. There was, as yet, no *Panorama*, no *Monitor*, no *Face to Face*. There were bizarre experiments such as a whole Elizabethan evening, with Philip Harben, the Delia Smith of his time, explaining the cooking of roast swan and syllabub. And the news was a joke. Tahu Hole, an austere New Zealander who had been in charge of BBC News for seven years, did not introduce news in vision at all until 1954, and then it was so plainly done that, as Asa Briggs records, the Director of Television wrote to him, 'Your division has acquired in sound broadcasting a reputation for accuracy, impartiality and integrity, and its subject matter is restricted in certain directions e.g. crime reporting. Given the same requirements and restrictions how would you devise a News Service for the viewer? Mine would not be anything like the present nor, I suspect, would yours. Should we start at that point?' The arrival of ITN was to be a violent shock to the BBC's handling of television news, with presenters like Christopher Chataway and Robin Day, who spoke directly to you and in an altogether more relaxed style.

So, in November 1955, I reported to Lime Grove. The BBC had bought Lime Grove – formerly the Gainsborough Studios where James Mason ravished 'The Wicked Lady' – in 1949 to accommodate the expanding television operation, hitherto crammed into Alexandra Palace. To this day, Lime Grove remains an unprepossessing place, squatting in a down-at-heel west London street, despite the fact that we spent a lot of money a few years ago renovating its interior. Thirty years ago, it was a maze of crazy corridors, bare concrete stairs, old scenery hoists and cavernous studios. We did not, however, suffer from rats. Grace Wyndham Goldie told me that rats were quite a feature of life in Alexandra Palace where, after working into the early hours of the morning, she was often accompanied along the dark corridors by an elderly one-legged telephonist who did not want her to be alone 'because of the rats'. No rats at Lime Grove, just squalor and overcrowding: with the result that the BBC had overflowed into the adjacent terrace houses and it was in them that we had our cramped offices, with the Central Line trains pounding past a few feet outside the windows.

I was taken to see Grace Wyndham Goldie. In the autumn of 1955, Grace was in her mid-fifties, Assistant Head of Talks under Leonard Miall. She was a small bird-like woman with a striking finely chiselled face (a portrait in her flat painted when she was a young woman was a regular reminder of how attractive she had been), a sharp, questing mind and great charm, though she did not deploy it on everybody or not always in equal measure. Women seemed to incur her displeasure more readily than men: 'Just a chit of a girl' was a familiarly dismissive phrase. Grace was the daughter of a civil engineer who built the spectacular West Highland Railway and so she was born at Arisaig, looking out on the jagged peaks of the Cuillin and the escarpments of Rhum and Eigg. Her father moved on to work on the strengthening of the Aswan Dam and when she returned to England to go to Cheltenham Ladies' College, they told her that her faulty foreign education would prevent her going to a university. She proved them wrong by getting a place at Bristol and then a degree at Somerville College in Oxford.

Grace had been the television critic of the *Listener* before the war and became a radio producer towards the end of it. It was Cecil McGivern, Controller of Television Programmes at the time, who had tempted her, against her better judgement, to come to television. She was reluctant. She had established a big reputation in radio and was content there. Once convinced, she flung herself into learning the craft of television with total commitment. She had pioneered series such as *Foreign Correspondent*, using film for the first time as a method of reportage on international affairs. With Chester Wilmott, a celebrated wartime correspondent, Grace had thought up the notion of presenting the general election results on television. She had recruited new young producers – Jim Bredin, Geoffrey Johnson Smith, Michael Peacock – and, from the Overseas Service, Donald Baverstock had recently joined the department. It was a time of great

8

creative activity and Grace, with her relentless energy, was at the heart of it.

Grace explained that she was attaching me to *Highlight* and that its producer was Donald Baverstock. I was taken along the corridor to the tiny office, right next to the railway, where Donald and his secretary, Anne Caro, were huddled together. Donald had reached television by way of being a navigator in bombers during the war, a period as a schoolmaster at Wellington, and an intensively active and fruitful time as a producer in the Overseas Service. He had worked with Grace on a television series called *We, the French* ('*Qui est-ce, cette dame formidable?*' President Vincent Auriol was heard to murmur to his aides when Grace was in full flood), and since September 1955 had been producing *Highlight*, a new and, for its time, a radical programme. These two people were to have a powerful influence on my professional life and were to remain lifelong friends of ours.

Highlight owed its existence partly to a need to fill a ten-minute gap in the early evening schedules and partly as a BBC response to the start of commercial television. It had virtually no facilities, no design, no film and very little money – £40 a night. We had the use of the presentation studio, but there was less than a minute before Presentation's last use of it, announcing the pattern of the evening's programmes, and the beginning of ours. We were poised like sprinters on their blocks to dash and rearrange the curtains and make the studio look slightly different before hustling in the speakers, cueing the titles and starting the programme. Five nights a week.

The hard core of *Highlight* was three interviews. We differentiated sharply between their nature – conversation, illumination, exposition, cross-examination, banter. As a rarity, we scrounged or borrowed the odd piece of film. We depended quite heavily on colleagues in the regions arranging for interviewees to appear in regional studios to be interviewed 'down the line', thereby establishing relationships which were to reach their full flower later on. Above all, under Donald's tutelage, we set about creating a new style of interviewing: new, at any rate, compared with what we saw as the soft and imprecise approach of programmes like *In Town Tonight*. In any ordinary edition of *Highlight*, there would usually be one serious interview; the cross-examination of a politician or the exploration of a complicated subject like the latest Defence White Paper or a conversation with a visiting American senator; a lighter item, perhaps involving a film actress or a comedian or an author; and the third item would probably verge more towards the eccentric, often with a regional flavour. Such people had appeared before, of course – celebrities in particular. What was new was that the programme was

9

nightly and that its approach was radically different. We strove to share with the audience the best that was in the speaker, to devise supplementary questions that would test the politician's ability to think on his feet, that would develop the banter with the actress or the skills of the raconteur, that would delight and astonish the audience with the range of human eccentricity.

Soon the *Highlight* production unit – or rather, Donald, Anne Caro and I – acquired a new recruit. Cynthia Judah had been working for *Picture Post* and got to see Grace, who fired a few questions at her and then took her down the scruffy corridor to the *Highlight* office. Cynthia described later how 'there in this little room was Donald, an incredibly shabby figure, and Alasdair, another incredibly shabby figure, and poor Anne Caro at the end. Donald said, "Sit down, girl. Take off your hat."' Cynthia had joined us. Cynthia brought a new element to the programme – a knowledge and love of the cinema, theatre and the arts.

The interviewers – first Macdonald Hastings, later as regulars Cliff Michelmore and Geoffrey Johnson Smith – were as involved as Donald, Cynthia and I in developing the techniques of interviewing as we became more confident in our ability to handle any subject in, say, three or four minutes. A possible edition of *Highlight* might have contained: Cliff trying to get past the guard of the late Krishna Menon, then Indian Minister of Defence, who foiled us all by replying to nearly every one of Cliff's most penetrating questions, 'That question is not cast in the mould of my thinking'; a conversation with Brigitte Bardot at the height of her power to dazzle and mesmerise; an interview with a man in Bristol 'down the line' who had by dint of great effort brought forth a bent egg. The audience reacted well to *Highlight*. It had a sprightly, bustling air about it. And we were all of us learning tricks that would give us a sure foundation for *Tonight* later on.

Then came Suez. Donald had gone off to America for a few weeks' break and Cynthia and I were running *Highlight*. The Suez Canal was nationalised by President Nasser of Egypt towards the end of July in 1956 and, since most other programmes that would have handled current affairs were off the air, we were left on our own to follow the developing events. We were soon caught up, too, in tense arguments involving ministerial broadcasts by the Prime Minister, Sir Anthony Eden, and the Labour Opposition.

Eden's first broadcast to the country about the Suez crisis was on 8th August. We were very short of studios and Grace and I had to produce the Prime Minister within the cramped confines of Studio P – the presentation studio where we did *Highlight* every night. It was a very close, hot night and there was no room for the Prime Minister's party to watch in the gallery. They had to watch the rehearsal off a 'feed' we arranged to a waiting room on the ground floor. Eden himself looked pale and strained. The lights in the studio also dazzled his eyes and he was very cross at having to wear glasses to read his speech. But he read it with conviction and we were relieved that in such circumstances it had passed off without more problems. A couple of days later we did have problems. Grace called me in and told me that No. 10 was pressing the BBC to allow Sir Robert Menzies, the Australian Prime Minister, to speak to the nation. In retrospect, it seems an odd idea, but Menzies had seen Nasser in Cairo on his way to Britain and was taking part in a conference in London to try and set up an international system for running the Suez Canal. Eden clearly felt that Menzies' voice would be a powerful aid to him. The BBC, in the person of Harman Grisewood, the Chief Assistant to the Director General, had refused the request.

By all accounts, the Prime Minister was furious. Grace felt that Grisewood did not perhaps realise that she had just transmitted a Press Conference programme where criticism of the Government's position had been voiced. To that extent, 'balance' had been achieved. She felt strongly that Menzies should be heard and she put that view to Grisewood, who changed his mind. I got a phone call from Grace, collected her in a taxi and together we went to see Menzies at the Savoy about the broadcast. We fought our way into his suite past the empty evidence of a really big Australian booze-up in the outer offices the night before, and met Sir Robert. He was not best pleased at having been originally turned down by the BBC and, in truculent mood, insisted that he would deliver his talk standing up. I equally insisted that he must sit down, otherwise he would be likely to sway on his feet and the audience would end up swaying with him. After a brisk altercation, we got agreement and he came to Lime Grove to do his broadcast in place of that evening's *Highlight*, saying much the same as Eden had said earlier: 'We can't accept either the legality or the morality of what Nasser has done.'

Eden asked for his second ministerial broadcast on 3rd November. By that time, Israel had attacked Egypt, British and French troops were preparing to land and the Prime Minister wished to explain our military intervention. As soon as he had spoken, the Labour Party demanded the right of reply, as was its privilege under an aide-mémoire agreed between the parties in 1947. We expected that to happen. But the essence of the aide-mémoire was that right of reply was not automatic but was allowed only if the Government's broadcast was 'controversial'. The Government thought it a magisterial appraisal of the situation; the Opposition found it highly controversial. They could not agree. The decision fell on the

11

broadcasters. To the fury of No. 10, the BBC quickly agreed that Hugh Gaitskell should have the right of reply. Gaitskell came to Lime Grove on the following day, 4th November, with another posse of advisers. He was as tense as Eden had been at the time of his original broadcast, which was not surprising since he was about to attack the policies of the Government when British forces were in action. The ceasefire followed two days later. A week or so later, when I was away on a short holiday, Cynthia invited General Sir Hugh Stockwell, the British commander at Suez who was back in London, to appear on *Highlight*. General Stockwell was already in Lime Grove preparing for the programme when a phone call from No. 10 stopped him. For René McColl of the *Daily Express*, who happened to be appearing on the programme that night as well, there was an unexpected scoop. It was only later that those of us who were producing the programmes learnt that Eden's anger with the BBC was so great that he had instructed the Lord Chancellor to prepare ways and means of taking the BBC over altogether. Both Harman Grisewood and William Clark, Eden's Press Officer, have confirmed that that was his intention.

At the very same time, *Highlight* was confronted with trying to cover the Russian invasion of Hungary. There was not much film and what there was, the News rightly wanted. For us, it became a matter of trying to explain a complicated and increasingly brutal situation. Our Bush House colleagues and one in particular, Francis Rentoul, Head of the Hungarian Section, were essential to that explanation. For a while, Francis appeared almost nightly on *Highlight* to tell us what he thought was going on in Hungary.

As 1956 neared its end, Donald and I were mapping out a new venture. The period between 6.00 and 7.00 p.m. had up till then been occupied by a blank screen since it was felt that mothers could more easily get their children to bed if there was no television. ITV wanted to breach the so-called 'Toddlers' Truce'. The BBC did not feel it could stand by and not compete. With the experience of *Highlight* behind us, we wondered whether we could create an altogether more ambitious programme to fill a large part of this early-evening time-slot. Five nights a week again, but running at forty minutes' length with better resources and wider scope. We worked flat out on possible ingredients; together with Grace, we rented a studio – the Marconi studio in St Mary Abbot's Place in Kensington – thereafter known to us as Studio M. We were halfway down the road to the *Tonight* programme.

2 TONIGHT

Towards the end of 1956 Cecil McGivern, then Controller of
Programmes for BBC Television, agreed that we should go ahead.
The programme we still called *Man Alive* (no disrespect to a later and
very successful programme of that name) was the right BBC offering
to fill the Toddlers' Truce through the weekdays.

McGivern has been described as 'the true architect of BBC
Television'. With a distinguished background in radio feature
production, he was a true producers' leader and enjoyed nothing
more than watching a programme, calling in the producer and
dissecting the result over a drink. His office was on the ground floor of
Lime Grove, quite close to the entrance and opposite the rooms
where we briefed the speakers. McGivern was there every night and
all night, peering from behind thick-lensed spectacles, always a
cigarette between his fingers, nearly always a glass in his hand. He
could be ferociously destructive in criticism and no less inspirational
in praise. Later, when he had been in charge of BBC Television
programmes for more than fourteen years, he found himself
appointed to the non-job of Deputy Director of Television, boxed in,
as Grace Wyndham Goldie records, 'between a Director of Television above him and a Controller of Programmes beneath him, who
increasingly saw eye to eye, but not with his eyes'. Cecil left the BBC,
joined Granada as a scriptwriter and shortly afterwards died tragically
in bed from a fire caused by a cigarette.

McGivern had given the go-ahead. Although *Tonight*, as it soon
became, went on the air with only about six weeks' preparation, we
had eighteen months' experience of *Highlight* behind us, and we had
a nucleus of people who had all worked on *Highlight* together. By the
end of 1956, both Cliff Michelmore and Geoffrey Johnson Smith
were seasoned performers. By then, they had certainly presented
more television programmes than anybody else in the country. And
they were an excellent contrast. Cliff, after starting in broadcasting
with the British Forces Network in Germany, had worked as
producer and presenter in sports and children's programmes before
Donald brought him into *Highlight*. He is a big, apparently easy-

13

going man with an infectious grin and an instinctive sense of rapport with people of all kinds; Cliff has a sharp head and was always extremely quick on his feet, one of the few people I have known in television who could appear to enjoy and surmount chaos in the studio.

Geoffrey Johnson Smith had gone from Oxford on a debating tour of the United States, had done some radio and the odd television interview and ended up sharing an office with Donald Baverstock, who plunged him into introducing *Highlight*. Geoffrey, now a Conservative MP of many years' standing and a former Vice-Chairman of the party was, and still is, sandy-haired, charming, urbane.

Macdonald Hastings, the very first presenter of *Highlight*, was also available. 'Mac', equally content in the bar of the Savile or the Savage or with rod or gun in hand, had worked on *Picture Post*, at that time the leading British picture weekly magazine, had been Editor of the *Eagle*, a famous children's comic, had broadcast for *Woman's Hour* but freely confessed that he had found his first association with Donald Baverstock on *Highlight* 'too much of a strain'. Donald, however, greatly admired Mac's instinctive approach to a story; he often recalled with relish Mac's introduction to camera for the *Highlight* item on the BBC's killing-off of Grace Archer: 'And now,' said Mac, leaning dramatically into camera, 'and now for a slight case of murder.' That ability to, as it were, grasp the audience by the scruff of the neck was something we happily developed in the very important linking material of the *Tonight* programme.

Cynthia Judah brought to us Derek Hart – the third of our regular *Tonight* presenters. Derek, a thoughtful actor with a good, dry wit, had included among his performances two years as Bob Dale in *Mrs Dale's Diary*, though he did not enjoy being reminded of it too often.

So there were Cliff and Derek and Geoffrey, and Mac Hastings. On the production side, there were the 'originals' – Donald and Cynthia, and Anne Caro and me. All of us were inured to producing ten minutes a night; could we really take on forty?

Two Tonys then came to join us. Tony Jay, a lean Cambridge graduate, quick of quote from Horace or Shakespeare, had been briefly with us on *Highlight* but the chemistry was somehow wrong for him there. It had not been much better in a brief flirtation with *Panorama* and Tony came downstairs to the scruffy end of Lime Grove with an obvious sense of relief. And the other Tony – Tony Essex – was a no less important influence in all that followed. Tony, eyes darting restlessly, cigarette crooked between his fingers, had worked in the commercial film world and had then joined the BBC. He edited the film for Donald on a series about British industry, fronted by Aidan Crawley, called *The Edge of Success* or, as Donald preferred it in his more sardonic moments, 'The Brink of Failure'. Nobody at Lime Grove at that time seemed keen to work with Tony Essex – perhaps he was too uncompromising, too individualistic for most producers to feel settled with him. But Donald wanted him, and this truly great film editor joined us shortly before we went on the air.

Then, just two weeks before we started the programme, over a drink in the pub at the top of Lime Grove, we recruited Gordon Watkins, a highly emotional but experienced journalist who wanted urgently to leave *Picture Post*, then in its death throes. Following Cynthia, Gordon was the second of a *Picture Post* cohort who brought *Tonight* great strength and renown. More would follow.

So there we were, a mere handful. Some of us had eighteen months' experience of television, others had a few days. What *Tonight* was going to look like and what it was going to contain, Donald had outlined in a note to Grace Wyndham Goldie early in January 1957, about a month before we were due to go on the air. 'Basically,' he wrote, 'the new programme should have a style similar to the many daily programmes of equivalent length which are transmitted in the United States.' (Donald's visit to America had been both a shock and a stimulus to him – a shock that American television studios were far more competently run than ours by people of apparently less calibre than we had available; and a stimulus that Europe had just as much to offer in terms of ideas as the United States. 'That place,' he said to me, 'confirmed to me that I was a European.')

The aim would be [he went on] to get on to a level of conversation with the viewers which means that the presentation and the manner of the people appearing in the programme would be very informal and relaxed. Many attempts have been made in weekly half-hour programmes to give an air of actuality and spontaneity to the arrangements in the studio, e.g. by installing monitors in vision, telephones on the desk for unexpected instructions. These have always looked contrived simply because one weekly programme put out at a specific time must have been prepared in detail in advance. In this programme every night, as in the general election marathon, there would be every reason to introduce those elements and they would add rather than distract from the impact on the viewers.

The facilities, obviously, would have to be better than those of *Highlight* which didn't really have any. For a start, *Tonight* was four times as long. In terms of today's operations, though, what we did have seems grotesquely inadequate. Studio M (the little one in Kensington, a mile away from all the offices and main technical operations with, for example, no possibility of seeing the film leader running through the gate when it was cued: counting in your head or even the use of a stopwatch is no help by comparison with seeing a leader run to achieve a smooth mix to the next picture); one heavy 35mm Mitchell sound camera originally developed for shooting movies on Hollywood sound stages and wholly unsuitable for the kind of fast countrywide reportage we were aiming for; the use of a couple of silent cameras; the benevolent willingness of the Head of Design, Dick Levin, to turn a blind eye to our design costs, which were minimal anyway; and a budget of £300 a night. Today it looks like lunacy!

On *Highlight* we had virtually no film, except what we could borrow or purloin. We had to have film on *Tonight* to get us out of the studio, to change the rhythm of the programme, and, above all, to involve the audience with whom we would be in conversation every night. Up to the mid-1950s, the live Outside Broadcast camera had been king. Even before the war, in the very infancy of television, OB cameras had been present at the Coronation procession of King George VI and it was their coverage of the Coronation of our present Queen that started the television explosion in this country. It was the OB cameras, too, that covered all the great sporting occasions, as they still do in this country. Film was essentially confined to the nightly *Newsreel*, based on the old cinema formula and used otherwise for *Panorama*'s expanding foreign reporting and for film documentaries.

But we intended to take film cameras all over the country; later all over the world. We needed directors and we needed reporters. Donald had worked on film a little, though his basic training and skill was in talks production. Apart from the film editors, the rest of us had hardly laid a finger on a frame of the stuff. Tony Jay was our first film director and the sensation of humping the mighty Mitchell from location to location must be engraved on some part of his anatomy. As for reporters, Mac Hastings had experience of picture journalism; by a happy agreement, we pointed him in the direction of being our resident countryman, shooting silent film with descriptive commentary on country matters. As he did most memorably in his first report on the behaviour of starlings in Berkshire, the screen black with wheeling, shrieking birds. Otherwise, for a while, we relied for reporters on actors like Derek Bond who knew something of film, and hardened journalists like Sam Pollock whose short piece on the affairs of the London Cattle Trough Drinking Association remains an early classic in my memory. And then there was Whicker.

16

Alan Whicker had been working for some years for the Exchange Telegraph, a news agency now long defunct. He had covered the Korean War for them, he had covered royal tours. He and I met for the first time on *Going Places, Meeting People*, run by a peppery and energetic producer called Ronnie Gibson. I was still a General Trainee at the time and quite properly treated as a lowly dogsbody. Alan, moustache sharply trimmed, a veteran of wars and royal confrontations, seemed chirpy and cheeky and very much a man of the world. When, in the very late autumn of 1956, Donald and I were talking about possible film reporters, I was asked to go along one evening and watch an aspiring television producer doing his production exercise. These exercises were the culmination of the television production course and, since there was no money available to pay the participants, it was a case of leaning on friends to help out. I had a bad bout of flu at the time and was in two minds whether to go or not, but go I did and there, to my surprise, was Whicker!

If my memory serves me right, Alan was interviewing a hair-dresser; not on the face of it the most exciting prospect, particularly when you have the flu. But the way Alan handled the interview, his sharp approach to the subject matter came strongly through the screen. I said to Donald the next morning, 'I think we ought to try Whicker.' We met Alan, sent him out to talk to Oxford Street traders and Ramsgate landladies. And when we saw the results, we booked him properly and he became part of the history of *Tonight*. Alan thereafter disappeared into the hinterland of Britain and, later, the world. On rare visits to Britain, we managed to entice him into the studio. I filmed with him twice in totally contrasting circumstances: in the Highlands of Scotland in January where our teeth so chattered with the cold we could hardly communicate; and in New York and then the Bahamas where he did all the swimming (for the cameras, of course) and we seemed to do all the work. His commitment to the job is best enshrined in memories of a New York hotel room which we had to share. He was still bashing away at his typewriter when I fell asleep at 2.00 a.m. I woke at 3.00 to hear him splashing in the bath; when I came to at 5.00 a.m. he was already sitting bolt upright in bed watching early-morning television! It's been much like that the world over ever since.

Sadly, in May 1957, three months after we began *Tonight*, Hulton's *Picture Post*, the leading British, and possibly world, picture weekly, finally stopped publication. But already we had garnered some of its finest reporters: Fyfe Robertson, 'Robbie' to all who knew him, the Glaswegian with the rakish taste in hats and a keen nose for uncovering bureaucratic muddle (it was Robbie who blew the

Tanganyika Groundnuts Scheme); Trevor Philpott, a Northampton-shire man with a deep understanding of industry and a natural liking for people, who had also been Assistant Editor of *Picture Post* for a time; Slim Hewitt, the Cockney with the permanent cigar butt in his mouth, an Army Film Unit photographer in the war, who became one of *Picture Post*'s star still photographers and quickly graduated to film, working with Trevor all over the world for *Tonight*. And later that elegant, tortured man and very considerable journal-ist, Kenneth Allsop. All came as to a haven from the dying *Picture Post*.

Add to them our lone girl reporter, the delightful Polly Elwes, and we had recruited a formidable team. We needed, too, our own resident engineer, not least because we were isolated from the main electronic operations in our Kensington High Street studio. This was quite alien to BBC regulations at the time; when Norman Taylor joined us, his colleagues looked on him with pity and gave him short shrift. Studio M was 'genlocked' (that is to say, it was electronically synchronised) to Lime Grove, but not very well. We had, as I have said, no way of previewing film; our connections with BBC regional studios, which were very important to the programme, were ram-shackle. Our willing studio crew were not even on the BBC payroll: they came as part of the package hired from Marconi. Yet Norman achieved miracles and brought off things in one afternoon that would normally have taken an engineer a week's work.

Leading us all was Donald Baverstock. Much has been written about this man: about his rudeness, about the wild, voluble Welsh-man with his broken nose, chewing his nails, thumping the table. All of that is, or was, part of Donald. Derek Hart once said, 'It's true that Donald has all the social graces of an untrained Labrador.' I had worked with Donald at very close quarters for eighteen months and knew that side of him well: the curtness arose not from innate discourtesy but from single-minded commitment to his work and from his very singular view of television. Ideas tumbled out of him in a flood, some of them useless, but many hugely exciting. Surprise was Donald's trademark based, I believe, on the vast amount of reading he did at Oxford where he found himself, the son of a Welsh shopkeeper, sharing the Peckwater Quad at Christ Church with the riotous living of contemporary Etonians.

Something of that surprise comes back from a vivid memory of one desultory afternoon when the *Tonight* programme was not coming together. It looked dull on paper. We needed an element of the unexpected, something that would lift what otherwise looked like being a thoroughly prosy programme. Sitting opposite Donald, as I did for four years, I tried some half-hearted thoughts on him without

18

any great enthusiasm. Suddenly, he said to me (these were the dog days of summer), 'Why do you think the British are so besotted nowadays with the sun and getting sunburnt? They didn't used to be. Pale skins were all the rage in the twenties. I think there's an item here. I remember a marvellous piece by Cyril Connolly on the obsession with the sun and getting a tan. Let's get him.' And soon he was on to Connolly, who was far from keen to come up to London from the country in the middle of the afternoon, but Donald persuaded him and that night we enjoyed a wonderfully turned piece of conversation on sun worship.

Donald was a great editor and a great inspirer of people. He was also merciless in criticism without always appreciating the damage he could inflict. Tony Jay wrote of him some years later:

> Although he is professionally expert in the craft of television production – writing, film direction and so on – he was no better than many others in the *Tonight* team and not as good as some. His strength was not so much in his ability to do things himself (though without it, he could not have commanded our professional respect) as in his extraordinary creative vision of what we ought to be doing and his power of making us improve sufficiently to achieve it.

Donald, someone said, created the context in which the rest of us could have ideas.

So, at 6.05 on Monday evening, 18th February, 1957, the first *Tonight* went on the air from Studio M in Kensington. We had, every night, to make our way the mile from Lime Grove to a short camera rehearsal and to meet our speakers. The control gallery was tiny and the only place to brief the speakers was a glass box that was even tinier. Quite early on I ran foul of Mrs Eleanor Roosevelt. I was trying to get the camera rehearsal completed, there was nobody to look after her and she complained to Grace about 'that young man in his shirt-sleeves blowing cigarette smoke in my face'. We didn't always have time for the niceties of life.

We had a title – *Tonight* – but only just. Leonard Miall, Head of Television Talks, thought it only courteous to write to NBC, the American network who also had a show called *Tonight* to tell them what we were up to. In due course, the Americans said they had no objection to our using the title, if we paid them $10 every night. Leonard remembered that NBC were running a programme called *Home* and reminded them that the BBC had broadcast a regular television programme of that name back in 1937. If they cared to pay retrospectively for their use of our title . . . So *Tonight* we got. We also had a new signature tune, 'Tonight and Every Night' and there

19

were frequent occasions when it was the only thing we had ready when we went on the air.

The first night we had a kind of television scoop. The FA Cup draw was televised live from the studio. We were exultant at pulling this one off. The other ingredients in the programme that night were a pointer to the programme's future shape. Cy Grant, the West Indian calypso singer (alternating with the late Rory McEwen, who with his brother Alex, folk singers both, contributed so much to the programme) sang a topical calypso – Cynthia's idea – written by one 'Taper' of the *Spectator*, alias Bernard Levin. John Metcalf presented a miniature *What the Papers Say*. Derek Bond reported on film about a statue that was causing offence to the citizens of Richmond. Derek Hart interviewed the famous American broadcaster Ed Murrow, who had made his name reporting for CBS from London during the Blitz and was now the undisputed doyen of American current affairs reporters. There was an interview with the Dame of Sark, and a few feet of film of the island, and Amalia Rodriguez, at the height of her fame as a Portuguese fado singer, sang a sad song of the sea on film.

There was, too, Jonathan Miller, fresh from his success with Peter Cook, Dudley Moore and Alan Bennett in the revue *Beyond the Fringe*, giving a very personal impression of shops in the West End of London: he was particularly entranced with a boot that stood in water in a well-known shoe shop to prove its eternal qualities. It has to be said that the good Dr Miller's participation in *Tonight* was shortlived. Each Saturday morning, for a few weeks, Grace Wyndham Goldie convened a meeting to thrash out the past week's work with the *Tonight* production team. I think it was on the third Saturday that she found grievous fault with Jonathan's performance a couple of nights earlier. A hilarious turn, in highly questionable taste, where he impersonated Nelson fumbling for the fatal bullet inside his waistcoat. It was no help that Jonathan, at that time uncontrollable in terms of studio discipline, had lurched past the cameras in his enthusiasm and so disappeared from view altogether for a while. It helped even less that the following item was an interview with Commander Kerens, RN, whose famous exploit in bringing his ship, HMS *Amethyst*, down the Yangtze, running the gauntlet of the Chinese shore batteries all the way, had just been made into a feature film. Jonathan, said Grace, must go. Donald and I demurred strongly, and when Grace started shouting, 'Shut up, Donald,' and talked of issuing instructions, we departed mutinously.

The newspaper critics did not greet the new programme with unqualified praise. They thought it promising, but Leonard Marsland Gander of the *Daily Telegraph* caught their general mood: 'It had variety, some spice and reasonable pace, but it lacked compelling interest and gaiety.' Lukewarm douches of that kind had little effect on us; we somehow knew we were creating something quite new. We theorised endlessly about what we were doing, even at times a bit pompously. To us it seemed that much of the television of the late fifties patronised the audience. We were determined to be on their side. If we failed to communicate, that was our fault, not the audience's lack of understanding. 'There is no such thing as a boring subject, only boring ways of looking at things,' was one of Donald's texts. Everyone outside the programme talked about it being a programme of topicality, but in truth it was not. At times, we almost stood on our heads to avoid chasing the news. We said it was about 'relevance', by which we meant that it was involved in ideas which were surprising or revealing and which themselves could become a kind of news because the viewers could be invited to feel that they were relevant to their lives on that particular day.

To that end, the 'links' – the words linking one story or interview to another – were of the essence. Donald and I spent as much time on the links late in the day as we had earlier in shaping the general programme content. And we developed the interviewing techniques originated on *Highlight* to a high level of skill, scrupulously mapping out the ways in which an interview might develop, noting the key supplementary questions, working over the material with the speaker and interviewee in pre-programme production in order to be as sure as we could that we helped the interviewee to give of their best. Live television interviews are edited in 'real time', as it were, and so the preparation of the questions and the production of the speaker were crucial to success.

The actual daily mounting of the programme was frantic in the early days, though we soon settled to a kind of routine. The pattern that emerged was a morning of discussion, argument, constant telephoning to contact speakers or to arrange for them to be brought to studios all over the country (how best, for example, to get a gifted tinker from his shack close by Rest and Be Thankful in Argyll to the Glasgow studio sixty miles away); a viewing session at 2.00 p.m. of all the available film which had been put into 'rough-cut' form during the morning – searing sessions those, with Donald at his most severe and some of the directors, briefly touching base, at their most tender; decision then on the final shape of the film for that night, an afternoon of commentary writing, interview preparation, of rough studio rehearsal; a late afternoon dubbing session to put the commentary and effects soundtrack on to the film, once a week made more difficult by the heavyweight *Sportsview* team of Paul Fox, Ronnie Noble and Bryan Cowgill who stood their ground like Sherman tanks, refusing to leave the dubbing theatre, and often had to be forcibly evicted! Even on days when they were not around, the dubbing frequently was not completed till after the programme started going out on the air.

In those days, there were additional technical hazards, quite apart from the 'blind' film cueing. There was, for example, no 'rock and roll' dubbing technique as there is now, whereby, if you make a fluff or the commentary does not fit, you simply go back a few feet and retake the sequence. Then you had to go right back to the beginning and do it all again, your eyes closed in prayer. Because of these inevitable problems of time, there was no point in trying to conceal our production agonies from the audience. Donald's prophetic talk of 'actuality and spontaneity' was, in fact, unavoidable. Cliff Michelmore was often seen on the phone talking to the studio director and then explaining to the audience candidly what kind of trouble we were in. Not infrequently, the talk to the studio director was simply to fill in time because the next guest had not arrived (Motor Show time at Earl's Court was an annual nightmare for traffic hold-ups) or because the next film sequence was not yet laced up and ready to run on the film machine.

In August, back on the air after a short break, we enjoyed brief notoriety when we interviewed a murder suspect who had been released by the police, and were duly disowned by the BBC: this on the eve of Donald's wedding! By the time we did our hundredth programme in September, we had got into our stride. The viewers were watching in large numbers, the production team were beginning to show the very great talent they possessed. Tony Jay, soon to come 'off the road' as our first film director (and to be followed by a tough Lancastrian, Don Howarth, who has since made his name as a director of fine documentaries and a prolific writer of radio plays), was refining his techniques of film commentary writing which for fluency, perfect match to film and speed of execution were unrivalled at the time and I doubt have been matched since; later, he pushed the bounds even further, writing easily to film in verse and producing an unforgettable elegy the night Dr Beeching closed down half the country's rural stations. Tony Essex and his fellow film editors were growing increasingly expert at 'synching up' (synchronising the separate sound tapes to match the lip movement on film), cutting and dubbing at speed large amounts of film; to see Tony or Jack Gold or Mike Tuchner (both of whom have since become movie directors of note) tackle several hours of raw film just in from a roving team and reduce it to manageable proportions in two or three hours was an education.

Cynthia Judah and Gordon Watkins (and later Liz Cowley who joined us in 1958 from *Reveille*) were experimenting with film and still

22

picture sequences that gave the programme changes of pace and style. In December 1957 the Guild of Television Writers and Producers gave Donald the award for the Best Factual Programme of the year. 'The success of *Tonight*,' said the *Sheffield Star*, 'is that it belongs to us.'

As our confidence grew, we raised our eyes from the grindstone and realised what riches we could find outside Britain. Making television programmes overseas was, at that time, confined to the occasional *Panorama* and the odd documentary: the world was waiting for us. In the autumn of 1957 canteen intelligence alerted us to the fact that the *Sportsview* mob of Peter Dimmock, Paul Fox, Ronnie Noble and Bryan Cowgill were going to Morocco to cover a Grand Prix event on film. We borrowed their camera and in three crazy days Derek Hart and I filmed three stories for *Tonight*: one on the Djna el Fnah, the great square in Marrakesh, was snatched in three hours after a long and troubled car journey from Casablanca. Our difficulty in the Djna arose from the fact that an American film company had been there a few weeks before us and the musicians and snake charmers and toothdrawers had recognised the advantage of a high dollar fee. They got nothing from us though we got much abuse from them, but we did not complete that assignment too well either, our ancient Ford finally collapsing on us after midnight in the middle of a field outside Casablanca, so disturbing what seemed like the entire Moroccan dog population.

In 1958 we became even more ambitious. We did complete editions of *Tonight* live from the Brussels Exhibition (a near disaster that one, since we only got access to the Belgian cameras an hour before transmission); from a park beside the lake in Geneva; from a Copenhagen restaurant where Karen Blixen, 'Isak Dinesen' of *Out of Africa* fame, made what I believe was her only British television appearance, Nina and Frederick, the folk duo who became so famous later, made their British television début and Fyfe Robertson decided that Danish arrangements for looking after their old folk suited him down to the ground. Our last extravaganza that exciting year was a complete programme mounted in the Piazza San Marco in Venice. On that occasion, my degree in Italian at last proved its value in directing the Italian crew live on the air, except that five minutes after we started the programme the field telephone – an ancient, tired machine – rang in the Outside Broadcast van. It was Presentation in London asking us to start the programme all over again as the picture had only just got through to them! It was in the same year, 1958, that we sent Alan Whicker out on the first of many memorable overseas trips that were to be the foundation of *Whicker's World*.

It was also in 1958 that the BBC Television Service sank to the nadir of its fortunes in competing for the audience's attention. In the early days of ITV, senior BBC figures looked down their noses at what they saw as the vulgar attempts of the hucksters to woo the audience away, even though the ranks of the hucksters contained some former eminent BBC people like Norman Collins and some very sharp operators like Sidney Bernstein of Granada and Lew Grade of ATV. By 1958, however, disdain had given place to near panic. The BBC's percentage of the audience had slumped to twenty-eight. Admittedly, ITV had gone in for some fairly questionable programming, like *People are Funny*, which lost no time in making the participants look as stupid as they could; and Asa Briggs records that Cecil McGivern was very critical of what he called 'ITA's addiction to wiggle dances, give-aways, panels and light entertainment': the truth remained that the audience had deserted the BBC in droves. In later years when asked, as one frequently was, why the BBC should pay any attention to its ratings, it seemed worth reminding the questioner that no government could possibly sustain a licence fee for a broadcasting organisation which two-thirds of the population totally ignored. The more recent experiences of the CBC in Canada and the ABC in Australia, struggling to cling on to minority audiences, would seem to lend weight to that argument.

The BBC Television management, led now by Gerald Beadle, was under heavy pressure. Beadle, who was famed for his choice of claret and his after-lunch naps at the Savile Club, which not even the DG might disturb, was, I have since been told, a more astute figure that we recognised at the time. He had had a hand in reorganising the administration of the BBC during the war and had apparently done the job well. But he had been brought back to London from a comfortable post as Controller in Bristol to be Director of Television, and I doubt if he knew what he was in for. The staff felt angry and betrayed, without sense of direction or leadership. A staff meeting was called at the Hammersmith Odeon and, though we were busy on *Tonight* and could not go, the canteen at lunchtime was buzzing with stories of Grace rising to her feet and calling for 'heads to roll'.

At Lime Grove, with *Tonight* as the nightly shock troops, attracting an audience of eight million which would eventually rise to ten, and with both *Panorama* under Mike Peacock and *Monitor* under Huw Wheldon gaining reputation weekly, we had no real cause for anxiety. But everybody thought BBC Television News, under Tahu Hole's guidance, pathetic. ITN was winning the audience's appreciation hands down by its fresh and open approach, fronted by new faces such as Robin Day and Ludovic Kennedy, compared with BBC News Division's stiff and solemn demeanour.

Then the first breath of change stirred: in early autumn 1958 Hugh

Greene was appointed Director of News and Current Affairs, while Tahu Hole went off to administration. One of Greene's first acts was to accept the advice of Donald Edwards, whom he had brought over from Bush House, and commission a report on television news from three television producers – Ian Atkins, an experienced drama producer, Michael Peacock and Donald Baverstock. They saw with stark clarity that as long as people who had little or no first-hand experience of working in television news continued to control the output (with Tahu Hole, I imagine, much in mind) then most of the obvious faults would continue. Later, and particularly when Hugh Greene succeeded Sir Ian Jacob as Director General, that report led to dramatic change, including the disappearance of Hole from the BBC and the appointment of Michael Peacock as Editor of Television News.

Two incidents enshrine for me the changes that struck the BBC when Greene took over from Jacob, though there are those who would argue that Jacob had begun to ease the windows open before Greene arrived and claimed he had let the fresh air in. Late in 1956, 'Jake' came on a tour of inspection of Lime Grove and, as befitted a former Chief Staff Officer to the Minister of Defence, a number of us were lined up in Leonard Miall's office, almost at attention and with our thumbs down the seams of our trousers. By contrast, Greene came in 1959 when he was Director of News and Current Affairs to see a *Tonight* programme go on the air and afterwards disputed with us vigorously over much gin until late in the night. We thought, being cocky, that we won the exchange but he clearly enjoyed it!

In 1959 my daily dose of *Tonight* was suddenly disrupted by the calling of the general election. Leonard Miall had me in and told me the Labour Party wanted to shape their election broadcasts somewhat after the pattern of *Tonight* and had asked for me to be seconded to help them for the duration of the election. How did I feel about it? he asked. I had had no direct involvement in handling party material since Suez and was very uncertain, but agreed to go and see Anthony Wedgwood Benn (as he then styled himself) at his house in west London, since he apparently was the co-ordinating figure for the broadcasts. We met, and there too were Christopher Mayhew and Woodrow Wyatt, both experienced BBC television performers. They wanted, they said, a magazine programme with the pace and sharpness of *Tonight*. I demurred. I doubted whether the *Tonight* formula was adaptable to disseminating party propaganda. In the end, we worked out a scheme with Tony Benn as presenter, Christopher Mayhew handling graphs and displays (at which he was very effective) and Woodrow booming into camera in inimitable polemical vein.

25

As we were coming up to our first broadcast, we had the luxury of seeing the first Conservative programme. It was repeated quite recently in a programme about television and politics, with Ted Heath, who was Tory Chief Whip at the time, describing it as 'a disaster'. There sat Harold Macmillan, with his Cabinet all gathered around him on sofas at Birch Grove, all looking slightly shifty and uncomfortable. He explained to the viewers that he intended to give them an end of parliament report and then called on each Minister in turn to speak. 'Derry,' he said, turning to Chancellor Heathcoat Amory, 'a word about the economy. I think we're doing quite well, don't you?' And so with each Minister. It was hilarious, and the press were very severe on the Tories about it.

The Labour Party programmes, by contrast, were quite sharp. Two days before polling, the *Daily Mirror*, with a huge splash headline 'LABOUR EXPECTS VICTORY', talked of 'the impact of Labour's TV programmes which have been way ahead of Tory efforts', and Keith Waterhouse wrote in the *New Statesman*, 'Labour's programmes have been called slick, which I am glad to say they were . . . But the real point is that the team came over not as politicians but as broadcasters.'

Hugh Gaitskell travelled the country a great deal in the 1959 election and was only occasionally involved in the programmes 'down the line' from regional studios. When he arrived to take part in the final broadcast, there was a great fuss because he complained that the desk provided for him (the biggest we had in Lime Grove) was not big enough. At twenty minutes' notice, I had to send to the Television Centre for the mightiest desk ever seen, which could only, with difficulty, be fitted in the hoists to get it to the studio.

In the last forty-eight hours of the election, the Tories abandoned the BBC's production support and went down the road to Norman Collins at ATV where Macmillan pulled off his famous theatrical performance, spinning the globe and talking impressively about his involvement in world affairs. It was a masterly turn. The Conservatives won the election resoundingly. I got a nice letter from Hugh Gaitskell, thanking me for 'all the hard work you put into the production of our party programmes. As I am sure you must be aware, the programmes were the subject of much favourable comment everywhere.' And from Leonard Miall I got a note that was even more important professionally: 'You have confirmed the ideal kind of relationship between a party and a BBC producer. You do not tell them how to run their business or let them tell you how to run yours.' It had not been easy, but all seemed satisfied.

Back on *Tonight* we continued to ride high. Slim Hewitt and I undertook one unforgettable assignment together when we set off for the north-west of Scotland to film Gavin Maxwell and his otters at the time of the publication of *Ring of Bright Water*. Slim's smart city shoes were no match for the mile and a half of Highland bog that had to be traversed to Camusfearna, the name Maxwell gave to his lonely cottage at Sandaig on the Sound of Sleat. Nor were Slim's ankles a match for Teko, one of the otters, who pursued him relentlessly for two days, nipping his ankles and chirruping with delight.

Quite the maddest filming venture we undertook occurred immediately after the 1959 general election. British Airways (BOAC as it was then) had decided to reopen the South American routes on which they used to fly and to use the new Comet 4 as the bait to bring the passengers back. (The original Comets had been withdrawn from service after three of them crashed mysteriously. My brother, Iain, was killed in 1953 in the first crash over Calcutta. The planes had then been tested to destruction in water tanks at Farnborough where metal fatigue had been proved to be the cause.) Now, redesigned and remodelled, the Comet was back in action and someone had the bright idea to ask *Tonight* to go with it on its proving flight. There were, as I recall, a dozen captains on board and two dozen of BOAC's most attractive stewardesses; and us: Derek Hart, our cameraman Dougie Wolfe, a veteran but testy Australian, our recordist Frank Dale and me. We had no proper research for stories except the odd Reuters' briefing background we had picked up. We did, however, know where we were going – Brazil, Argentina, Chile, Peru, Brazil again and home. All in a month. We knew, too, that South America was largely ignored by Fleet Street and, therefore, we could rely on little support from Fleet Street stringers there. Bush House had, of course, its own support in South America and we came to rely on them heavily.

We stopped off in Lisbon before crossing the Atlantic to Recife in Brazil. In Brazil the reception had a very special flavour. Pan Am had a virtual monopoly of international flights into Brazil at the time and were intent on making the new interloper's life as much of a misery as they could. They managed to manoeuvre the authorities into preventing us landing at Rio's main airport; we ended up at 2.00 a.m. at a military airfield seventy miles from Rio, almost pushing the aircraft into its hangar and certainly unloading all the baggage ourselves. The customs arrangements were intentionally protracted. It was after dawn by the time we were bussed into Rio.

What to film in twenty-four hours before we took off again for Buenos Aires? We put together a story contrasting the glamorous life on Copacabana Beach with the miseries of the *favellas* – the shanty-town huts of Rio. In Buenos Aires, we tackled the traffic which was horrendous and included some of the most bizarre and

27

overdressed hearses I have ever seen. We heard that strange things sometimes turned up in the endless, winding waterways of the River Plate delta; and we did indeed discover an old lady from Stoke-on-Trent who had once been a nanny to an Argentinian family and now lived alone miles from the nearest neighbour. When the floods came, she told us, the water level rose to ten feet and she took to the roof. She had never seen a camera before.

In Chile, we left the Comet and set about real filming. We shot in Andean mines at eight thousand feet where every breath was an effort. Virtually the only story for which we possessed some research details concerned a Belgian priest working in a tiny oasis in the Atacama Desert at the foot of the Andes in the far north of Chile. He, it was said, had discovered remains that put the date of the arrival of the Indians in the Americas twenty thousand years earlier than had been previously estimated. We determined to go and film him and arranged for the Chilean Air Force to fly us early the following morning to the great copper mine of Chuquicamata which was only four hours' drive from his village. That night we supped off a gruesome-looking gruel which rejoiced under the name of Soup Sancho Panza. By 3.00 a.m. we were all in a pathetic state. We staggered to the airport in the morning where I explained our condition to the Air Force captain in my strange mixture of Italian and Spanish. We must, he said, have injections of atropine to 'paralyse the stomach'. I protested that we did not want our stomachs paralysed, but he insisted and so, heavily doped, we bumped our way north through the desert thermal currents. At Chuquicamata we recovered enough to get up at 3.00 a.m. and drive across the desert while the sun came up over the mighty Andes. Our priest told us his story and showed us his museum, where there were rows of figures, mummified by the absolute dryness of the atmosphere. They were set out like dolls in trays, most still with Davy Crockett-like hats on their heads. It was an extraordinary journey.

In Peru, with only three-quarters of an hour before the Pacific sun set, we knocked off a story among the myriad screaming sea-birds who produce the rich fertiliser called guano. It had taken nearly all day to reach this distant shore from Lima because our villainous driver lied to us consistently about the distance. As he drove us back in the dark, with one faint light bulb to confront the blazing lights of the oncoming lorries on the Pacific Highway and a thousand-foot drop on our right into the ocean, we shut our eyes and prayed. We filmed the great Inca ruins at Sacsuaman and Machu Picchu high in the Andes; we filmed the booming city of São Paolo in Brazil. We met up with our captains and stewardesses again in Recife and flew home on Christmas Eve, having shot fourteen stories in twenty days.

The greatest joy at the end of a pulverising month was to be met at the airport by Sheila and the boys; Seumas, sixteen months old, proudly demonstrating to the onlookers that he could walk.

In the spring of 1961, Donald Baverstock was promoted to be Assistant Controller of Programmes under Stuart Hood, the Controller; and I took over the editorship of *Tonight*. By then, new names had joined the programme's credit list – Chris Brasher, Liz Cowley, Peter Batty, Derrick Amoore, Tony Smith. When we reached our one thousandth programme in September of that year, some three thousand people had been interviewed in the studio, another ten thousand outside and we had screened some two million feet of film: seven hundred and fifty hours of television in three and a half years. That evening, I got a telegram from Hugh Greene. It read, 'Congratulations to you and your colleagues. *Tonight* has not only been a professionally skilful and most enjoyable programme, it has contributed enormously to the new face of the BBC. One reason why I hope we get a second television programme is that there could be a late edition of *Tonight* at a time when people like myself could see it more often.'

But with the warming plaudits came the increasing pressure from the older hands to be free to spread their wings. In August of 1961, the first Tonight Productions documentary was screened – *Whicker Down Under*, a compilation of Alan's Australian *Tonight* stories. We moved on rapidly from there, becoming a separate production department two years later. Mac Hastings did a six-part series about criminal cases where the evidence of Churchill the gunsmith had proved conclusive, partly dramatised with Wensley Pithey playing Churchill and directed by Jack Gold. It had a good title originally, *The Other Mr Churchill*, until Churchill looked likely to die and we called it, rather tamely, *Call the Gunsmith*. Whicker worked with Jack Gold on a film on the Quorn Hunt, with Kevin Billington in Spain and Mexico, with Michael Tuchner in Texas. Kevin and Malcolm Muggeridge, as the first of a tentative series of films on Malcolm's varied life, caught a real flavour of the last days of the Raj in *Twilight of Empire*. Even the tireless team of Trevor Philpott and Slim Hewitt, covering the world from Lima to Laos, wanted room to breathe and extend their work. And, almost at the same time, Ned Sherrin, who had been directing *Tonight* in the studio for three years, was at work on a new idea – *That Was The Week That Was*. Tonight Productions was absorbing an increasing amount of our energy.

Tonight itself went on, but wearying slowly. Tony Jay followed me as Editor but was deeply unhappy. Gordon Watkins did a few months' stint for old times' sake. Peter Batty followed him but the changes he introduced seemed to me unfortunate and I worried that morale was slipping away. Peter said at one time that there were too many ex-editors hovering around *Tonight* and he was probably right. The problem, however, did not go away. At all events, I moved him out of the chair and took over the programme myself again with Liz Cowley standing in for me when the many works of Tonight Productions needed my attention. *The Great War* alone, twenty-six forty-minute films on the 1914–18 war, a mammoth series on a scale never before tried in this country, was a daily absorption, though brilliantly handled by Tony Essex and Gordon Watkins.

The last Editor of *Tonight* was Derrick Amoore. By then, both Brian Redhead and Magnus Magnusson had joined the studio team and Derrick's perverse attempts, as it seemed to me, to promote Magnus and demote Cliff in terms of studio presentation were the cause of a huge row on the programme's first night back on the air in the late summer of 1964. Tempers cooled in due course, but the atmosphere remained strained and difficult for some weeks.

Tonight came to an end in June 1965, shortly after Donald Baverstock and I had left the BBC. Perhaps that was the right moment. For five nights a week, over a period of eight years, we had followed the Reithian formula of 'educating, informing and entertaining' not, perhaps, in a way that Reith would have envisaged possible, but in a way that I hope he would have enjoyed. (When, just before his death, I asked him if he had ever seen the programme, he was too deaf to hear the question. Also he was never a great television addict, though he made two very revealing programmes about himself with Malcolm Muggeridge.)

I know that we gave millions of people insight and pleasure over hundreds of programmes: and we – the *Tonight* team – struck up a relationship that has remained indissoluble over the years. When we met on the thirtieth anniversary of the programme on 18th February, 1987, some, alas! had gone – Mac, Robbie, Slim, Derek, Tony Essex and, since then, Polly too; for the rest of us, it was as if we had never parted.

3 THAT WAS THE WEEK THAT WAS

By late 1961, *Tonight* was in its maturity. It commanded a nightly audience of around ten million. Its presenters – Cliff Michelmore, Derek Hart and Kenneth Allsop – were among the best known household names in the country. Its film reporters – Alan Whicker, Fyfe Robertson, Trevor Philpott – were no less famous. The directors working with them – Jack Gold, Michael Tuchner, Kevin Billington, Derrick Amoore – were all to achieve wider public recognition later. The studio and film team at base in Lime Grove – Cynthia Judah, Gordon Watkins, Tony Jay, Tony Essex – had the assured touch of success. There were no signs of the staleness that can so easily infect long-running television programmes.

Ned Sherrin, who had been with us earlier as Studio Director, had returned after a spell with Light Entertainment that worked for neither of them. Ned's relaxed and faintly flippant approach wholly fails to conceal an extremely sharp intelligence, allied to a skilled use of words, especially in a dramatic context. Shortly after leaving Oxford, he had begun what turned out to be a long and fruitful writing collaboration with the late Caryl Brahms.

When Ned came back to *Tonight*, we very soon began to see intriguing developments. He used the 'dead hours' of the studio during the afternoon to rehearse and record seven- or eight-minute dramatised adaptations from novels – something we had done before but only rarely and usually to preface an interview with a performer or author. Under Ned's hand, these became 'set pieces' which, if they didn't always work, invigorated and refreshed the programme. At the same time, Donald Baverstock and I had been talking almost nightly at Hampton, where we both lived, about the possibility of tackling a new programme venture for Saturday nights.

Saturday was then, and still is, the BBC's key occasion for entertaining the population – for comedy and variety shows, for popular drama, for easy relaxation. The arrival of BBC-2 made it possible to present much more challenging material on the second channel, but I see no reason for apologising for trying to entertain the audience as best we could on BBC-1 on a Saturday night. Long afterwards, Mrs Thatcher took me to task because she could find, she said, nothing worth watching on Saturdays when she had finished her boxes. When it transpired that she did not finish the boxes till 10.30 p.m., I think it was Bill Cotton who pointed out to her that television had virtually finished by then!

We were keen, then, to provide something different from the regular diet of light entertainment and comedy and films, something towards the end of the evening that was characterised by intelligence, good humour and good words. Shortly before *That Was The Week That Was* (the title, Ned Sherrin reminds us, should be attributed to John Bird) went on the air in November 1962, Donald Baverstock described to Stuart Hood, the Controller of Programmes, some of the thoughts we had refined with Ned over the preceding months. He wrote:

> Late on Saturday night people are more aware of being persons and less of being citizens than at any other time of the week. It is, therefore, the best time to hang contemporary philosophy on the hook in the hall, to relieve the pressure of earnest concern and goodwill which presses down on us throughout the rest of the week. To abandon what Mary McCarthy calls 'the slow drip of cant'. One key to this programme must therefore lie in the language used in it. It must be more vital and vigorous than the common run of communication offers. Another and most important key to its success will be the humour and wit with which opinions and observations are expressed. We are contemplating the world, not our navel [a favourite Baverstock expression].

That forecast was written on the verge of the first transmission. In the meantime, there had been management upheavals in the Talks Department where we were all working. Leonard Miall was suddenly removed by Hugh Greene from the position he rejoiced in as Assistant Controller of Talks and Current Affairs; and after days of being threatened with Hugh's particular form of Siberia – Scotland – ended up as Assistant Controller of Programme Services, charged with the business of setting up the staffing of the fledgling BBC-2. Grace Wyndham Goldie became Head of Talks and Current Affairs in his place. I was suddenly advanced from being Editor of *Tonight*, which everybody understood, into one of those strange BBC title jobs, Assistant Head (Current Affairs), Talks, Television. Which meant, after close study, that I still supervised *Tonight* (though Tony Jay succeeded me as Editor) but that I was also responsible for *Panorama* and other current affairs activities. And for the new Saturday night programme. As Grace recorded in her book *Facing the Nation*, she knew full well that Donald, Ned and I were going to put this one together and, though nominally it fell under her control, she had little part in it. The formal BBC control of the new programme was laid firmly on me. Donald confirmed this to Stuart Hood, the Controller of Programmes: 'I have therefore asked Alasdair Milne to regard his responsibility for this programme as an absolute priority over all his other duties until the New Year. In case of doubt about policy or taste, it will be his responsibility to refer to me.'

Ned Sherrin had been busy through the early part of the year. He has written himself that before the first pilot

> we had the active support of the Director General (Hugh Greene) and the late Kenneth Adam, Director of Television. Both had their own idea of the sort of show that might emerge. Greene's view was coloured by his experience of political cabaret when he was a correspondent in Germany, during the early years of the Nazi régime. On the other hand, the memories which coloured Adam's vision were of Herbert Farjeon and the Gate revues, small theatre shows in London in the late 1930s.

Since there was much talk of Berlin cabaret and Gate revues after the end of the first series, I must record my clear memory that neither Greene nor Adam had the slightest notion of what kind of show would emerge until they saw the first one. We, ourselves, were a bit hazy about the final form, though we could clearly see the way things were developing.

What Ned did, first, was to find the people. He found David Frost at a nightclub called 'The Blue Angel'; to this day, Ned relates that he went to see David and was told that as his act had not been going too well, David was unlikely to appear that night; at which point, a 'formidable old agent and booker' intervened, saying, 'Give the boy a chance,' and so David took the stage. David insists that he had been paid for the week and so was bound to appear. There is no argument between them about the place or the time. This was, of course, shortly after the great success of *Beyond the Fringe* and the time when Peter Cook's Establishment Club was flourishing. Millicent Martin had done several *Tonight* appearances and was a natural choice. Ned 'booked' Lance Percival, Bernard Levin, Willie Rushton, Roy Kinnear and Kenneth Cope. Next, he involved a small army of writers, many of them journalists who saw possibilities in the show, and kept adding to them through the run of the programme as they saw what they might offer. Then he settled for a show with an audience in the studio (something we had all felt was an essential ingredient if it was to feel like an entertainment) and a loose, unstructured camera plan with no attempt to conceal the studio surround or the cameras themselves. Though, when I say 'unstructured', nobody should imagine there was not much art and skill to achieve the feeling of being unstructured at the pace at which the show was conducted.

So we set about the first pilot. It lasted nearly three hours. Ned records that Millie Martin, who sang the opening number then as she did throughout the life of the show, had taken off from Heathrow for a Spanish holiday before the programme was even finished in the studio. Bernard Levin's role in the pilot was to debate with twelve Conservative ladies whose appearance had been organised by Liz Cowley, one of our key *Tonight* producers. Some of the ladies wrote sternly after the experience that they wished to disassociate themselves from what had taken place and did not think it reflected the political impartiality they expected from the BBC. Sentiments that were to be repeated more heatedly on many occasions during the life of *TWTWTW*.

The pilot was recorded on 15th July. Donald, Grace and I viewed it a little later with Ned. Grace didn't care for it much – in her book she says she found it 'amateurish in its endeavours to seem casual, and politically both tendentious and dangerous'. I think the last remark must refer to Levin's joust with the Conservative ladies which Grace did not like at all. It was very long and very different; but talking about it afterwards, Donald and I were sure there was the germ of something really original in this first effort. We decided to make another pilot. That happened at the end of September and was very close to the shape of the programme as it first appeared on the air.

The first *That Was The Week That Was* went out live on Saturday, 24th November, 1962 from Studio 2 at the Television Centre, at 10.50 p.m. To Ron Grainer's jazzy tune, Millie Martin sang the opening lines:

> That Was The Week That Was
> It's over, let it go
> But what a week it was
> On the Stock Exchange the tea shares hit an all time low.
> A time study group's asking questions at court
> And who'll get his finger out when they report
> At Brussels Ted Heath has the world at his feet
> He got tariff reductions on kangaroo meat
> Sir Keith Joseph's lady gave the homeless a break
> They called to protest, she said – 'Let them eat cake'.

34

There was a wonderful sketch by Keith Waterhouse and Willis Hall about private soldiers putting themselves forward as parliamentary candidates, delivered by Roy Kinnear. Over a caption of a soldier in tropical kit, Roy said,

Policy. What is our policy? It is as follows. Number one – Commonwealth. Our Shadow Secretary for Commonwealth Affairs is Provost-Sergeant Macmichael J., who has done extensive tours of the Commonwealth under discussion and is in fact married to a wog bint. So what Jock does not know about these hot countries is not worth knowing. Get your knees brown, Lord Home.

And later,

I would like to introduce to you tonight our European expert, Fusilier Geordie Woollerton [caption: picture of Fusilier Woollerton, apparently drunk, clutching a bottle]. Without swinging the lamp, Geordie has had more hours in Minden than Mr Heath has had hot dinners. He outlines our Common Market policy quite simply and succinctly: you cannot trust the Krautheads. Also, if the price of a bottle of lager at Helga's Bar, Windelstrasse, is indicative of Common Market trading, you can stuff it.

We were on our way.

The budget for the show was £3,000 which, even in those days, was hardly munificent for an entertainment programme. The first audience research returns showed a viewing figure of around three and a half million. For late on a Saturday night we were well pleased. We expected no more for a show we were certain would not have mass appeal. We had not the faintest idea of what was to happen to the audience in the weeks ahead.

Simply getting the programme on the air was work enough. Ned used up most of his prepared material early on and the pressure, therefore, was to commission new ideas, interest more writers. Keith Waterhouse and Willis Hall, Peter Lewis and Peter Dobereiner, David Nobbs and Peter Tinniswood, Christopher Booker, Dennis Potter, Herbert Kretzmer – all were regular contributors to the programme. Gerald Kaufman (then a humble journalist) came up with a marvellously crafted piece on The Silent Men of Westminster – thirteen MPs who had not spoken in the House for ten or even fifteen years. That got us into trouble but it remains in the memory as a moment of pure joy. As does the feel of the studio every Saturday night. Mulled wine to get the audience in the mood, Ned's witty

35

warm-up, his return dash to the gallery, Millie's opening signature tune. The tension – would such and such a sketch work as it had done in rehearsal? How would the audience respond to this or that crack? Oh God! We're overrunning again! I had been directing and producing live television for eight years when we started *TWTWTW* but there was nothing quite like the intoxicating effect of that show in its early days.

How to try and convey what *That Was The Week That Was* was like to somebody who may never have seen it? It was, of course, in black and white since we were not yet in colour then. It was fast, directed by Ned at a cracking pace, with the cameras moving freely in vision. As to its content, it is impossible to conjure up words and performances of twenty-five years ago, but I picked up, at random, the script of the fourth edition broadcast in mid-December 1962 to see if it provoked memories. After the opening song from Millie Martin, there was a piece about Robert McNamara, who had just left the Ford Motor Company to become American Secretary of Defense. It took the form of a telephone conversation between him and Peter Thorney-croft, our own Minister of Defence, whose name he constantly mispronounced. The pay-off was: 'Don't worry, Thorneygold. If you carry on the way you're going, you'll soon be an underdeveloped country. Then you'll qualify for all the aid we can give you.'

There followed a piece about northern writers moving to the south to write about the north from a safe distance. Roy Kinnear doing a stand-up turn as a veteran comedian trying to catch up with the satire age, written by Waterhouse and Hall. A Lewis and Dobereiner sketch about trade union demarcation. Bernard Levin's confrontation that night was with a dozen farmers, his opening remark being the memorable, 'Good evening, peasants.' A piece based on that week's announcement of a new batch of Nobel prize winners. One of Millie Martin's brilliant 'patter' songs delivered at breakneck speed. Concluding with a mildly satirical piece about *The Times* – 'What a splendid thing it is to read a newspaper which eschews the trivial' – the opening quotation being, 'Now, here is an important and illuminating article in Monday's edition about Countess Anna-Maria Cicogna Volpi di Misurata and her friend, Countess Teresa Foscari Foscolo. It says that each recalls that as girls they were tomboys. And goes on – Countess Cicogna's tree climbing and other unfeminine early pursuits were the despair of her mother.'

A reasonably average edition of the programme, I suppose, with lots of laughs and a good deal of the unexpected. It was, of course, the combination of good writing and good performance that made *TW3*, at its best, such an electrifying experience and quite unlike any other programme before it and, maybe, since as well.

For me, with *Tonight* happening five nights a week (I had by now acquired the clearer role and more sensible title of Head of Tonight Productions) and a whole range of big documentaries to plan and oversee, the pattern of *TWTWTW* was straightforward. Ned got cracking on Tuesday, we talked occasionally through the week, I got a copy of the draft script on Friday night or early Saturday morning at home and then went into the afternoon rehearsals. By that time things had, as often as not, changed quite radically with fresh news coming in or new angles turning up; they would change again during the early evening and often right up to transmission, just as they did on *Tonight*. Ned and I had known each other at Oxford and worked together on *Tonight* for some years. He was meticulous in alerting me to anything he thought might be tricky and equally meticulous, after due discussion, in cutting material I thought would damage the show. It was a very good working relationship.

To my mind, the show really took off with the edition in early January 1963 which included the Consumers' Guide to Religion. It was a powerful piece, applying the language and standards of consumer guides to various religions and, therefore, calculated to offend nearly everybody. It was introduced by David Frost thus:

This week your Consumer Guide presents its reports on religions. Of the dozens of products on the market, we investigated the following five: Judaism, the Roman Catholic Church, the Protestant Church, Islam and Buddhism. We ruled out Hinduism. It embodies a caste system which we felt was alien to the British consumer. However, the Hindu does believe that animals have souls, every bit as good as human ones. In this sense, it could be said that every Englishman is a Hindu at heart.

We began by applying three basic tests:
a) What do you put into it?
b) What do you get out of it?
c) How much does it cost?

It was a long and carefully structured sketch but this extract, I think, gives an authentic flavour.

We next tested the Roman Catholic Church. The vigorous new ideas of this splendid corporation were largely pioneered by the previous group [Judaism]. But a superb sales organisation has enabled it to far outstrip the parent company with three hundred and forty million current users. Applying the tests we found:
a) What do you put into it? Belief in only one Godhead operating on a troika basis. Belief in the infallibility of Angelo

37

Guiseppe Roncalli now known as John XXIII, who was elected Head of the Organisation in 1958. We must stress here that the idea that the Head (or Pope as he is called) claims infallibility in all matters is a fallacy. The Pope cannot tell you which books are the best. His infallibility is strictly limited to matters of faith. He can only tell you which books you cannot read.

b) What do you get out of it? Principally, the new Christianity. The confessional mechanism is standard; the rule here is 'Don't', but if you must, confess as soon as possible afterwards. We found this very useful. A comprehensive 'Life and Death Advisory Service' is available from a priesthood unencumbered by family ties. With Roman Catholicism comes a guarantee that it is the *only true faith* and exclusive personal survival in heaven is assured. On the whole, we found this product deeply satisfying.

c) What does it cost? A drawback – it is very expensive. During a visit to Head Office in Rome, a rosary or aid to prayer cost 100 lire; devotional pictures 40 lire a time; we were charged 200 lire to see the catacombs; 300 lire to enter the Sistine Chapel (which is very dark) and a tour of the ante-rooms of St Peter's Basilica cost 300 lire in tips alone. We found it impossible to obtain a divorce.

Explaining its purpose, I wrote at the time, 'It originated from an idea that hardly a day goes by without some progressive cleric talking about bringing the Church down to earth, or making the faith available to ordinary people – attitudes which are in themselves no doubt sincere, but are increasingly likely to have religion promoted like any other product.'

The night of transmission Kenneth Adam, the Director of Television, happened to come into the room at Television Centre where we and the artists had some supper. I said to him, 'I think you ought to have a look at this. I am not asking for a decision because I have already decided it will go out. But it will cause a row and you ought to know what it's about.' He read it, turned on his heel and walked out without a word. Already, the programme was beginning to cause strain in high places.

Hugh Greene was the first to applaud its irreverence and said to us, 'Tell them I take my hat off to them', but some Governors were not happy. Quite early on there were tales of disquiet within the Conservative Party which was not really surprising since Conservative Ministers tended to be the targets. Even Donald occasionally became jittery. He wrote to me sharply after the edition which contained the Consumers' Guide to Religion. There were, he said, 'strong reasons for thinking that this item did have a place in the context of this programme'. But he was highly critical of the use of swear words and obscene gestures in a football sketch. He also wanted the programme to stick to the planned length of fifty minutes, whereas, being at the end of the evening, it tended to sprawl and overrun.

By the time we came to the end of the first season in April 1963, we had also been savaged by our own Light Entertainment colleagues within the Television Service. Six weeks into the programme, Kenneth Adam, clearly under pressure from senior heads of department, called a special meeting of programme makers to discuss *TWTWTW*. Kenneth, tall, bespectacled, episcopal in bearing, not the strongest man I have met (Malcolm Muggeridge, who had known Kenneth in Manchester in the 1930s, described him waspishly to me once as 'a man of straw, dear boy'), called on the colleagues to express their views. Tom Sloan, then Head of Light Entertainment, declared in a prolonged attack that, because of the programme, he had never been so ashamed of the BBC in the twenty-five years he had worked for it. It was not a cheerful occasion. We, by contrast, found ourselves the centre of a national interest that brought us between ten and twelve million viewers every Saturday night and made it, apparently, an occasion people did not wish to miss.

Distant echoes of worry continued to reach me through the summer of 1963. In his biography of Hugh Greene, Michael Tracey records that the Governors asked Stuart Hood and Kenneth Adam to appear before them in July to discuss future editorial control of the programme. Thus far, I reported direct to Donald Baverstock; neither Adam nor Hood, as far as I knew, were closely involved. But things were now to change. Tracey writes, 'Hood and Adam promised them [the Governors] that measures would be taken to prevent the return of smut, that the Deity would be spared in the future and that attacks on mere mortals would also have to be properly chosen as to target and judicious in execution.' That is his description of events of which I knew nothing.

What I did know was that 'smut' figured prominently at a press conference Stuart Hood held in Blackpool in September to launch the autumn programmes. Clearly, somebody felt that 'smut' had gravely marred the first run of *That Was The Week That Was*, though I confess that, the odd bad joke apart, it wasn't something that concerned me much. But the Chairman, Sir Arthur fforde, had been heard to say, 'It would be a pity to spoil the ship for a ha'porth of dirt,' and the charge stuck.

At his press conference Stuart said, 'The programme was criticised towards the end of the run for smut and this is something which we will be keeping a very sharp lookout for.' He added, 'The programme will be fifty minutes long and there will be a programme after it. We have seen what the mistakes in the last series were and it will be my hope that those mistakes will not be repeated. This does not mean it will not continue to act as a gadfly and when a gadfly stings you, it hurts.'

These remarks from Stuart, a strange, private man, were a puzzle to us. Stuart came from Edzell in the Howe o' the Mearns, and had the strong Angus lisp which marked his every statement. He had come up through the news tradition, after being a prisoner of war in Italy, the experiences of which formed the basis of his remarkable novel *Pebbles in My Skull*. But he was never content with the corporate life, lived through a difficult period working with Kenneth Adam above him and Donald Baverstock below him, and one day left to join Rediffusion and changed every aspect of his life, including his haircut. He was later to become a media guru figure, who advocated the restructuring of all broadcasting institutions.

Stuart's remark about the programme's length and particularly about its not being the last programme of the evening provoked Ned to write sardonically to me,

Can the Director General and the Director of Television be reminded that when they invented *That Was The Week That Was* they also invented a special time for it and that all their detailed planning was directed towards providing a show suitable for the closedown hour? No one would deny the success of their creation, but I do think in all friendship that one should point out the possibility of jeopardising that success if the programme is followed by a piece of trash like *The Third Man*.

It has to be admitted there was nothing good to be said of *The Third Man* (not the Carol Reed film), a second-rate piece of co-production work that could not even be safely buried late at nights on Saturdays. Within a month of our return to the air at the end of September, Stuart Hood wrote to me that Hugh Greene himself decided that *TW3* should be the last programme on Saturday evenings.

When we came back on the air, expectation ran too high. In fact, the first three or four shows weren't very good. They seemed contrived, strove too hard for effect. Perhaps also the atmosphere created in the country during the summer by the Profumo affair and the Denning Report that followed it was no longer so receptive to a programme like *TW3*. At all events, there were many complaints and few voices in support. It was criticised for being vulgar, smutty (again!), infantile, stupid, boring and dreary – quite a catalogue. Moreover, the nervousness at high levels in the BBC was character- ised by my having instructions 'to undertake a rather stricter

40

responsibility when the programme returns and Ned Sherrin and those most intimately concerned must also be aware of this'. Since all of us had worked our legs off to make the first series work, I found this sort of talk affronting. Grace Wyndham Goldie had been wheeled into the act. 'I was dismayed,' she wrote. 'I felt I was being asked to ride a tiger.' The Director General himself now became involved editorially and insisted on being consulted personally if I had any anxieties. He also came to the Television Centre every Tuesday morning for a detailed post-mortem of the previous Saturday's programme.

Doubts were endemic on *TW3*. Doubt certainly arose on 19th October when Christopher Booker wrote a piece about Lord Home's emergence as leader of the Conservative Party. The piece was written as if from Disraeli and was to be delivered by David Frost made up to look like Disraeli. It was certainly hard-hitting. 'My Lord,' it began, 'when I say that your acceptance of the Queen's commission to form an administration has proved, and will prove, an unmitigated catastrophe for the Conservative Party, for the constitution, for the nation, and for yourself, it must not be thought I bear you any personal ill will' – and so on in a similar vein for another two pages. It ended, witheringly:

If you are prepared at last to accept one lesson from history, let it be this. That of all the men who have held your office in the past sixty years, there have been but two kinds. Such Ministers as Mr Gladstone, my rival, Mr Lloyd George and Macmillan, your predecessor, who understood and mastered their office but grew jealous and held on too long. So that they were eventually hustled out, more vilified than they deserved, their exercise of power turned sour by over-use. And on the other hand, such tiny men as Eden, Bonar Law and Chamberlain, who may have promised much but proved no better in their offices than would the meanest of their supporters. For these men, history has no gratitude, no honour and no mercy. Reflect for a moment, my Lord, in this hour of your triumph, into which of these two categories your Ministry is likely to fall.

The item concluded with a typical Frostian crack, 'And so, there is the choice for the electorate, on the one hand Lord Home, on the other hand Mr Harold Wilson. Dull Alec versus Smart Alec.'

This was obviously strong stuff, but it seemed to me a proper item to include. If *That Was The Week That Was* were to exist at all as a vehicle for political comment, it must have the freedom to use occasions as they arose, like a cartoonist contributing to a newspaper.

You do not expect the cartoonist to balance his drawings or to restrain his pen as long as he makes his point – which he does by exaggeration. But clearly we had to expect a violent reaction to this item. I thought it right to ring Hugh Greene at home and he asked me to read the script to him. This was, of course, an impossible way of conducting a programme. Since he did not have the opportunity of reading the script himself, he kept asking me to go back and re-read certain sentences, and then would try and suggest cuts which ruined the sense. It was not fair to him or any of us. In the end, we broadcast the item. There were nearly six hundred calls and three hundred letters of protest. By now, the Governors were rattled and the Vice-Chairman, Sir James Duff, close to resignation. At the General Advisory Council meeting on 23rd October, at which both Sir Arthur fforde and Hugh Greene were, as usual, present, the programme was slated for being offensive, venomous and increasingly unfunny. Greene argued that the GAC should remember that *TW3* was only one part of the output, that it was in contrast to other programmes such as *Panorama, Gallery* and *Tonight.*

In November, out of the blue, the BBC announced that 'The present run of *That Was The Week That Was* will end on 28th December, 1963 and not continue, as had originally been intended, until the spring.' The reason given was that 1964 would be an election year and 'the political content of the programme, which has been one of its principal and successful constituents, will clearly be more and more difficult to maintain.' 'Election year? Tell that to the Marines,' one viewer wrote. This time the storm of protest was the other way round, seven hundred letters of protest at taking it off, only two hundred approving.

For Hugh Greene, the programme had caused many problems. He openly encouraged it; his biographer, Michael Tracey, records that '*TW3* was the only issue on which he would systematically go round the Board of Management asking each member what they had felt about the previous Saturday's programme,' and that has been confirmed since. By the second series, in which he had involved himself editorially, the pressures had become so heavy on him that time off at home with flu brought him to believe that the stability of the Board was threatened by it. It seems he then decided to take it off and so advised the Governors, to their evident relief. For us, it was a shock but perhaps not a complete surprise. Grace Wyndham Goldie has written that *TW3* died not so much from excessive censorship as from confusion of purpose with too many different instructions coming from too many people at too many levels. There certainly were a great number of us worrying over it during its second run. But I prefer to side with Ned Sherrin when he said that 'it was as though we had set out to build an aeroplane and come up with a rocket. When the rocket had run its course, it fizzled out.'

The programme had one moment of glory to come. On 22nd November, many of us were at the Dorchester for the annual Guild of Television Producers' Ball where *TW3* was to get an award. Suddenly, the whisper began to run around that President Kennedy had been shot and was badly hurt. *Tonight* had closed down ten minutes early, there were blank screens and then, when it was known Kennedy was dead, near pandemonium as people tried to contact senior politicians for obituary statements. When Ned had got his award, we travelled back to the Television Centre together. Clearly, we couldn't go ahead with the existing script which, not surprisingly, did not mention President Kennedy. But could we come up with an entirely new show in twenty-four hours and could we strike the right note? Ned has told how he spent half the night phoning writers and checking reactions. The next morning Donald told me he felt sure we should aim for something like a funeral oration; words were the stuff of *TW3* after all, and the occasion called for the best words we could find.

We had one run through and it was hard to hold back the tears. No jokes, no mulled wine tonight; we went on the air with a twenty-minute show with Millie Martin singing a poignant song written by Herbert Kretzmer and Dave Lee:

> A young man rode with his head held high,
> under the Texas sun,
> And no one guessed that a man so blessed
> would perish by the gun.
> A shot rang out like a sudden shout, and
> heaven held its breath,
> For the dreams of a multitude of men rode
> with him to his death.

In cold print, the words look a little maudlin today, but the show had tremendous impact that night, even greater the following day in the States. Donald had the bright idea of arranging for it to be recorded on the American line system so that it could be flown there next day. It was shown, many times, all over the States and Senator Hubert Humphrey called for the entire script to be entered in the Congressional Record.

It was back to party time for the last show on 28th December. Nostalgia was our theme as we re-ran some of the best items from the past. We knew by then that we had made broadcasting history and we enjoyed the feeling. But now we had a problem: where to go next?

43

When the election was out of the way, Greene was insistent that we should dream up something to take the place of *TW3*. Tonight Productions was by this time in a turmoil of activity. The reporters and film directors were enjoying attempting bigger ventures than *Tonight* film reports; Whicker and Gold and Philpott and Robertson were hard at work making fifty-minute documentaries. Tony Essex and Gordon Watkins were in the final stages of the massive twenty-six-part history of the Great War. *Tonight* had a new Editor in Derrick Amoore and a new presenter in Magnus Magnusson.

Now there was Saturday night to be filled again. We toyed with trying a late-night show five nights a week, but British viewers tend to go to bed at 10.30 p.m. on week days and there might just, we thought, be nobody there to watch. Discussing it with Donald (Ned was away in America) we hit on the notion of doing a programme the three weekend nights, that would give it some shape and continuity. But were we overstretching ourselves? How could we fill that amount of time properly weekend after weekend?

We both had a bad attack of nerves which was finally resolved over a dinner at Glenfinnan in the West Highlands where I was on holiday. And so, when Ned got back, it was on to the pilots again. We did six; when we started on the air, nobody liked *Not So Much A Programme* a lot. There were some excellent things in it – funny sketches, good talk, fresh faces in Eleanor Bron and John Wells, John Bird and John Fortune, Paddy Campbell and Michael Crawford. But it never caught the fine rapture of *TW3* – how could it? An error of judgement over a piece about the Duke of Windsor blew up in our faces and put paid to any future run in the autumn.

By the spring of 1965, my own career was to undergo a violent change. Donald Baverstock's position was being destroyed by management movement at the Television Centre. The previous year, Stuart Hood, the Controller of Programmes, had suddenly upped and gone to Rediffusion. Donald naturally expected to get his job. Nothing happened for some months. When he asked to see Hugh Greene he was told there was too much animosity against him in the Television Service. He could take up a new assignment in charge of Special Programmes, or he could run BBC-2, or he could go to Paris and run the office there. He was stunned and began to talk of leaving the BBC. I was tired and also ill at the time, and I felt he had been shabbily treated. I needed a break and it looked as if the time had come. Huw Wheldon's appointment as Controller of Programmes sealed matters for Donald. I decided to leave with him and set up our plate elsewhere.

4 BELOVED SCOTLAND

Were we the first independent producers? We were certainly among the first and, for a time, it was a chilling experience. In fact, it was almost like being members of a new species in an alien planet.

Tony Jay, who had left the BBC after an unhappy period as Editor of *Tonight* and then head of a ragbag production department, had established links with ICT (ICL as it now is), Britain's leading computer company at the time. ICT wanted expertise in handling press conferences and seminars. They wanted films to be made to explain to their own staff and customers what ICT computers and tabulators (yes, tabulators still existed then) could do for firms and institutions ranging from big Government departments to high-street grocers. In particular, they were about to introduce a new series of computers – the 1900 series – on which they pinned a great deal of faith. It had a wide range of applications and they saw it as being of critical importance to them as they struggled with IBM and other overseas giants to secure a reasonable share of the UK and world computer market.

Tony had made a contract with them. Donald and I joined him and we set ourselves up in modest offices in Kensington Church Street as Jay, Baverstock and Milne – JBM. Shortly afterwards, Elwyn Jones who, as Head of Drama Series at the BBC had been a key figure in the creation of *Z Cars* and was now a regular scriptwriter on its successor *Softly, Softly*, joined us too. Apart from our computer work for ICT we felt there must be work we could undertake for the BBC. After all, Donald had been in charge of BBC-1 for more than a year and both Tony and I had been heads of departments. Very shortly after we set up shop outside, we had a meeting at Television Centre with Huw Wheldon, the new Controller of Programmes, Mike Peacock, the new Controller of BBC-1 and David Attenborough, the new Controller of BBC-2. They were all new in their jobs, they were all friends of ours. But they were uncompromising, as I imagine I would have been in their place. The BBC was staffed, they said, to produce all the programmes it required; there was, therefore, no room for outside intervention or involvement, certainly on the scale

45

we had in mind. That door was shut. We retired stung, but not beaten.

We worked hard to learn about computer systems and applications and how to make sense of them in terms of films. We worked in ICT offices and factories. We worked with potential customers like mail order firms or Government departments. I found myself crossing Checkpoint Charlie in Berlin for the first time since I was a subaltern in the Gordon Highlanders in 1950 and walking down Unter den Linden to make contact with a man from Zeiss of Jena who were said to have an interest in ICT computers. On another occasion I found myself in a Swedish forest trying to interest a paper manufacturer in filming their ICT computers. We drafted plans for seminars and rehearsed and produced the executives who were to participate in them. I think we did a decent job for them.

We were also active in television, or tried to be. Elwyn was writing regularly for the BBC but he and I also set out to make a hugely ambitious, and only partly successful, programme about the Norman Conquest for the nine hundredth anniversary in 1966. I filmed the detail of the Bayeux Tapestry from a replica which was on display in Bournemouth – in the middle of the night because we were told that was the only time we could avoid inconveniencing the local citizenry. Jack Gold and I filmed scenes from the Battle of Hastings on the ground at Battle Abbey in pouring rain and with the smallest army imaginable – a dozen footmen and two mounted soldiers. We put it all together for Southern Television in their studios in Southampton and we called it *The Last Invasion*. The critics were not greatly impressed, but it earned the partnership a fair sum. When Jeremy Isaacs left *This Week* to go and edit *Panorama* for the BBC, Cyril Bennett, a witty and highly amusing man who was Controller of Programmes for Rediffusion, asked me to go and run *This Week* for a while. The money was highly attractive so I agreed, and there struck up friendships with Alastair Burnet and George Ffitch, and Cyril himself. I also ran their political programme called *Division*, where the late-night hour caught many politicians on the wrong foot, not least George Brown.

We began, midway through 1966, to be tickled by the forthcoming review of the ITV franchises. It was widely recognised that Granada, who had for ten years enjoyed the franchise for the whole of the north country except for Tyne Tees and Border, were bound to have Yorkshire carved away from them and a new company created to operate the Yorkshire franchise. There was feverish activity: Lord Goodman was invited to lead one faction, the Telefusion people (more solidly based in the north) led another. There was fierce competition as to who could sign up this Yorkshire knight or that

Yorkshire company. Donald and I got sucked into this maelstrom – as did many other broadcasters. There was hardly a senior member of the BBC whose name was not being written down covertly on applications to the IBA. There were meetings here, there and everywhere.

I realised after a while that this was not for me. I knew little of Yorkshire; I felt I had little to contribute to whichever group emerged triumphant. But Scotland was different. I came from Scotland, I felt deeply involved with the country and Scottish Television was thought to be vulnerable. It was not many years since Roy Thomson, that well-known Canadian entrepreneur, had picked up the STV franchise without opposition, and even fewer years since he had injudiciously told the world that he had acquired 'a licence to print money'. What's more, everybody I spoke to in Scotland told me STV's programmes were awful.

I talked to Alastair Burnet, then Editor of *The Economist*, over an early-morning dram. He was sure *The Economist* would come in and he was very happy to participate personally in drawing up the application. I talked to David Astor, then Editor of the *Observer*, and his General Manager, Tristram Jones; they were keen. I talked to Esmond Wright, then Professor of Modern History at Glasgow University, but also a man with a lot of experience of political broadcasting for BBC Scotland. Gradually we put together a consortium. I happened to be with Ludo Kennedy at his wife Moira's birthday party the night Jo Grimond gave up the leadership of the Liberal Party. Ludo rang him there and then, and he said yes, he would consider becoming Chairman of our consortium. Others spoke to Tom Taylor (now Lord Taylor of Gryfe) who was then at the Scottish Co-Operative and Wholesale Society and he agreed that his name might go forward as Managing Director. (Later, Tom became a Director of STV, so he arrived there by a more direct route!) With Grimond as Chairman, Esmond as Vice-Chairman, Tom as Managing Director and me as Director of Programmes and with the finance secured, we seemed to have a genuine chance of wresting the franchise from STV. We brought in Dame Jean Roberts, a former Lord Provost of Glasgow, to add west coast weight. Alastair and I wrote the introduction and programme pages of the application. The financial and engineering pieces looked solid to me.

We attended in force for the IBA interview in the Old Brompton Road. The Scottish member of the IBA, McFarlane Gray, was thought by all of us to be sympathetic to STV and neither he nor, I thought, Lord Hill, the IBA Chairman, made any bones about us being interlopers. Charles Hill has since told me that he took a particular dislike to Dame Jean, who did set about STV in the most uncompromising manner. Moreover, Hill felt, he told me, that STV had taken steps to burnish their image by promoting Bill Brown to be Managing Director shortly before the franchise renewal and by bringing in Francis Essex (the brother of the Tony who worked on *Tonight*) as Director of Programmes. I have a feeling that we came within a whisker of unseating them, but we didn't. I was deeply disappointed and returned my thoughts to the south wondering what to do next.

The Yorkshire franchise, meantime, had gone the way of the Telefusion group and Donald was, therefore, out in the cold. The IBA then engineered a merger of interests and within a few weeks a number of us, I am told, were propositioned to join the new Yorkshire Television company as Director of Programmes. I certainly was but declined. The job finally went to Donald Baverstock and I was delighted for him, though his move meant that JBM was fast disintegrating.

I refused the Yorkshire job principally because I was discussing going back to the BBC. One summer's afternoon Huw Wheldon and I were playing golf at the Royal Mid-Surrey – he with his strange corkscrew stance and diabolically accurate putting – when he said to me, 'Why don't you come back and run Lime Grove? Things aren't going too well in Current Affairs.' But I had the taste of Scotland in my mouth. I knew Andrew Stewart, the incumbent Controller, was due to retire soon. Moreover, I had itched for a move north ever since applying for the job of Head of Programmes in Scotland when I was Editor of *Tonight*. That application produced strange responses. James Kemp, the News Editor in Scotland and a man prone to see conspiracy all around him, was said to have written my name on a slip of paper and deposited it with his bank for later proof that the job had been fixed for me. At the appointments board in Glasgow, Andrew Stewart catechised me sternly about the ballads, about Scottish history, about my recent lack of experience of Scotland. But Stuart Hood, Controller of Programmes for Television and a fellow Scot, was also on the board and there was an impasse. Andrew would not have me – 'a young man in a hurry' was the phrase reported back to me. Stuart would have no other. For nine months there was an interregnum until Hugh Greene, having failed to transport Leonard Miall into the job, loomed over one James Millar, a Glaswegian, at that time living a peaceful existence in the French West African Service in Bush House. A reluctant James was despatched north to work with an equally reluctant Andrew Stewart.

So I wanted to return to Scotland. Nowadays, the Governors of the BBC have established a fairly elaborate system for appointing Controllers. Then, I was seen by the National Governor for Scotland, May Baird, and by Hugh Greene alone. Hugh then phoned me and

BELOVED SCOTLAND

confirmed that the Board had agreed my appointment. I was to rejoin
the BBC on 1st October, 1967 but, since Andrew did not retire till the
following July, it was agreed I should spend the intervening months
familiarising myself with Scotland again. Not a wholly agreeable
prospect over a period as long as nine months, but there seemed no
alternative.

The news of my appointment caused a predictable stir. Allen
Wright, the arts correspondent of the *Scotsman*, wrote under a
banner headline: 'MILNE: A TIGER AT THE GATES. *TW3* man is new
controller of BBC Scotland. Headlines like this, announcing Alasdair
Milne's appointment, must have sent shivers through some people.
Apparently, the last bastion of Lord Reith's decorous empire was
being stormed.' So I toured all the buildings. I met as many people as
I could. I visited transmitters – in those days transmitters were
manned whereas now they are nearly all automatically operated.
They were run on a strictly hierarchical basis, too. When, for
instance, I had admired the gleaming brass of the old medium-wave
transmitter at Burghead, polished to a brilliance any naval seadog
would have been proud of, lunch was served in the wardroom, as it
were, with only the Engineer-in-Charge and his assistant present.
Back in London, I was given an introduction to an exiled Scot who
started to improve my rudimentary Gaelic. We began to house hunt
in the Glasgow area though it seemed there was plenty of time for that
kind of decision.

Events then took a sudden and wholly unexpected turn. Hugh
Greene discovered that Andrew Stewart had agreed to become a
Director of Scottish Television, the commercial opposition, on his
retirement the following summer. There was a barely concealed
antipathy between the two men and Hugh fell upon Andrew like
Sennacherib; retirement was hurried forward. I was now due to take
over BBC Scotland (one of my first acts was to add the word Scotland
to BBC on the façade of Queen Margaret Drive) on 1st January,
1968.

Which, being an ass, I did. New Year's Day remains a very public
holiday in Scotland. Indeed, like the majority verdict for juries, we
have recently exported it to England. At just thirty-eight, I was the
youngest Regional Controller in the BBC's history and I confess I
felt it. I flew to Glasgow on New Year's Eve, went to the traditional
Hogmanay programme which that night came from Cumbernauld
New Town and next morning John Maclean, who has been driver to a
generation of Scottish Controllers, collected me early from the Lorne
Hotel. I climbed over the recumbent bodies and went to Broadcasting House in Queen Margaret Drive where there wasn't even a
commissionaire to be seen. My secretary, Elizabeth Sutter, who was

49

to guide me over the next five years, was there. I had asked James Millar, the Head of Programmes, and Douglas Stewart, his deputy, to join me for lunch. Otherwise, it was a day for solitary meditation.

I came home to Scotland at a time of great political upheaval. The son of an Aberdeen surgeon and an Edinburgh mother, I was born in India where my father ran a hospital for fourteen years, but was brought up from an early age, like a number of my cousins whose parents were also overseas, by my grandparents in Edinburgh. My grandfather had been Headmaster of Heriot's, a famous Edinburgh school, for more than twenty years. He was author of *Clark's Logarithms* which was in common use in schools, certainly till after the war, was a senior figure in the city and an elder of the kirk in Morningside. Both he and my father shared the east coast Scots' contempt and dislike of the west and, above all, Glasgow. My grandfather was there once in 1903 and warned me sternly against having anything to do with the place. My father took me there for the Empire Exhibition of 1936 in Bellahouston Park and vowed he would never go back. And here we were about to live and work in Glasgow!

The political excitement at the time of my return to Scotland stemmed from Winnie Ewing's victory in the Hamilton by-election in 1967 for the Scottish National Party. The youth of the country seemed fired by nationalist aspirations. The cry went up that neither of the major parties had done much for Scotland as her major industries such as shipbuilding and steel went into terminal decline. North Sea oil was on the horizon – 'Scotland's oil' – and only a reversal of the Act of Union of 1707 and a separate, independent Scotland would satisfy her people's longings. That was the SNP case and it was heady stuff indeed. At every rally the Lion of Scotland and the bagpipe cried out for freedom.

Three months after my arrival, we produced a big two-hour programme called *Where Do We Go From Here?*, the theme being the impact of the Hamilton by-election and its effect on Scottish politics. Two hours before transmission, I had a phone call from Tam Dalyell, younger then but no less radical in his views, who warned me that if we went ahead with the programme 'the effect would be more drastic than Hiroshima'. We did go ahead and the building stood. But there were great political strains. I was invited to a friendly lunch by Sir Gilmour Menzies Anderson, Chairman of the Conservative Party in Scotland, and George Younger, an old friend and then a young MP, to be given a polite wigging; the Labour Party was even more jittery, and I had some bitter arguments with some of their MPs. Both parties clearly believed there was a strong SNP cell in Queen Margaret Drive – which at least made an interesting deviation from their normal judgement of the BBC. Still, the nationalist tide ran strong. There was loose talk of Jo Grimond becoming President of the SNP. Ludo Kennedy wrote that he had a vision of an independent Scotland as he walked down Princes Street in Edinburgh. I was counselled by some to consider how much better Scottish broadcasting would be if we broke away from the pestilential English. Norway, Denmark, even the Faroes were quoted to me as excellent examples of independent small nations with strong indigenous broadcasting operations. Not, I am sure, that my interlocutors had seen much of Norwegian or Danish television, even less did they understand the financial structures and pressures of the broadcasting world. But wild words were freely spoken and the SNP fever ran strongly on through the 1970 election. Though it was not until 1974 that they could field a decent mini-coachful of MPs for the Thursday night train home to Scotland.

Politics apart, there was a vast amount to learn and much to do. One had, first, to try to understand Scotland's relationship with the rest of the BBC. Some years later I came across the wise words of one Hywel Davies, a much loved and respected Welsh Head of Programmes, in a lecture he gave about the role of the regions in British broadcasting. (Scotland and Wales are, of course, nations: 'regions' is a BBC form of shorthand!) He said:

At worst, a region can look upon itself as the repository of the resigned second-rate and the restive first-rate; at best, as a lively centre for people of involvement and ambition. One way or another, it relates itself to the metropolis; and a proper relationship between London and the regions is of vital importance. The worst picture one can draw is of an unhappy family whose members dislike, distrust and resent each other; of London looking upon the regions as a necessary but expensive nuisance, full of people whose methods are amateurish, whose judgements are irresponsible, whose attitude generally is chauvinistic; hempen homespuns swaggering near the cradle of the fairy queen; people whose demands are insatiable and any satisfaction of them a diversion of effort from the main task of the organisation. Or of the regions looking upon London with envy and resentment because its people are superior in their attitudes, maliciously derisive in their criticism, totally lacking in understanding and sympathy. But the success of the BBC is founded on a high standard of professionalism and a deep sense of involvement; and both qualities are there to be admired and emulated.

And in another memorable phrase, 'The things we [in the regions] are broadly concerned with are the excitement and frustration, the satisfaction and resentment, the inspiration and the vanity of those who are not at the seeming heart of things. We are concerned with the joys and the tribulations of being off-centre.'

Bearing in mind that no true Scot would accept we were not at the heart of things, we certainly had our fair share of the 'resigned second-rate'. For a start, I thought the Scottish television news poorly done. Within three months, we made a move to link up the Glasgow, Edinburgh and Aberdeen studios to combine in *Reporting Scotland*. The facilities in these small studios were poor, all of them still in black and white and very cramped. But we had a big, new colourised studio in Glasgow, capable of the most complex drama and light entertainment programmes and we had excellent technicians and some first-class cameramen and film editors. It seemed to me that we should concentrate on offering to the television networks programmes in the high-cost areas of drama, light entertainment and documentary. We already had outlets in these and other programme areas on the radio networks. It was essential, though, that Scottish work should be seen on the national networks, and not just through the one instance of *The Kilt Is My Delight*; though the demands of our mainstream work for Scotland did not leave us much room for a high volume of network programming. The work, therefore, had to be distinctive and very well done. We had, too, to rebuild a mutual trust with London – echoes of Hywel Davies again. Scots are rightly sore at the occasional insensitivities of the English ('The Queen of England' is a favourite red rag north of the border) though they can make a fetish out of it. There had been one or two 'invasions' by English production crews that drove Andrew Stewart near to closing the border to the rest of the BBC. The atmosphere between BBC Scotland and London was not happy. Indeed, at my very first meeting of the Broadcasting Council for Scotland, which has very considerable powers within the BBC structure, being, in effect, in charge of the standards and taste of programmes made for Scotland, I had to sit and listen while their suspicions of English manipulation drove them to give May Baird a roasting for not consulting them about my appointment. I knew all the people in London; I set out to try and repair the relationships and I think things improved in time.

When our first major serial, an adaptation of Lewis Grassic Gibbon's *Sunset Song* reached BBC-2 screens alongside a number of well-made plays and documentaries for both networks, I felt we had made our mark. In the mid-seventies, the relationship with London was again to go through a damaging change and I, unhappily, was in the middle of that. Like all family connections, this relationship needs constant tending.

As Controller, I was naturally expected to travel widely throughout Scotland and appear often at public occasions. There were great ceilidhs in the islands, noisy public meetings when the clamour from small communities for immediate television provision nearly overwhelmed us. The big set pieces – extremely formal dinners in the Merchants Hall in Edinburgh – could be very daunting, but our first reception by the Lord High Commissioner in Holyrood was an unforgettable experience. Lord Reith was Lord High Commissioner, representing the Queen, at the General Assembly of the Church of Scotland.

For those not familiar with Scottish custom, it should be explained that the General Assembly of the Kirk is the parliament of the Church of Scotland and is held in Edinburgh once a year in the month of May. It is presided over by the Moderator, who holds office from one Assembly to the next, when a new Moderator is appointed. Throughout the period when the General Assembly is in session, the Lord High Commissioner holds court in Holyrood Palace and normally attends the Assembly's deliberations at some point during the day. Since he or she represents the Queen, the Lord High Commissioner is attended by a high degree of formality; a Purse Bearer accompanies him everywhere, he is addressed always as 'Your Grace' and in every way is treated with vice-regal respect. It was rumoured about the town that one day Lady Reith made to get out of the official car before him and Reith thrust her aside saying, 'Woman, do you not understand that I am the Queen's representative in Scotland?'

For Reith, this office was made to measure. There was an early moment of anxiety when Bill Jackson, the Head of Engineering, reported to me that they had wired him for sound to speak with a neck microphone – only to discover that he had had a pacemaker inserted and alternative arrangements had speedily to be made to avoid the resultant interruptions. When it came to the Lord High Commissioner's reception at Holyrood, it was magnificent: it looked as if this was the nearest Reith could get to his avowed ambition to have been Viceroy of India. He himself looked splendid. He wore green strapped trews, a gorgeous tunic and a great feathered bonnet on his head. He towered above all his guests, seeming at least seven feet tall. By sharp contrast, I saw sitting in a window seat an extraordinary figure: bald-headed, with a full white beard to his waist, dressed in full Highland dress of a peculiarly Victorian nature, hung with dirks and studded with cairngorms. Introducing myself, I asked tentatively who he was. 'I,' said he, 'am the MacNab of MacNab.' And proceeded to tell me that he had aspired to be the MacLeod of MacLeod, being a relative of that family and indeed had at one point changed his name to MacLeod in expectation; an expectation not fulfilled because Dame Flora chose her grandson to succeed her as the Chief of MacLeod.

Our own entertaining in Queen Margaret Drive had its moments. Lord Hill, the new Chairman of the BBC, arrived on a state visit and I did my best to arrange a good dinner party for him. In his broadcasting memoirs, Charles touched upon this visit: 'Alasdair Milne, the Controller, clearly eyes me cautiously. He was, after all, the proposed programme chief of the Jo Grimond group which did not get the Scottish ITV contract. Dinner of local worthies. Not a great success. Mrs Alasdair Milne tried to pump me about the BBC and my intentions.' Having overhead that particular exchange, I can record that Sheila simply asked him some questions about himself and his past. 'All in my book, my dear,' said Charles, 'called *Both Sides of the Hill*. Get it in any public library.' I fear he was rather bored.

By contrast, I wanted to give a dinner for the cast of *Dr Finlay's Casebook* which was being recorded in Glasgow for the first time; previously, the filming had all been done round Callander ('Tannochbrae') but the programmes had been recorded in London. Andrew Cruickshank, Bill Simpson and Barbara Mullen were all enthusiastic and it was arranged for a Monday night. We worked diligently at the guest list because Elizabeth, my secretary, who knew about actors and their superstitions, drummed into me that we must under no circumstances end up with thirteen at table. If we did, she said, the actors would all get up and walk out. Through various accidents, by 6.30 on the evening of the Monday, we were down to thirteen again. I saw a producer minding his own business in the corridor, ordered him to come to dinner and welcomed our guests, peaceful in the knowledge that the numbers at least were right. Until Barbara Mullen, who played the inestimable Janet, walked in alone: 'Where's your husband?' I asked in a strangled voice. 'Oh, he's filming seals in Harris,' said she. Somehow, they never noticed we were down to thirteen again.

There were other joys. I learnt Gaelic from a marvellous teacher, a Skyeman, 'Jake' MacDonald, former Senior Tutor in Gaelic at Jordanhill in Glasgow, and so was able to enjoy occasions which had passed me by before, and to understand what my Gaelic Department was up to! As an enthusiastic piper from my boyhood on, I was once more back in the mainstream of Scottish playing and musical study. I was lucky enough to become friendly with the late John MacFadyen, a great player and certainly the best piobaireachd player I ever heard. When he died tragically early, some friends of his and I formed a trust in his memory which is active in promoting the playing and understanding of *ceòl mór* – the great music, the classical music of the Highland bagpipe. In short, I immersed myself in Scotland.

Then, in September 1972, when I had been in Scotland a little less than five years, Huw Wheldon told me in his garden at Richmond that David Attenborough wanted to give up his job as Director of Programmes at the Television Centre and, as it were, return to the jungle. Would I take the job? Paul Fox was then a vigorous Controller of BBC-1, Robin Scott had been running BBC-2 well since he came over from Radio 1. 'Is there a proper job as Director of Programmes?' I asked Huw. Of course, he said, a very big job. He urged me to take it on. Back home in Scotland I had long days of doubt. I loved my job, I was only just beginning to feel that we were getting things straight. I did not want people to feel I had used Scotland as a stepping-stone because I never had any such intention. We had a fine house set beautifully in the Campsie Hills outside Glasgow. Kirsty, our daughter, was only eight and had just gone to school in Glasgow. Ruairidh and Seumas were at school at Winchester but were used to travelling back and forward. Sheila and I had lots of friends and life was full of variety. On the other hand, I was not yet forty-three. Could I really see myself, from the point of view of the BBC or, indeed, from my own, staying on as Controller Scotland for another seventeen years? It seemed we must return south. And so I told Huw, though the decision tore my heart.

5 HARD TIMES

The BBC Television Service I returned to in January 1973, and where I worked for nearly ten years, had gone through a period of great change. During Donald Baverstock's time as Assistant Controller of Programmes and then when he was chief of BBC-1 and Michael Peacock of the new BBC-2, there was a clear recovery of confidence and a consequent flowering of programme activity. New comedy series like *Steptoe and Son, Till Death Us Do Part* and *Dad's Army* were created and won quick audience appreciation. In current affairs, *24 Hours* took over from *Tonight* after its demise in 1965 and was, itself, succeeded by the bold and complex venture of *Nationwide. Panorama* was joined by *Gallery* for more extensive treatment of topical matters and a whole new range of programmes such as *Man Alive* sprang up on BBC-2.

In particular, the BBC hit a rich seam in its drama output. Sydney Newman had been brought in from ABC in the early sixties as Head of Drama, with a reputation for backing new, contemporary drama in *Armchair Theatre*. The controversies surrounding many of his *Wednesday Play* productions (*Cathy Come Home, Up the Junction* etc) were matched by the way in which popular drama series such as *Maigret, Z Cars* and *Dr Finlay's Casebook* enriched the schedules.

Above all, the arrival of a second BBC channel in 1964 gave all production departments and producers room to breathe, to spread their wings and try new programme formats and experiment with fresh ideas. As the audience share between the BBC and ITV gradually settled at around 50:50, the traumas of the 70:30 ratio of the late fifties were soon forgotten.

The management which took over the running of the Television Service in 1965 – Huw Wheldon, David Attenborough, Michael Peacock – had vast practical experience of television production which their immediate predecessors, Donald Baverstock apart, did not. Wheldon had produced and presented children's programmes after joining the BBC from his post as Publicity Officer for the Festival of Britain and a spell of doing similar work for the BBC. He had worked extensively with Sir Brian Horrocks on several series on

56

the Second World War and on battles generally. He had edited and presented the first regular television programme on the arts, *Monitor*, for eight years and had built up a team which included such famous names as John Schlesinger and Ken Russell, Humphrey Burton and Patrick Garland, and whose loyalty to him and reputation in handling their material was unqualified.

David Attenborough not only had a number of series of his *Zoo Quest* natural history programmes behind him (who can forget the first sight of the Komodo dragon advancing squatly but surely on the goat David and his people had hung in the trees for him?), he had also had wide experience in producing other talks series – J. B. Priestley on books, for instance.

Michael Peacock had edited *Panorama* with a sure hand for a number of years, had brought new life to Television News as its Editor, and had worked in Outside Broadcast Television experimenting with new formats such as *In the Lion's Den*.

They were a formidable trio. And when Peacock left to be the Managing Director of the new London Weekend Television consortium in 1968, there was the burly figure of Paul Fox ready to step into his shoes as Controller of BBC-1.

Huw Wheldon brought to his job as Controller of Programmes and later, when Kenneth Adam retired, as Managing Director, a true feeling for leadership and an enormous zest for programme making. He talked much about 'command' and having served with distinction as an infantry officer throughout the war, he knew what he was talking about. He knew a good programme when he saw one and he also knew that good producers did not grow on trees (a favourite expression of his) but had to be nurtured and cherished. With his gargantuan laugh and his inexhaustible fund of stories, he exuded confidence, which was just what the Service needed and relished. Some were surprised that he was passed over as Director General when Hugh Greene retired and Charles Curran succeeded; in his book, Charles Hill says that he was the only member of the Board who was enthusiastic for Wheldon and attributes their antagonism to Huw's loquacity. It was certainly true in my own experience that few Governors warmed to Huw. They seemed to find his personality overwhelming. He responded cheerfully by referring to them habitually as 'the sodding Governors'.

David Attenborough, first as Controller of BBC-2 and later as Director of Programmes, was the ideal counterpart to Huw: equally loud of laughter, equally irrepressible, equally confident. Charles Hill, who visibly doted on David, says, 'It was generally agreed [amongst the Governors] that Attenborough was a man of unusual brilliance.' So the leadership was strong and confident. And though the BBC was not awash with money (I remember Hugh Greene complaining as far back as 1964 when the licence fee was increased from £4 to £6, that it was too little and too late), nevertheless, inflation was low and every year there was some room for expansion, for programme development. Drama and comedy were still very strong. Major documentary series emerged when Attenborough, with great persistence, wooed Kenneth Clark to undertake *Civilisation*; and the tradition was developed by Aubrey Singer's Features Group with Alistair Cooke's *America* and 'Bruno' Bronowski's *The Ascent of Man*.

There were the inevitable crises. There was one in 1967 when the BBC Chairman, Lord Normanbrook, died and Harold Wilson switched Charles Hill from the chairmanship of the IBA to the BBC: 'It's like sending Rommel to take command of the Eighth Army,' commented David Attenborough. There was an even bigger one when the blazing row broke out with Harold Wilson in 1971 over the film *Yesterday's Men* and the questions put to him by David Dimbleby about the money he received for his book *The Labour Government 1964–70*. I was in Scotland at the time and so not closely involved; but Huw Wheldon told me that Charles Curran, the DG at the time, was called to the phone from a Television Centre dinner he and Huw were attending to speak to a fulminating Lord Goodman, Wilson's lawyer. They agreed to meet at Goodman's flat to discuss the crisis, the only problem being that neither Curran nor Wheldon knew the number of the flat, and spent the small hours wandering up and down Portland Place with a torch in search of the blessed Arnold. With hindsight, though, we can see that *Yesterday's Men* marked a watershed in the BBC's relationship with politicians and government. The Conservatives' disenchantment with the BBC can fairly be dated to Suez and the critical, sometimes jeering, tone of programmes like *That Was The Week That Was*. Labour's shock, on coming to power, at finding the BBC allowing criticisms of them as sharp as anything that had been directed at the Tories, was profound. *Yesterday's Men* compounded that feeling and was a major step along the road to today's perception by the politicians of 'the media' as a hostile political force rather than a necessary channel for dissemination of news and participation in political debate.

None of these crises, however, seemed to affect the onward, confident march of the Television Service. When Attenborough departed to return to programme making, I found morale at the Television Centre still high, but there were signs of trouble ahead. Money really was tight now and inflation was rising. ITV, able of course to manipulate its advertising rates to its best advantage, seemed to enjoy significant percentage increases every year whereas the Television Service was standing still financially, if not in fact going backwards. This was to be the pattern throughout the seventies and one which caused us increasing pain.

Huw Wheldon had told me that being Director of Programmes was a proper job. I confess that at first I was not at all sure he was right. In Paul Fox and Robin Scott, we had two highly experienced Channel Controllers and the production departments effectively worked to them because they dispensed the money and the airtime. Huw Wheldon, as Managing Director, presided over the Service and represented it in the higher councils of the BBC, but the Director of Programmes – it seemed to me – was a kind of readily available wet nurse for the programme staff, who found himself giving interminable annual interviews, chairing the weekly programme review meeting but otherwise was ground between the upper and the nether millstones. For the first few months, I did not really enjoy myself and wondered again at the wisdom of leaving Scotland.

But almost immediately we were plunged into preparing for the Annan Committee hearings. There had been committees of inquiry into broadcasting before, of course – Ullswater, Beveridge and Pilkington. Now, once again, the roots of broadcasting were to be dug up and examined under the microscope. In particular, we in television were enjoined to prepare the third of the BBC's many submissions – the one on programme policy. Huw was very keen to involve as many of the production staff as possible. To that end, he convened a series of meetings on sixteen successive Monday evenings, as I recall. Huw was a man of known frugality, and so the menu was the same every Monday – a trout, beer and an apple. The fare did begin to drag after a while. He took a special delight in introducing producers from other departments to each other feeling certain that they would probably never have met before. It troubled him not at all that he often got their names wrong himself. And since he was a voluble conversationalist, he found it very difficult to refrain from haranguing the troops. It has to be said that they did not, some brave souls apart, have much opportunity to speak. As against that, I do believe that those who came to these strange soirées felt they had some small part in the creation of the programme document.

When it was finished, we thought it a reasonably good attempt at explaining our programme policies though there was widespread apprehension that much of the BBC's evidence to Annan was smug and dull. We were not, however, prepared for the scenes that occurred when the Annan Committee, which comprised some familiar broadcasting names like Marghanita Laski and Phillip Whitehead, and also my old friend and colleague Tony Jay, came to the Television Centre for their first formal meeting. Things did not go well. For the first hour, Huw went on his own with Michael Checkland (then Chief Accountant, Television) in support. We programme people were invited to join the meeting after a short coffee break at 11.00 a.m., but when Mike came out of the room and I asked him how it had gone, he said, 'Not well'.

It appeared that Huw had tried to lecture Lord Annan on the principles of broadcasting and that Noel Annan had not responded well and had spoken sternly about what he saw as management deficiencies at the BBC. *Pari passu*, that had not gone down well with Huw. Our programme session passed off reasonably well, though members of the Committee appeared to think that we were weak on the news and current affairs front. ITV, they thought, was much better, especially on news.

It was difficult to comment helpfully on such judgements. The lunch that followed was a genuine disaster. Huw had thrown all caution to the winds and laid on the most exotic fare. Lord Annan and attendant members of the Committee munched their lobster but in a mood that registered their disenchantment with the way BBC Television was being run. At the least, they reserved judgement.

When the report was published, it came as something of a shock to the BBC. Beveridge had been warm, even though Selwyn Lloyd's minority report eventually brought about the breaking of the monopoly. Pilkington had flattered the BBC, some thought to the point of embarrassment, while cheerfully flaying ITV. Annan was altogether cooler about the BBC and its performance, particularly in the current affairs field. We were treated to phrases like: 'We agreed that some affliction of feebleness had struck the current affairs output. Time and again people in the BBC attributed this palsy to the effect of the row over *Yesterday's Men*.'

The Committee then warmed to their work. We were told that we were disinclined to go in for investigative journalism, that Fred Friendly, the American broadcaster, was particularly scornful of the BBC's handling of news and of its failure to examine in depth the origin of the situation in Northern Ireland, that the quality of individual programmes was patchy, sometimes dull and, on occasions, 'superficial to the point of banality'. They said they had the impression that the fault lay at the top. The younger generation of producers, Annan claimed, was bubbling with ideas which were not allowed to surface. He felt that the Television Service had 'lost that clear sense of direction which it had in days gone by'. For good measure, they announced that 'at times the Television Service was in danger of forgetting that BBC-1 and BBC-2 existed to serve the

60

public. Here is an instance [quoth they] of that tendency detected by Professor Burns [*The BBC: Public Institution and Private World*] of the ethos of professionalism replacing to a large extent the ethos of public service in the BBC. We felt,' they thundered, 'this could be seen in the Television Service.'

Huw was furious. The rest of us certainly bruised. But, meantime, dramatic things had taken place at the Television Centre. One day shortly after I arrived back from Scotland, Paul Fox came to tell me he was leaving to join Yorkshire Television. I knew the job was falling vacant as Donald Baverstock was obviously being eased out by Yorkshire. But I never thought Paul would grab the fly. Huw gave Paul a military dressing-down and then Paul left. Huw was disconsolate. David had gone, now Paul, a robust and excellent Controller of BBC-1, had defected. I told him that I would like to act as Controller of BBC-1 for a while as well as being Director of Programmes (the same situation as was arranged for Michael Grade in 1986). Above all, the double function would give me the opportunity to learn about the Service at the coal face because I would have to handle the autumn Offers Meetings for BBC-1. After a word with Charles Curran, Huw agreed.

To this day, though there have been subtle refinements over the years, the Television Service depends on the Offers Meetings. These take place in the early autumn. They involve all twenty or so production departments and they are conducted separately by both Channel Controllers. At these meetings the departmental heads put forward their plans for continuing existing strands (another run of *Bergerac*, another series of *Mastermind*) and they draw across the Controllers new programme ideas, though these will have been bruited and discussed informally over many months previously as well. These formal Offers Meetings are fully minuted and agreements reached as to finance and resource allocation.

The Programme Planning Department are present at all of these meetings. It is their job to record the Controllers' decisions and then run the financial and resource allocations through the computers to present a clear picture of the outcome. At the end of the year, the ritual 'Cutting of the Plan' takes place. At that time, the Controllers have to confront the truth that their programme aspirations probably cannot be met by the available resources. When that exercise is finished, 'The Plan' forms the basis for the next production year of BBC Television (and, nowadays, with lead times being so far ahead, for some projects for the next three years or more) and hence for its transmission plan also. Of course, things continually change and alter in the creative complexity of making some ten thousand programmes a year, nearly all of them different from each other, but the framework has lasted for many years and remains a solid and sensible one.

With Paul Fox gone, I embarked on my first round of Offers Meetings carrying the added authority of Director of Programmes for the whole service. The drama meetings, especially, brought home to me how things were going adrift. We simply could not any longer afford the budgets and the resources that Shaun Sutton, the Head of Drama, and his departmental heads thought necessary to do their job properly. Naturally, they overestimated to cover themselves and, equally naturally, the planners pared back the estimates to what they thought reasonable. But it was clear to me that in this very high-cost area of production we were slipping backwards. In cutting our coat, we were beginning to depart from the numbers of programmes set in the more affluent sixties, if not yet from the standards established in those years.

The pressures became increasingly acute as inflation soared and the Labour Government introduced its incomes policy. Although the BBC was not a nationalised industry in the strict understanding of the term, the Treasury deemed the BBC to be in the public sector and so subject to incomes policy restraint. ITV was not so constrained, and we began to lose skilled people in growing numbers. That had happened, of course, when commercial television started because the ITV companies had nowhere else to turn to acquire skilled staff. It had also continued to happen in a small way over the years because the BBC was the only part of the broadcasting industry that ran comprehensive recruiting and training schemes. But suddenly a trickle became a flood. We lost over a hundred engineers in eighteen months, all BBC trained. We lost fourteen make-up artists (each of whom takes four years to train) in six weeks. And with the worrying losses of skilled people, incomes policy brought with it difficult salaries and wages problems. For the first time in our history, we found ourselves compelled to provide company cars to selected staff because they could no longer afford to buy their own. The unions became increasingly vexed as their members' standards of living declined and we were involved in long-drawn-out and grinding disagreements. Those came to a climax in the 1978 strike which was settled on Christmas Eve by reference to an obscure piece of legislation primarily designed to protect the wage differentials of Cornish clay workers.

Yet for all those problems, they were rich and exciting years for programmes. We surely had the best of Morecambe and Wise and of Mike Yarwood too. Saturday night entertainment was sewn up year after year with Bruce Forsyth and *The Generation Game*, followed by Jimmy Savile and by popular drama like *All Creatures Great and*

Small. There were marvellous adaptations like Jack Pulman's version of Robert Graves' *I Claudius* or *Tinker, Tailor, Soldier, Spy*, the first of our John Le Carré adaptations. There were new series of great originality like *Days of Hope* or Freddie Raphael's *The Glittering Prizes* or Dennis Potter's *Pennies From Heaven*. Penny Keith and Felicity Kendall came from the stage play *The Norman Conquests* to delight us all with Richard Briers and Paul Eddington in *The Good Life*, and the same Paul Eddington was brilliantly cast as the Minister to Nigel Hawthorne's civil servant in Tony Jay and Jonathan Lynn's acutely observed *Yes, Minister*.

There were, too, brilliant documentary dramas such as Chris Ralling's *Search for the Nile* and, even better in my opinion, his series on *The Voyage of Charles Darwin* with its haunting Wilfred Josephs' score. And – some said with more than a touch of hubris – in the late seventies we tackled the complete cycle of Shakespeare's plays. A first in world television which is still being sold by BBC Enterprises all over the world.

It has to be said that we also had some stunning failures. When I arrived from Scotland, Paul Fox had commissioned twenty-six single plays to celebrate the centenary of Winston Churchill's birth. Loosely based on his book *The History of the English Speaking Peoples*, they were to be called *Churchill's People* and to be wholly studio based. One day Bryan Cowgill, who had been appointed Controller of BBC-1, came to tell me that he had seen the first of the programmes, *Pritan*, written by David Rudkin. 'I think we've got trouble,' he told me. 'I don't think it's transmittable in its present form.' When we saw the second one, in which a Gaulish prisoner had his hand cut off by a Roman governor and the hand crawled across the floor apparently by muscular contraction, but in fact by a brilliant piece of design effect, we had trouble of a different kind. *Churchill's People* gave us a long six months. I remember two out of the twenty-six being quite good.

And later came the *Borgias*. With Mark Shivas, who had worked on the *Six Wives of Henry VIII* and had been producer of *Elizabeth R*, in charge, we felt sure we had a winner on our hands. It looked marvellous but, in truth, it was poor stuff. It was also the most expensive serial the BBC had made up to that time. Things did not always go well.

We became, too, increasingly involved in the developing discussion over taste and standards on television. Hugh Greene had had early clashes with Mrs Mary Whitehouse and her National Viewers and Listeners Association to the point where she identified the cloven hoof in him and he refused to speak to her or correspond with her. An odd stance, I always thought, on his part, because you did not need to agree with a word Mary said, but you could still have an agreeable exchange with her.

What worried us far more than Mary Whitehouse's complaints about this programme or that was the increasingly violent nature of many cinema films in the early seventies. We had our own fairly stringent guidelines for handling difficult programme material, but films like *Straw Dogs* and *A Clockwork Orange* were posing acute problems for the British Board of Film Censors, never mind the BBC. Indeed, early in 1973 the Governors became so concerned about the trends in cinema explicitness that a private session was arranged for them by the Secretary at the Censor's office in Soho Square. Few Governors, after all, could claim to be regular cinema-goers.

Picture to yourselves a windy evening in the month of March. We gathered, a little conspiratorially, in the Censor's office, sitting on rickety cinema seats in front of a projection screen and, after being handed a warm glass of gin, Stephen Murphy, who was Censor at the time, gave a graphic description of his problems which included a cut he made in *Straw Dogs* which some argued had turned an act of rape into one of buggery. Then the Governors were regaled with his special 'difficult' selection: the masturbation scene and burning at the stake from *The Devils*, the rape and mutilation scenes from *Straw Dogs*, the gang rape from *A Clockwork Orange*, topped up with the latest German import called *Massage Parlour*. When it was over, someone had arranged for us, most aptly, to have dinner at the Gay Hussar.

The Governors were stunned: indeed, two lady Governors who were present were speechless. The Chairman, Michael Swann, newly arrived from being Vice-Chancellor at Edinburgh University, was moved to articulate their anxieties. But we reminded the Governors that we already had pretty tough guidelines to help us handle our own productions. It was Hollywood and, indeed, the new freedom in the British theatre which caused us the biggest problem. Directors moved easily now from theatre to cinema to television and objected strongly to disciplines in television that were not enforced in the other media.

Quite early on as Director of Programmes, I had a tricky case to deal with. Simpson and Galton, the writers for Hancock and creators of *Steptoe and Son*, had written a new comedy series called *Casanova 73*. It filled the key slot after the main news. But after the first transmission Bill Cotton, the Head of Light Entertainment, told me he was worried about the series. He felt it was tasteless and would not work, and should be cancelled. We duly cancelled it and an obscure late-night programme called *Mastermind* was rushed in to fill its place, which is still doing wonderful business after fourteen years.

Again, in 1976 Bryan Cowgill referred Dennis Potter's latest play *Brimstone and Treacle* to me. He was worried, he said, about the piece. It concerned the devil in the guise of a young man who worms his way into the affections of a couple whose daughter has been reduced to the level of a vegetable by a car accident. The devil finally rapes the girl and so restores her understanding to the realisation that it was her own father who knocked her down as he hurried away from the bed of her best friend. As was often the case, the play had been referred very late with only a day or two before *Radio Times* went to press.

The BBC recently transmitted the play; at the time, I found it repugnant. It has always seemed to me that it was the broadcaster's duty at times to shock, but that he must take care not to outrage his audience; otherwise the dialogue between them would become wholly one-sided. But outrage was, it seemed to me, what Dennis had achieved; such was the brilliance of the acting, particularly by the girl with her swollen tongue and slobbering grunts, that the act of rape made me feel almost physically sick. I decided that we would not transmit *Brimstone and Treacle*, most reluctantly, because Dennis's work had brought great distinction to the BBC and has again since. I wrote to Dennis and explained my reactions to the producer and Head of Department. There was, of course, a great row.

Public anxiety about the possible effects of violence on the cinema and television screen had, as early as 1970, induced the Home Secretary of the day, James Callaghan, to call in the Chairman and Directors General of the BBC and the IBA for a discussion of the matter. The BBC responded by setting up a special advisory committee on the social effects of television which I inherited from David Attenborough. Those anxieties have been aggravated by much that has happened since, and in the most spectacular fashion by the awful massacre at Hungerford and shortly afterwards, the senseless killings in Bristol. Quite early on, the Surgeon-General's report in the USA had suggested a possible causal connection between screen violence and social behaviour. The brutal violence in the cinema was a constant reminder to us that this was not something that could or should be shrugged off. Our responsibilities, broadcasting direct into the home, to audiences of varying ages, were stark and clear.

It is, in my judgement, absurd to talk about 'sex 'n' violence' on television as is often the habit of the tabloid press and even too often the language of Ministers. Different difficulties arise; different solutions are predicated; and, anyway, this silly and easy formula seems to ignore something that research shows offends the viewer much more than the odd sexual encounter or moment of violence: bad language on the screen.

One must, however, confront the arguments and try to deal with them. They have, after all, been part of my professional life for twenty years anyway. For a start, there is very little explicit sex to be seen on television. One thinks immediately of the woodland love-making scene in Dennis Potter's *The Singing Detective*, of the rape and other scenes in Granada's *Jewel in the Crown*; I remember shortening a scene in an adaptation we did of *Sons and Lovers* some years ago. And, certainly, we have made cuts in feature films where the latitude for erotic celebration is much greater. But the erotic, surely, has a place in television; it is a central part of the human condition and there should be no part of that condition that television cannot discuss. We could, perhaps, understand the virtues of reticence better.

When we approach the question of violence, there is no doubt that certain programmes in the early seventies tended to glorify the nature of physical violence. I think of some of the early *Starsky and Hutch* episodes; of *The Sweeney* and our own *Target* series. We soon learned where programmes had gone too far; but programme makers needed a more exact definition of the arguments and I asked Monica Sims, then Head of Children's Television, to lead a group of senior programme makers in mapping out some detailed guidelines. The document they produced addressed itself to the matter in great detail, though public concern was not wholly allayed. We revised the guidelines again in 1986, and this time I invited viewers to write to me and express their views. A large number did so and I read them all before passing them on to the group working on the guidelines.

I had already had an indication of the Prime Minister's anxieties on this front when she kindly invited me for a drink at Downing Street shortly after I became Director General. We were chatting about the effect of the new technology when she suddenly asked, 'Have you read the report by a group of teachers about violence on television? It was in my box over the weekend and I found it very good. Have a look at the recommendations – I don't expect you'll agree with them!' An aide was sent to bring the report and I duly glanced through the recommendations. They seemed fairly draconian; in fact, I thought they were excessively severe and said so. She urged me to have a talk with Sir Keith Joseph and he, in due course, came to lunch. The only problem was that Sir Keith, as he had told me before, does not possess a television set and that made the conversation distant and unhelpful.

But the argument over censorship and control took a more difficult turn when Winston Churchill MP introduced a Private Member's Bill to bring the broadcasters within the remit of the Obscene Publications Act. Hitherto, the broadcasters had by general consent been excluded from the provisions of the Act because of the assurances given regularly by the Governors to the Home Secretary and because the provisions of the IBA's Act were thought adequate for them. I met Winston at the House and we discussed the matter. We had tough guidelines, I pointed out, much tougher and more detailed than the provisions of the Act. So why should you worry, he queried? It was tricky ground on which to stand; but I was sure that we would very soon be subject to vexatious litigation and end up with the courts deciding on matters of artistic judgement. Although the Bill fell, others will pursue the matter. I understand the argument about broadcasters not being seen to be accountable for their actions, though of course they are, to the organisations which employ them. Certainly it is the daily duty of broadcasters to exercise constant vigilance in these difficult programme areas, and horrific events like the Hungerford massacre are bound to inflame public opinion. But I continue to believe that the law is a crude instrument by which to regulate taste and standards in cultural matters. The producer's conscience should be the guide in programme making, not fear of prosecution in the courts.

By the spring of 1977, when I had succeeded Ian Trethowan after his brief tenure of office as Managing Director, we were still going through a period of great industrial difficulty; but the programmes were strong, the audience balance with ITV was healthy (we had, of course, two channels still to their one) and we had found ways of balancing our programme expenditure exactly to our budget. Significant changes had also occurred in senior management: when Robin Scott retired as Deputy Managing Director, Bill Cotton succeeded him and his job as Controller of BBC-1 was filled by Alan Hart. Aubrey Singer, after a rich and boisterous period as Controller of BBC-2, had gone off to be Managing Director of Radio and was succeeded by Brian Wenham. No less importantly, I brought Michael Checkland back from his position at Broadcasting House as Controller of Finance to be the key figure in programme planning at the Television Centre in a new job as Controller of Planning and Resource Management. In 1980, I myself was appointed Deputy Director General while still continuing in my job as Managing Director of Television.

Two further matters in this period demand record. The first is co-production. Although there have been all kinds of new ways of approaching such deals developed over the years, what Aubrey Singer and Huw Wheldon and others who started this process described was very simple. The BBC invited from 'programme producers or companies of good standing' money up front before production started in return for well-defined overseas sales rights. We insisted that we made the programmes for consumption by the audience in the UK. There were to be no mid-Atlantic compromises as there had been earlier. We hoped that overseas audiences would enjoy the programmes as we made them.

Of course, there were arguments, particularly with early American co-producers. They wanted certain star figures (Robert Wagner's appearance in *Colditz* is a famous case in point, where we were happy to involve him). They often argued for script changes or modifications. But, despite rumours of rows in cutting rooms and on location, we stuck to our guns and increasing sums of money arrived to support the more expensive programmes, drama in particular. In the early 1970s we were bringing in around £3 million a year in co-production. Now the figure is nearer £10 million. Few major drama ventures that I can remember in the last fifteen years did not have co-production money involved and the same was true for many documentary series. At times, departmental heads complained that they spent more time raising co-production money and doing deals than supervising their output. Aubrey Singer, a great co-production funder in his time as Head of Features Group, even spent a fruitless week in Ulan Bator to squeeze co-production money out of the Outer Mongolians!

The other event was our entry into breakfast television, almost my last act before leaving the Television Service to become Director General. We had, for some years, planned to develop early-morning television, but it was not as high a priority as enriching drama, strengthening our regional news operations and opening up daytime television, until the IBA suddenly proposed a franchise for breakfast television. They fixed a date for their hearings and for the start of the franchise. We had a number of options – should we leave it to them, should we compete, or should we find some halfway house? There was no extra money and no question of suggesting to the Government a supplement to the licence fee. There were many inside the BBC and even more outside who thought we had overextended ourselves anyway, and now we were contemplating a further act of expansion. I was sure myself that the morning hours were going to be very important to us in the future, particularly from the news point of view. North America went to bed later than we did and if we left ITV a free start in the morning, it seemed possible that, in due course, people would automatically start with the commercial channel for their morning news and stay with it for the rest of the day. But, again, if we went into breakfast television, what would be the effect on radio and on Radio 4's *Today* programme in particular?

For a time we hesitated. BBC Scotland tried a simple 'radiovision' experiment: in effect, televising a radio programme. Monica Sims, by now Controller of Radio 4, worked with a group on a more sophisticated version of television and radio working together. I remained convinced it would not work and that we should tackle breakfast television in our own way and, in the end, the Board and the Director General backed me and we announced, over a breakfast for the press, that we were going ahead. Naturally, much was made of this being a spoiling tactic against TV-am and when they later ran into trouble, even more mud was flung at us, not least by those who had an interest in the troubled commercial station.

We funded BBC *Breakfast Time* by organisational savings made at the Television Centre and by increased overseas sales. That brought in the £6 million we needed. We fought our way through tricky union negotiations for late-night and early-morning working, though we had to indulge in some eleventh hour threatening tactics. We put Ron Neil, a Scotsman who had worked with me in Scotland and had won his spurs in Lime Grove thereafter, in charge of this new venture and, apart from the inclusion of the astrologer Russell Grant who proved hugely popular to all but me, Ron and his team got it right from day one. We had taken the first major step since the start of BBC-2 more than fifteen years earlier in the expansion of BBC Television.

6 Governing The BBC

The last letter I received from Grace Wyndham Goldie was a note to wish me luck at Christmas time when I had been in the job of Director General a little over two years.

> I have always thought that the job of being Director General of the BBC was one of the most important and difficult in the world; it can never have been so difficult as it is now, what with cable, the increasing use of satellites, pressure from advertising interests for the BBC to take advertising in order to meet some of its ever-rising costs, and the attitudes of politicians, many of whom seem to want to use television in the short term for their own purposes while not, apparently, having much understanding of its nature nor any adequate policy for its long-term future.

If Grace thought the job difficult, some went even further than that. William Rees-Mogg, shortly after I left the BBC, expressed the opinion that the job was an impossible one.

So what is this very taxing job? What, in fact, does the DG do? In bald terms, he is responsible, as Chief Executive and Editor-in-Chief of the Corporation, for the output of two television channels, four radio networks, more than thirty local radio stations in England, the special services for Scotland, Wales and Northern Ireland, and the External Services of the BBC. It goes without saying that he is responsible to the Board for the proper handling of finance, personnel, engineering and general administrative matters affecting a staff of some twenty-nine thousand people. Obviously, no single individual can encompass the vast range of that sort of broadcasting output – it is like being editor of all of Fleet Street, most of the provincial press, and then a great international service, publishing round the clock in English and in more than fifty vernacular languages as well. I doubt if John Reith, who effectively presided over one radio channel, knew of everything that was going out on his air. The sheer volume of broadcasting now makes it a wholly different process to guide from the contrastingly narrow, traditional methods of the Fleet Street newspaper editor.

There being so much broadcasting, over the years sensible devolutionary steps have been taken. There are Managing Directors in charge of the three 'output' directorates – Television, Radio and External; there are Directors of Engineering, Personnel and Finance and what was until recently called Public Affairs – the regions, the educational services, the religious output, the BBC's information services. There has usually been a senior individual responsible to the Director General for the BBC's manifold journalistic activities and for its standards in that field. These people make up the BBC's Board of Management, a group established by Sir William Haley shortly after the war. Part Cabinet, part sounding board, part advisory group to the DG. All major policy initiatives in the BBC are examined and discussed by the Board of Management before going forward to the Governors for ratification, alteration or rejection.

If you asked me what were the primary functions of the Director General, I would answer: first, to do his utmost to engineer a harmonious relationship with the Chairman and with the other Governors, because if that relationship goes wrong, horrors can follow in its wake; secondly, to strive to promote a climate of confidence wherein programme makers can do their best work without having constantly to look over their shoulder at threats of penury, pusillanimous leadership or political arm-twisting.

The DG must also make every effort to be seen throughout the Corporation, visiting the outlying stations as often as possible in order to pass on the thinking of Governors and management and get in return the stimulus of the ideas of those working at the sharp end. It is he, too, who must speak for the BBC; as the chief executive and professional head of the BBC, he is bound to be listened to with more attention than any part-time Chairman or Governor.

That is the way the system has worked for a good many years, though the passage of time has brought both accretion and change and each new DG will adapt the methods of working to his own personality. Thus, my first job as Director General Designate was to form a new management team. Any period of five years or so in broadcasting will leave scars on the existing management.

Quite early on after my appointment, it became clear that the Governors were going to be very involved in the choice of the next management. Even before Christmas 1981, there was a long meeting at which they discussed a paper prepared by the previous Vice-Chairman, Mark Bonham-Carter, about the relationship between the two boards and about the workings of the Board of Management. George Howard was of the view that the Annan Report had been an important catalyst in the relationship between the Governors and the management of the BBC. Annan had, in a very clear sense, called for

71

the Board of Governors to be more involved in detail and George Howard thought this had driven both boards to become more introspective. William Rees-Mogg, continuing a theme he had opened up at his first Board meeting, propounded a different diagnosis. The BBC's programme tradition, he argued, was a strong and living one and the Governors' role in that field was a delicate one. What he called 'management' he felt quite differently about – the Director General needed as strong an executive team as he had a programme team. Ian Trethowan remonstrated gently with Rees-Mogg; he wondered if he wasn't likening the BBC to a newspaper and reminded him that the traditions were very different. The discussion lasted for a long time. There were to be more long meetings in the New Year before any decisions about the new management team were reached. In the meantime, I was invited to prepare papers on my thinking about the top jobs.

Over the Christmas break, I worked out the pattern I wanted and talked to the people involved. I had in mind to promote Aubrey Singer from his job as Managing Director of Radio, where he had bravely grasped the nettle of reducing the number of house orchestras employed by the BBC to those we actually needed, but had earned considerable opprobrium from the strike by the Musicians' Union that followed that decision. I wanted Aubrey to be Deputy Director General with immediate responsibility for regional affairs, education and religion, but also to take charge of our sales branch, BBC Enterprises, and our publications activities; most importantly, to be the BBC's chief activist in the field of cable and satellite where I thought his entrepreneurial experience would bring us handsome returns. Aubrey, however, was not happy with this disposition. He wanted airtime and money – the two crucial limbs of a successful broadcasting executive – and, above all, he wanted to be Managing Director of the Television Service where he had, with great success, spent most of his broadcasting career, whereas I was planning to move Bill Cotton, who was my deputy at the Television Service, to be its Managing Director.

There was a further difficulty. In Ian Trethowan's administration, Dick Francis held the post of Director of News and Current Affairs (revived for the first time since Hugh Greene's tenure in the late 1950s) which carried with it the responsibilities of being line manager for the News Division, but also a broad remit to intervene in both radio and television current affairs. This seemed to me an unsatisfactory way of running things from my own day-to-day experience because, effectively, the Television Service was not answerable for its news, and only partly for its current affairs output. It was not unknown for the buck to disappear without trace of any kind. The alternative – the creation of a separate News and Current Affairs Directorate – removes at a stroke a large segment of Television and Radio's responsibilities and carries within it the seeds of dissension and disharmony over scheduling and expenditure. I felt it important that both news and current affairs programmes should be delegated to the Television and Radio directorates; but I knew I also needed somebody with clout and with the authority of a new post, which I called Assistant Director General, to oversee all the BBC's journalism, to protect its standards and to be my right hand in that often contentious area.

The man I wanted for that job was Brian Wenham, but Brian was not to be persuaded. He had come to the BBC from ITN to run *Panorama*, had suffered a heart attack in his thirties, but had recovered quickly and run Current Affairs well, only to have his department's work singled out for special criticism by Annan and his fellow committee members. Brian was now enjoying a very successful period as Controller of BBC-2, where his flair for seeing the gaps in what was being offered elsewhere had brought forward some good innovative programmes. And I do not just mean snooker, though he remains a keen devotee. Many in the business regarded Brian as a confirmed cynic without any real commitment – a judgement which I always thought harsh, though he did nothing to alleviate it by the sharpness of his tongue. I thought him a skilful operator who could tiptoe his way through the minefields with ease. Moreover, he had frequently taken a hand in planning other people's careers and, certainly, spent much thought on his own and I, therefore, argued that being Assistant Director General would offer him good scope for following me in due course. No, said Brian, he wanted (like others) to run the Television Service. He had had his bellyful of overseeing current affairs when he was in charge of Lime Grove. The job was too exposed and would bring nothing but trouble. My arguments made little impression on him.

Nevertheless, that was the scheme – with Dick Francis to replace Aubrey as Managing Director of Radio – that I put to the Governors at a special meeting early in the New Year. They were acutely anxious about the devolution of news to the output directorates. Would this not surely lead to a different appreciation of overall standards? Not, I said, with a strong man as Assistant Director General. In the end they acceded, though I think with some reluctance; they were clear that they did not wish a 'free-standing' Deputy Director General because, by dint of circumstance, the Managing Director of Television was the most powerful available deputy. And that job, they insisted, must go to Aubrey Singer. The Chairman, George Howard, was particularly vocal on this point. I discovered later that he had promised Aubrey he would fix it for him.

The Governors were definitely taking a hand in making up my cabinet for me. We finally settled on Aubrey for Television and Deputy Director General, Dick Francis for Radio, Bill Cotton to be Director of Development in charge of our new satellite operations (after the announcement of the new dispositions, Bill asked me if he could stay on at the Television Centre doubling up as Director of Programmes, and after a late-night phone conversation, Aubrey reluctantly agreed; later Bill moved full time into the satellite world as Managing Director, Direct Broadcasting by Satellite). We agreed that Brian Wenham should become Assistant Director General, and that if he continued to refuse, Alan Protheroe should be approached. We also agreed that Michael Checkland should be promoted to the new post of Director of Resources for the Television Service.

These were long and exhausting meetings. I had, I confess, expected a speedier acceptance of the plans I had put forward. In the event, Ian Trethowan and I saw all those involved after the formal Board proceedings were completed and everybody was happy with the new arrangements. But not Brian. He would not budge. He would not take the job. Even George Howard could not shake his resolve. So we sent for Alan Protheroe who was then languishing somewhat after having been moved out of the Editor's chair at Television News. He was made Assistant Director General, with responsibility also for overseeing the BBC's press and publicity affairs. Alan was dumbfounded but thrilled. Brian remained, sulkily, as Controller of BBC-2.

But should the Governors intervene in senior appointments in this way? Should they continue to insist that their voice is dominant in the choice of the top fifty or so BBC posts as they have done since Charles Hill's time? Certainly, in the case of some of the more specialised positions, the outcome can be dramatically unhelpful as occurred when the Governors, at George Howard's insistence, voted to reject the management's first choice for Controller of BBC-1 in January 1981. Nobody could dispute that one of the Governors' most important decisions is to appoint the Director General; and they have every right and need to be informed about and fully discuss subsequent management moves. Whether they should manipulate them is another story, and raises the whole complicated question of the governance of the BBC.

From the earliest days, there have been passages of strain between the Governors of the BBC and the Director General. I think it was Mrs Snowden who recorded when she joined the Board in the late 1920s that 'few Governors were speaking to each other and none to the Director General' – who was, of course, John Reith. Things came to an even prettier pass. Asa Briggs, in his book *Governing the BBC*, writes: 'At a Board meeting in July 1929, Clarendon [the Chairman] wanted to insert a rebuke in the minutes about the Director General's behaviour. "Unfortunately, he has given us all the impression that he wants – if he does not agree with the Board – to override us."'

By then, Briggs goes on, the Governors were lunching together as a group after Board meetings at the Savoy Hotel, and infuriating Reith by never inviting the Director General to join them. They were also prepared to issue ultimata. They demanded the right to attend all advisory meetings, to call on heads of departments and ratify all appointments and resignations. When Reith objected to this approach, the Chairman read the terms of the Charter to him: 'The Charter makes clear the supremacy of the Board of Governors,' he exclaimed. 'Like the commander-in-chief on a battlefield, their status and powers are unquestionable.' 'Surely,' Reith replied, 'the Board holds an authority equivalent to the Cabinet, with the chief executive in the position of commander-in-chief.'

Later, in 1932, Whitley, the new Chairman, and Reith drafted a document defining the rights and duties of the Board of Governors which remained definitive for more than thirty years.

> The Governors of the BBC act primarily as trustees to safeguard the broadcasting service in the national interest. Their functions are not executive. Their responsibilities are general and not particular . . . With the Director General they discuss and then decide on major matters of policy and finance, but they leave the execution of that policy and the general administration of the service in all its branches to the Director General and his competent officers. The Governors should be able to judge on the general effect of the service upon the public, and subject as before mentioned, are finally responsible for the conduct of it.

The post-war Chairman, Lord Simon of Wythenshawe, thought nothing of this document and argued strongly against its philosophy before the Beveridge Committee of Inquiry into broadcasting. What's more, they agreed with him. They felt the Governors should be altogether more active, and even recommended that the Chairman should attend meetings of the Board of Management which Sir William Haley, the Director General, had just set up. Simon was deeply resentful when he was not so invited. Thereafter, relationships proceeded on a smoother path. Sir Ian Jacob apparently got on well with his Chairman, Sir Arthur fforde, who became Chairman in 1957 after retiring as Headmaster of Rugby School.

But there were the problems between DG and Board which I and others have referred to over *That Was The Week That Was*. There were voices from outside the BBC calling for greater gubernatorial influence. Reginald Bevins, a Postmaster General of the time, is on record complaining that 'the Governors were governed by the professionals. In my time and before I am sure that the real power was wielded by the Director General, Sir Hugh Greene, and the top professionals. They knew all the answers.'

But the Governors, on several notable occasions, exercised their influence in programme matters. Simon cancelled the repeat of a television play, overriding Haley's objections, apparently because he thought it might upset the Labour leadership of the day. Lord Normanbrook, former Cabinet Secretary who succeeded fforde as Chairman, refused to allow Ian Smith, then Prime Minister of Rhodesia, to appear in *24 Hours* in 1965, despite his recorded view that Governors should not interfere in programme decisions in advance of the event, but make their opinions known afterwards. The classical position of gubernatorial involvement.

In the very same year, Peter Watkins' *The War Game* was seen by both Greene and Normanbrook, and both felt that 'the responsibility for its showing was too great for the BBC to bear alone'. Greene then went off to West Africa to a Commonwealth Broadcasting Conference, and Normanbrook took the highly controversial decision to invite the Secretary of the Cabinet, Sir Burke Trend, and representatives from the Home Office, the Ministry of Defence and the Chiefs of Staff to see the programme, as Briggs records. That invitation was much resented by those involved in the production of the film, and though *The War Game* was made available for cinema screening by the BBC, it was never shown on television until I decided to screen it, together with our new productions *Threads* and *On the Eighth Day* on the anniversary of the bombing of Hiroshima. The only dissenting voice among the Governors on that occasion was that of Sir William Rees-Mogg. Not that he spoke up when I told the Governors of my intention. But later he complained to the Secretary, David Holmes, that he had never been told, until he was shown the minutes of the Board meeting at which he had been present.

In 1965 again, the entire Board previewed a television programme – the last occasion, as far as I know, they did so until the *Real Lives* episode. Ironically, it was one of my last commissions before leaving the BBC, a Tonight Production documentary made by Alan Whicker and Kevin Billington about the famous young Spanish bullfighter, El Cordobes. Bullfighting was a topic which, at the time, caused great audience anxiety. Having seen the film the Board, as Asa Briggs records, was divided. Some wished it had never been made. Normanbrook said that if it had been referred to the Board in the first instance they would have withheld permission. Greene's position is not recorded. *Matador* went out in January 1966 and seemed to cause little offence. It is interesting to recall Sir Charles Curran's words about the relationship between Sir Hugh Greene and his Chairman, because Charles was Secretary of the BBC at the time and, therefore, privy to most confidences. He wrote in his book, *The Seamless Robe*, 'The public thought that Sir Hugh, a bold editor and a great publicist, was the dominant force. That was not the reality. The Chairmen were in charge on the major issues.'

When Charles Hill was switched by Harold Wilson from being Chairman of the ITA to the BBC, relationships soured sharply. Greene was furious and there was much talk of resignation. Hill has recorded the freezing reception with which he was met on arrival in Broadcasting House. Hill has never made any bones about his intention to be 'an active Chairman' though he claimed he did not want to adopt 'the management responsibilities of the Director General'.

An active Chairman Hill certainly was. It was very much on his initiative that McKinseys were brought in to examine the BBC's operational methods in the late sixties, leading to the structural changes of Broadcasting in the seventies. Active enough, anyway, for Greene soon to leave, nor did his odd period as a Governor last very long. Charles Curran has written candidly about some of his exchanges with Charles Hill, in particular the occasion when Hill wanted to insist that a full-time Deputy Director General should be appointed. In the event, after much wrangling, the Board could not agree either upon the function or upon the individual. And a curious compromise emerged whereby the Secretary was redesignated the 'Chief Secretary'. In that context, Charles Curran writes a telling sentence, 'The Director General should not be required to submit to the direction of the Board when he is convinced that the proposed appointment is wrong.'

Many of these historical events I was only dimly aware of, if at all, though the strains between Curran and Hill were common gossip at senior levels within the BBC. And I personally witnessed, at a retirement dinner for a Governor where, by tradition, the Chairman spoke first and the Director General second, the peremptory tones with which Charles Hill sat down and said, a sharp edge behind the fruity tones, 'Get on with it, Charles. Don't want to be here all night.'

But on my return from Scotland, a new Chairman travelled south with me, as it were. Ted Heath had appointed Sir Michael Swann, Vice-Chancellor of Edinburgh University, to succeed Lord Hill as Chairman, believing, as he told Swann, 'that the BBC is rather like a university'. Though Leonard Miall also records that when an American correspondent asked at 10 Downing Street why Swann had been appointed, he was told, 'To re-establish the position of the Director General.' Swann himself used a skilful metaphor to describe his role: 'The Director General,' he said on the night of his appointment, 'will be doing the driving and the Governors and I will be reading the map.'

I had met Michael socially in Scotland. A big, apparently bluff man, with a highly distinguished scientific background, a very sharp brain and clouds of pipe smoke which he used to conceal a moment of rumination or a darting change of approach. Quite early on in his chairmanship, there was a great frisson in the Television Service because Michael and the Board appeared to rush to apologise to Shirley Williams who was miffed at being involved in a noisy *Man Alive* debate. But soon the Board visibly began to relax under his guidance.

My very first attendance at a Board meeting just before I took over as Director of Programmes for Television was characterised by an onslaught by a Board member, Tom Jackson, then General Secretary of the Post Office Workers' Union, on Huw Wheldon and David Attenborough whom he roundly accused of lying over what seemed a minor misunderstanding. That seemed odd behaviour; and in Charlie Hill's time, voting was quite often part of Board procedure. I do not remember hearing of another vote throughout Michael Swann's period as Chairman. His style was to encourage discussion to ebb and flow, sometimes at great length and then say, 'Look, we've got to get on,' and sum up to achieve the end result he desired. It was a very successful method of operation.

There were the occasional moments when the Board seemed to us to levitate, causing unnecessary alarm and confusion to all concerned. I am thinking, for example, of their knee-jerk response to the first reports of the Carrickmore incident. This happened in 1979, when a *Panorama* crew were telephoned while filming in Ireland and were told that if they went immediately to the village of Carrickmore, they would witness something of importance. They went, found masked IRA men parading the street of the village, flagging down cars and the like. They filmed these happenings, and next day told the police what had happened.

But the story leaked out through a Republican source, and highly coloured versions were being passed around Fleet Street the morning of a Cabinet meeting and a coincidental Governors' meeting. George Howard, then SOG (alias Senior Ordinary Governor) was called out of the Board meeting to take a phone call from Willie Whitelaw, Home Secretary of the day and a close personal friend of George's. The PM, said Willie, was hopping mad, and so was he. What were the Governors going to do about it?

One must remember that not a foot of film had been transmitted, or ever was. I doubt if it had even been processed for development by then. And it hardly seems a crime for journalists working on a story in Northern Ireland to have responded as they did to the call to Carrickmore. But a heinous crime was deemed to have been committed and the Governors issued a statement that an inquiry would immediately be set up. As ill luck would have it, Ian Trethowan was then recovering from a heart attack and I was in New York on my way home from a business trip to Australia and California. Gerry Mansell, the Managing Director of External Services, was deputising for Ian and Robin Scott for me. They had the unpleasant task of conducting the inquiry which, for a time, looked likely to result in the Editor of *Panorama* being removed to the Secretariat – the equivalent, in BBC terms, of being put in the stocks. There are still newspapers around who occasionally claim that this traitorous film was transmitted. Roger Bolton, the erstwhile Editor of *Panorama*, has received substantial damages to prove they are wrong.

Again, the problem of the 1980 Olympic Games caused the Board much pain. The US withdrawal from Moscow and our own Government's position had certainly made the political climate difficult, but the Games were going forward. We had spent many months of time and many millions of pounds preparing for them. Some Governors were for pulling out altogether, others for somehow sharing the exercise with the ITV companies. The latter was a position we had stoutly resisted for years on the grounds that the BBC devoted far more effort to sport of all kinds than the ITV companies had ever done – particularly athletics – and that the Olympics were the culmination of four years of preparation. In the end, we adopted a policy of 'maximum mutual avoidance', which didn't really mean a great deal.

In both cases, I feel the Board succumbed to an element of panic which more time for deliberation might have avoided.

So who are the Governors and what do they do? You might well ask. They are twelve in number – though the laggardness of governmental appointment procedures frequently leaves the ranks thinned. There is a Chairman and a Vice-Chairman. There are three National Governors speaking for Scotland, Wales and Northern Ireland each backed up by a Broadcasting Council with quite significant powers spelt out in the Charter, though they are also expected to take the overall good of the BBC into proper account. Then there are seven other Governors, one of whom will always be an academic, another a trade unionist, another representing the ethnic minorities, another interested in music and the arts, another with a

Foreign Office background to keep a weather eye on the External Services and its welfare, another (or two) from the City or the world of business. There should always be – and latterly there have been – at least three and probably four women. They tend, as with all such bodies, to be older rather than younger, but that is almost inevitable when they are poorly paid, are required to undertake much more than the fortnightly meeting that the Home Office used to specify, and probably have many other part-time activities to pursue. As to their duties, a recently retired Governor prepared, a few years ago, a revision of the Whitley-Reith document entitled 'Letter to a New Governor' setting down some fresh guidelines based on his eight years of experience.

> Legally, the Board of Governors *is* the British Broadcasting Corporation. They employ a staff of some twenty-seven thousand under the leadership of the Director General as professional head, Chief Executive and Editor-in-Chief. In conceptual terms, they have made a huge act of delegation by which they have entrusted the Director General and his staff with the implementation of the purposes for which the Corporation has been established. This is not just an academic concept. It is important, because it establishes that the Board and the staff of the BBC are parts of the whole, they are not countervailing, but complementary, and must live in partnership.
>
> Let me say at this point that it is not immediately perceptible to a new Governor what an immense and immanent authority the Board enjoys within the BBC. There are many staff members who will never meet a member of the Board in their working lives, and for whom the Governors must have an Olympian remoteness. Yet they will all say that the authority of the Board hangs over everyone. In a very real sense, the Board is apprehended by those working in the Corporation as the conscience of the BBC, and the ultimate guardian of its public service ethos.

Thus, a retired Governor writing to future Board members. And with most of what he wrote, I have no quarrel. Such a short extract might suggest he paid less than proper heed to the producers who actually make the BBC and the public service ethos what it is, but he spent a lot of time later encouraging new Governors to travel through the BBC and learn about its works. He wrote some time after the Annan Committee published their report. They, too, had a good deal to say about the Governors. They noted that 'in some of the evidence we received there was a growing ill-humour that the Governors were both judge and jury in their own cause, trying to combine the regulatory function with the managerial decision-taking needed to produce good programmes. As a result, their role had become hopelessly confused.' Annan went on to identify the changed relationship between the Chairman and the Director General, quoting Lord Hill as saying that over the years the Governors had come to be regarded 'as an advisory committee to the executive'. All that had changed, said Annan: 'Now when the BBC was publicly criticised the Chairman, and not the Director General, often spoke to the press. The Prime Minister would consult him rather than the Director General. The buck,' said Annan, 'stops at the Governors.' And then, quoting both Lord Hill and Sir Michael Swann as telling them how hard it was to get BBC top management to accept proposals put to them by the Governors, he pronounced that this was intolerable. 'It would do worlds for the reputation of the BBC with the public if the Governors were seen to govern.' Though, surely, that last statement continues to beg the question.

During most of my dealings with the Board, the Governors numbered amongst themselves people of real distinction: Mark Bonham-Carter as Michael Swann's Vice-Chairman; National Governors like Glyn Tegai Hughes and Alwyn Roberts from Wales and Lucy Faulkner from Northern Ireland. Governors like Sir John Johnston, a robust and highly literate ex-diplomat, formerly our High Commissioner in Southern Rhodesia, Malaysia and Canada; Roy Fuller, poet and mordant wit, and a gentle but passionate scientist from Sussex University called Christopher Longuet-Higgins. When Michael Swann gave up the chairmanship after seven years, he was, to most people's surprise, succeeded by George Howard. ('I knew,' said Michael, 'that something had happened when George came to tell me he was to be my successor, he had grown to twice his normal size!')

George was, indeed, an unmistakable figure. At that time, before his illness, he was a man of great girth, who wolfed down everything put in front of him, smoked incessantly and was much given to wearing very fancy suits and exotic kaftans. He announced to the world that he intended to adopt a 'high profile' and was seen around the town squiring a succession of youngish girls. He also travelled extensively overseas, turning up unfailingly at every one of the many overseas television festivals. He went to China with Aubrey Singer where, to his intense fury, he was given a dressing-down by a lady in the Chinese Foreign Service for some misdemeanour we were thought to have committed, and with me to America where he uttered the immortal remark about the very comfortable and extremely expensive Bel Air Hotel: 'I don't like cottage hotels.' It was also in America on that occasion that his health began to fail.

George's handling of the Board was also highly idiosyncratic. He seems to have intrigued a good deal, particularly during the private sessions that preceded the normal Board meetings, and took an especial delight in putting down his new Vice-Chairman, Sir William Rees-Mogg. At Mogg's very first Board meeting, William told us that he had the highest possible regard for the BBC's programmes but none for its management practices. We demurred strongly, pointing out that we had no division of editorial and management practice, such as was common in Fleet Street, and how could he know anyway, since he had only crossed the BBC's threshold that morning for the first time? Stuart Young told me later that George had put William up to it 'in order to stir the pot'. George sat beaming while William and we disputed his assertions.

William Rees-Mogg, former editor of *The Times*, antiquarian bookseller, director of the GEC and soon to be Chairman of the Arts Council, was to play an increasingly important role in the Board's relations with BBC management. His apparently shy and scholarly air, contrasting with sudden and surprising fits of the giggles, was accompanied by quite frequent and long periods when he did not contribute to the debate, taking voluminous notes the while. But when he spoke, he did so with great cogency and was listened to as someone with real authority. I remember a masterly and generous discourse on our coverage of the 1983 Brixton and Toxteth summer riots. He clearly thought that he had a highly developed commercial sense and pressed hard during his terms for an outsider to run the BBC's commercial activities, something we did, in the end, achieve. But I sensed that he was also, at times, factious against the management, and some of the events that follow would tend to confirm that feeling.

One other matter that must be recorded here was our growing anxiety about the politicisation of the Board. There had been rumblings on this front in the history of past administrations, but latterly the process began to assume worrying proportions. The same recently retired Governor whom I quoted earlier had this to say about party political affiliations: 'There is no place for party politics in the Board's business,' said he, 'and if Governors have party affiliations they leave them behind them when they enter the Board Room. It is our duty to ensure that the BBC, as the national instrument of public service broadcasting, remains unequivocally independent of any sectional interest.'

But time and again, the BBC has put forward what seemed to us perfectly proper names for consideration by Government, together with those from its own sources, for appointment by the Queen in Council to the Board. Time and again such names were rejected, usually, we were told, by No. 10, and people of obvious political complexion appointed. When Lord Allen of Fallowfield, formerly Alf Allen, a trade unionist of essentially middle-of-the-road views retired as a Governor, we got as his replacement Sir John Boyd, formerly General Secretary of the AUEW. John may have been Chairman of the Labour Party in his time, but he was a man of conservative opinions, unashamedly held and unequivocally expressed. It was a matter that concerned the Opposition parties, the BBC and, in the end, I believe, the Home Office itself. It is high time that a return is made to finding people of the highest standing as Governors of the BBC, not just those who are 'one of us'. I also believe that the Board, increased in numbers by Harold Wilson presumably to help stamp on Hugh Greene, is too big at twelve to be manageable for the Chairman, or thoughtfully clear about the BBC. At an early opportunity, it should be reduced again to nine.

I do not, incidentally, share the belief of those (and they have included, at one time, my predecessor Sir Ian Trethowan and, more recently, in his 1987 Dimbleby Lecture, Sir Denis Forman) that a mixed board of professional and non-executive directors, on the commercial model, would be advantageous for the BBC. Fewer and better Governors, properly distanced from the management but working with them in harmony and, I would hope, in their support is a better prescription.

In the summer of 1983 George Howard retired from the chairmanship and became Lord Howard of Henderskelfe, after the original name of the site on which Vanbrugh's Castle Howard now stands. We pressed hard for Stuart Young, who had been a Governor for two years, to succeed him. Stuart, a wealthy accountant who had built up his own firm from scratch, was also a director of companies like Tesco and British Caledonian, very active in the Jewish community in London and a leading figure in bodies like the Historic Buildings Society. With his smooth silver head of hair and his well-cut suits, he looked every inch the successful businessman. And in matters of finance or property movement, he was an aggressive and highly assertive figure. But in editorial discussion or in matters of public policy, he was altogether less sure of himself, handling the Board with kid gloves, urging them to debate at length, refusing to lead except from behind, cautious to a fault in his anxiety not to seem to suppress argument. He also believed that William Rees-Mogg had been instrumental in confirming his appointment and determined that debt would be fully repaid. Whereas George had been at times almost brutally careless of William's position, Stuart quite openly deferred to him. At all events, we in the management were genuinely delighted when Stuart's appointment was confirmed, though I wondered at the sense of nominating a man of his energy and comparative youth to be a non-executive Chairman for four days a week. Above all, we all liked the man, and he clearly loved the BBC and thought it the greatest honour to become its Chairman.

Within weeks, though, having hardly suffered an illness in his life, he was stricken with lung cancer. He was operated on and then underwent a course of chemotherapy. For the last eighteen months of his term, George Howard had been very ill and, indeed, did not survive for many months after he left the BBC. Now, once again, we had a sick Chairman and a leaderless Board of Governors.

Directing *Tonight* 1957.

The *Tonight* team 1957. BACK ROW FROM LEFT: Cliff Michelmore, Derek Hart, Geoffrey Johnson Smith. SIXTH FROM LEFT: Donald Baverstock AND ON HIS LEFT: Tony Jay, Alasdair Milne, Ned Sherrin. MIDDLE FRONT ROW: Cynthia Judah.

That Was The Week That Was
1962. LEFT TO RIGHT: David
Frost, Roy Kinnear, Kenneth
Cope, Lance Percival, Willie
Rushton.

Millie Martin – in typical pose.

Hugh Greene – the day Charles Hill became BBC Chairman, 1965.

Alasdair and Sheila
Milne – the day he was
announced as Controller
BBC Scotland, 1967.

Farewell to Scotland –
with Michael Swann and
National Governor, Lady
Avonside, 1973.

I Claudius – Derek Jacobi in the title role.

Brimstone and Treacle – the Dennis Potter play banned by Milne.

The Shakespeare canon – John Cleese as Petruchio.

Huw Wheldon's last meeting. BACK ROW LEFT TO RIGHT: Bob Longman, Chief Engineer, Television; Aubrey Singer, Controller, BBC2; Bryan Cowgill, Controller, BBC1; Michael Checkland, Chief Accountant; Peter Raleigh, Head of Planning. FRONT ROW: Leslie Page, Controller, Administration; Robin Scott, Controller, Development; Huw Wheldon, Managing Director, Alasdair Milne, Director of Programmes; Pat Ramsay, Controller of Programme Services.

7 THE FALKLANDS WAR

The Falklands War began in earnest just after 8.00 a.m. London time on Friday, 2nd April, 1982, when Argentine troops landed on the islands and the small force of Royal Marines there surrendered.

It is certain that British journalists had read the runes accurately enough to realise many weeks earlier that something was afoot and to take steps to deploy staff and crews to the Argentine. Much earlier than we, the Ministry of Defence had also read the intelligence correctly, but the Foreign and Commonwealth Office, occupied as it had been for some time in complicated negotiations with the Argentines, took the view that an invasion was neither probable nor imminent. The strange events in South Georgia when Argentines posing as scrap dealers set up their flag on the territory only served to confirm our predictions.

We already had Harold Briley stationed in Buenos Aires for the External Services and for our general radio operations. Television organised a sophisticated, and dangerous, operation in Buenos Aires because the city was obviously going to be a major centre of activity (dangerous because operating from the capital city of a country with which we were soon likely to be at war was not going to be easy). Further arrangements were put in hand in Montevideo, Uruguay, because we felt that it was likely to become a political staging post and thus an important source of news. And, in order to get as close to the Falklands as we physically could, we despatched a crew to Punta Arenas, on the southern tip of Chile.

But the crucial matter for the broadcasters was how we could conduct our coverage of the conflict from London; and what arrangements we could make to accompany whatever force might be sent to the South Atlantic. This campaign was going to be fought in bleak, inhospitable territory, eight thousand miles from Europe – a distance as far as that from London to Calcutta. When it happened, I had not yet taken over as Director General of the BBC. My time was due in July. Ian Trethowan was about to leave on a farewell overseas trip; Alan Protheroe had just assumed his new duties as Assistant Director General, supervising the BBC's journalistic activities.

It was not until ten hours after the Argentine landings that the Government was able to confirm that the islands had indeed been invaded. On the Saturday, 3rd April, there was an extraordinary debate in the House of Commons and the resignations of the Foreign Secretary, Lord Carrington, and his Foreign Office Minister, Humphrey Atkins, followed soon after. The news of the invasion and the decision to send a Task Force to the South Atlantic provoked a huge rush by television, radio and the press to demand places on the ships of the forces. A hurried lunch meeting convened by Mr Ian McDonald, the somewhat lugubrious and solemn spokesman for the Ministry of Defence, whose almost nightly appearances on television news programmes brought him brief national fame, established that BBC Television and ITN would be allowed to send one correspondent each, would share a BBC crew consisting of that well-known and much-campaigned team of Bernard Hesketh and John Jockel, and would be supported by an ITN engineer to oversee the technical problems. There was an unholy squabble for press places, including intensive lobbying of Ministers and a direct appeal to Bernard Ingham at No. 10, whose intervention clinched an increase in the number of correspondents to be carried. Though we argued loudly for a berth for an External Services correspondent whose voice would be clearly identified with the World Service, we failed. Instead, one of the provincial newspaper correspondents selected to accompany the fleet came from the *Wolverhampton Express & Star*, a town not noted for its maritime connections, to the exclusion, for example, of the *Portsmouth Evening News*. The confusion was pervasive.

For BBC Television, Brian Hanrahan, just back from a sailing holiday, was asked by his editor, 'How about another one?' and was told to be at Portsmouth at a few hours' notice to join HMS *Hermes*. Robert Fox, for BBC Radio, was at first refused a passage altogether but travelled four days later in a secondary press party on *Canberra*. In the general confusion of a sudden sailing to war eight thousand miles away, it is wholly understandable that tensions ran very high; but the Navy did not have as much familiarity with the media as the other services and the attitude of certain of the ships' officers ('Any trouble from you and I'll have you put in irons,' was one statement passed on to me) was openly hostile to all reporting. Hanrahan has written that he was told that anything he reported might be detrimental to the Task Force.

Such suspicions are not, of course, new. Frank Gillard told me recently that when he was reporting the invasion of Italy by the Allies in the winter of 1943, he was summoned from the Naples area to a dinner meeting with Field Marshal Alexander, two hundred and fifty miles away in the heel of Italy, to discuss 'the secret transmitter' he was thought to be operating. What is more, William Haley, who was only three weeks into his job as Editor-in-Chief of the BBC, had been brought all the way from Britain by a circuitous air route to attend the meeting. There was, of course, no secret transmitter; Frank was sending his material back to the BBC as soon as he could, whereas the field commanders were taking their time to send selected reports of their activities to Alexander's headquarters. The other side of that coin was that Haley struck up a·good relationship with Montgomery. As a result of which, the BBC had thirty-two reporters covering the invasion of Europe the following summer – and its own mobile transmitter! Nearly forty years on, we were not so well represented.

The difficulties faced by the television reporters in particular were unprecedented. It was three weeks before a still picture of the recapture of South Georgia reached the UK; in his book, *Gotcha!*, Robert Harris comments that for television 'the situation was marginally *worse* than it had been in the Crimea. In 1854 the Charge of the Light Brigade was graphically described in *The Times* twenty days after it took place. In 1982, some television film took as long as twenty-three days to get back to London, and the average for the whole war, from filming to transmission, was seventeen days.'

The American networks were incredulous at the lack of coverage, though they were to experience very similar restrictions (perhaps copied from the Falklands model) when their own invasion of Grenada took place in October 1983. Given the lack of pictures from our own crews, some viewers found it hard to bear seeing the welter of film provided by Argentine television from the islands and from Buenos Aires. For others, the regular appearances of retired soldiers and sailors speculating about future military moves was no less infuriating.

The reasons for our lack of pictures were both technical and complicated. Satellite transmission of pictures from *Hermes* would have meant using the Navy's own communications system which, understandably, they refused to allow. There was talk of using an American satellite but that too came to nothing. Film and ENG (Electronic News Gathering) coverage was available to us from the ground station at Ascension Island; but once the fleet passed on into the South Atlantic and was out of helicopter range for lifting material back to the island, we were entirely dependent on voice-only reports from our correspondents. Otherwise, pictures were put on the next ship returning to Ascension: hence the occasional twenty-three-day lapse. There was also the inevitable problem of MoD censorship – double censorship in fact, because material had to be vetted in the Falklands themselves, once the Task Force had landed, and again in London. Quite often, as we were to discover to our chagrin, one or other system would pass copy which the other would then stop. It made the news editors' job a nightmare.

Meantime, our tabloid newspapers, in particular the *Sun*, were having a jingoistic field day. Amidst talk of a negotiated settlement the *Sun*, on 20th April, roared: 'STICK IT UP YOUR JUNTA!' A week later, they screamed: 'IN WE GO' – three weeks before British troops actually landed on the Falklands. Their climax came when the *Belgrano* was sunk on 2nd May with the headline: 'GOTCHA! That even outdid the *News of the World*'s scorecard, 'BRITAIN 6 (SOUTH GEORGIA, TWO AIRSTRIPS, THREE WARPLANES), ARGENTINA 0 in treating war like a children's cartoon. In this hysterical atmosphere, it was fairly certain that some of the tabloids would manufacture some kind of campaign against the BBC. For the moment, they were too busy savaging each other. 'What is it but treason,' yelled the *Sun* about the *Daily Mirror*, 'for this timorous, whining publication to plead day after day for appeasing the Argentine dictators because they do not believe the British people have the stomach for a fight, and are instead prepared to trade peace for honour?' To which the *Mirror* responded in kind. Under the headline 'THE HARLOT OF FLEET STREET', it wrote: 'The *Sun* has long been a tawdry newspaper. But since the Falklands crisis began it has fallen from the gutter to the sewer . . .'

Then the BBC's turn for the lash came. It began with an attack on a *Newsnight* programme by Jack Page, MP for Harrow West. He took offence at phrases used by Peter Snow and claimed they were 'almost treasonable'. What Peter Snow said was this: 'There is a stage in the coverage of any conflict where you can begin to discern the level of accuracy of the claims and counter-claims of either side. Tonight, after two days, it must be said that we cannot demonstrate that the British have lied to us so far but the Argentines clearly have.' He went on to report an Argentine claim that *Hermes* had been disabled, roundly denied by Hanrahan. Later Snow continued: 'So what now? If we believe the British, and I have already pointed out we have good reason to . . .' As I said a little later, I thought the phrasing infelicitous, but treasonable? I authorised a statement pointing out that 'in its coverage of the situation in the South Atlantic, BBC Television and Radio have reported British, American and Argentine statements and reactions, while stressing the unreliability of Argentine claims.' (Ironically and coincidentally, the Argentines began jamming our Spanish programmes beamed to Latin America by the External Services, though they did not make a very good job of it.)

But by now the bandwagon was really rolling. Jack Page raised the issue with the Prime Minister in the House on 6th May when he asked her if she felt that 'the British case on the Falkland Islands is being presented in a way likely to give due confidence to friends overseas and support and encouragement to our servicemen and their devoted families?' Mrs Thatcher's rebuke was unequivocal:

> Judging by many of the comments I have heard from those who watch and listen more than I do, many people are very concerned indeed that the case for our British forces is not put over fully and effectively. I understand there are times when it seems that we and the Argentines are being treated almost as equals and on a neutral basis. I understand there are occasions when some commentators will say that the Argentines did something and then 'the British' did something. I can only say that if this is so, it gives offence and causes great emotion among many people.

It did not seem to cut much ice that Ian McDonald himself nightly used the phrase 'British forces'. In fact, we were following the same practice used during the war and again at the time of Suez. But the apparent even-handedness was bound to inflame passions, especially when the tabloid papers rejoiced daily in reference to 'our boys'. Anybody who did not follow them was to be accused of treason, as we shortly were to be ourselves. John Wilson, our Editor of News and Current Affairs in Radio, spelt out the policy we had decided on in a memo dated 26th April:

> Not Our Troops
> We should try to avoid using 'our' when we mean 'British'. When we say 'our troops', 'our ambassador' or 'our ships' we sound to some people as though we are a mouthpiece of Government. We are not Britain, we are the BBC; so 'our' should be reserved for 'our correspondent' and 'our reporter'. No listener should be in any doubt that when we refer to 'our man in Buenos Aires' we are talking about a BBC correspondent and not a British official.

It seemed the right approach, not least since we were broadcasting to a world which might feel sceptical about the Falklands conflict. Already, Ian Trethowan had written to remind Jack Page that 'our people wish to be told the truth and can be told it, however unpleasant it may be.' And George Howard in a speech on 6th May underlined that argument:

> It needs saying with considerable vigour that of course the BBC is not, and could not be, neutral as between our country and an aggressor . . . But apart from the fact that Argentina is an aggressor, one of the things that distinguishes us from that country is that we

have the good fortune to live in a parliamentary democracy whereas the Argentines are ruled by a military dictatorship. One of the greatest virtues of living in a free land is that our people wish to be told the truth.

All that fell on stony ground. The brave *Sun* screamed: 'There are traitors in our midst', and named Peter Snow and the BBC. Robert Adley, MP for Christchurch and Lymington, took issue with us over film of the funerals of Argentinian sailors, saying we had become 'General Galtieri's fifth column in Britain'. The temperature was rising fast. Even Francis Pym, then Foreign Secretary, joined the fray after a meeting of the War Cabinet. Speaking to the Foreign Affairs Select Committee, he said that 'I think all of us are aware of the criticism of the presentation [of the war], particularly by the BBC. The Government are very concerned about it indeed.'

Were we getting it wrong? As a matter of fact, there were very few complaints from the public until after the attack on HMS *Sheffield*. Then the charges began. We were giving too much time to Argentine views, to pictures from Argentina. In an interview I gave to the *Standard* at the time, I said I had sensed that if there were losses and the Government came under pressure, it would be likely to turn on the media and the BBC especially. It happened a little later than I expected, but with a ferocity I did not expect. We were all acutely aware of the sensitivities of the situation. Language, tone, pictures – any slip could inflame or wound. Ever since we screened a deeply moving interview with the mother of a sailor who had been killed on *Sheffield*, even though she clearly wanted to talk, I was worried about interviews with the bereaved and we stressed to our people the need for the utmost care in that area.

But things were now coming to the boil. *Panorama* on 10th May was a study of those who had doubts about the Falklands action. The previous edition of the programme had been given over to an interview with the Prime Minister. The introduction to the programme made it clear what the brief was. Robert Kee said:

At a critical moment like this, it's just worth remembering who started all this and how and the principle at stake. It was Argentina who unquestionably put herself in the wrong by acting unilaterally to settle this long-standing diplomatic dispute by military aggression . . . By this weekend it was equally clear we wouldn't be insisting on return to British administration and control and would be prepared to hand this over to the United Nations and the pledge to the islanders of self-determination and the paramountcy of their wishes had become much more ambiguous. Nothing could show more clearly than these really quite considerable concessions the Government's wish to avoid war, if possible. Opinion at home is now undoubtedly behind Mrs Thatcher if war seems necessary, but there are still reservations here at home. What weight do such voices carry, now that we may be poised for an invasion of the Falklands?

The programme contained five extracts from speeches and interviews with the Prime Minister together with other brief extracts from speeches by pro-Government Conservative MPs, and interviews with a retired Air Vice-Marshal, an Anglo-Argentinian opponent of the Junta, two Labour MPs and two Conservative MPs. The four MPs expressed doubts about Government policy. The film was followed by a live studio interview with Cecil Parkinson, who made no criticism of the film. I still believe it was a reasonable report to undertake, particularly as it was prefaced with a careful introduction; though with the memories of Suez nearly thirty years earlier still vivid in my mind, perhaps I should have known better.

All hell broke loose. There were some four hundred telephone complaints. In the House, Sally Oppenheim raised the matter claiming that 'for the most part it was an odious and subversive travesty'. The Prime Minister commented: 'I share the deep concern that has been expressed on many sides, particularly about the contents of yesterday's *Panorama*. I know how strongly many people feel that the case for our country is not being put with sufficient vigour on certain – I do not say all – programmes.'

Things were not helped when on the following day Dick Francis, Managing Director of Radio, made a robust response in a speech to the International Press Institute in Madrid. He argued that:

To suppress pictures of Argentine widows alongside British widows (as the London *Sunday Times* had on its front page this week) for fear of appearing unpatriotic would be ignoble at the least. The widow of Portsmouth is no different from the widow of Buenos Aires. Such suppression would fail to make clear the distinctions journalists must always make as between illegitimate, unacceptable means and legitimate, if debatable, ends, and between those responsible for the illegitimate use of force and its innocent victims. As we have already made plain, BBC journalists need no lessons in patriotism from the present Conservative Government.

Taken out of context as it quickly was, the phrase about the widow of Portsmouth poured oil on the flames.

91

The screaming editorials showed the way things were going. On the day after *Panorama*, David Holmes, then Chief Assistant to the Director General, brought a message to George Howard and me inviting us to an exchange of views with the Conservative Backbench Media Committee the following day. I asked David to nose around the House and try to get a feel of how many MPs might turn up. Usually these meetings attract a dozen or so. He said he thought about twenty-five. In fact, when we arrived at Committee Room 10 on the hot, sweaty evening of 13th May, there were nearer one hundred and twenty-five including, at the far end of the room in my direct line of vision, the impassive face of Ted Heath who, I was told, had not been seen at such a meeting for years.

The meeting was chaired by Geoffrey Johnson Smith, my old colleague from the *Tonight* days. He invited George Howard (who was at his full weight then and perspiring freely from the heat) to open up the subject, which George did, saying he understood the depth of feeling amongst members but did not believe the *Panorama* programme had been a mistake and would make no apology for it. At this the serried ranks of Tory MPs growled with fury. We were clearly for it and George's occasional tendency to perform like a great Whig grandee addressing his retainers was not helping. When he had spoken for ten minutes or so, 'Alasdair,' said he, 'will deal with your detailed complaints.' It was, I think, Bernard Braine who started. When I began to reply they barked, 'Speak up.' So I spoke up. 'Stand up,' they yelled. We were clearly in for a very special form of Star Chamber.

The descriptions provided to the press that evening (despite Geoffrey's assurance that the meeting was confidential and only he would speak to the press) were graphically lurid. We were 'roasted alive', 'there were blood and entrails all over the place'. It was, indeed, a very nasty meeting. Our defence was reported to have been 'appalling', 'disgraceful'. In truth, they had not come to listen. It was a ritual bloodletting which 'had to be gone through' as Willie Whitelaw, Home Secretary at the time, told us as he offered us a welcome whisky immediately after the ordeal. The meeting itself ended with one moment of high hilarity. A young Tory MP approached George and me as we were getting up to leave. He looked up at George and said, 'You, sir, are a traitor.' George jabbed a finger down at him, 'Stuff you!' he snapped.

The occasion seemed to have lanced the Tories' anger because when Ian Trethowan came back from abroad a week or so later, he enjoyed a very peaceful meeting at the House. And indeed, David Holmes passed on to me a message from one Conservative MP to say that the attack on us had been 'very nasty' but that, more important, he did not believe it was an attack which would carry credibility among the generality of the party.

When we came to discuss the *Panorama* programme with the Governors on Thursday 14th, most were reasonably happy about it, though both Stuart Young and William Rees-Mogg were critical. But *The Times'* correspondence column on the morning of the 14th started the rumpus all over again. It contained a letter from Robert Kee, of which he sent George and me a copy, dissociating himself from the programme's content. He thanked the Chairman and me for defending him and other colleagues against criticism of the film section of the programme; but, while agreeing it was wholly appropriate to examine the minority view about the Falklands, Kee felt it should have occupied a much shorter part of the programme and that, anyway, the film 'identified in a confusing way *Panorama*'s own view of the Falklands crisis with that of the minority view it was claiming to look at objectively'. When he finally saw the film on the air before interviewing Cecil Parkinson, he had, he said, 'momentarily considered dissociating myself from the film but in the interests of programme solidarity decided not to'. He concluded: 'Much as I would like to be able to maintain that solidarity now that the BBC is facing much ridiculous and hysterical abuse for what in general seems to me the exemplary exercise of its duty, the interests of that truth for which the BBC has always stood demand otherwise.' We were all greatly saddened by this, not least because it emanated from a distinguished journalist and broadcaster who had brought the BBC much distinction over the years. It seemed inevitable, however, that he should not continue presenting *Panorama* and he shortly asked us to terminate his contract. His letter provoked some of the tabloid papers to another bout of BBC bashing, but by the end of the week other papers came to our defence, *The Times* writing: 'The BBC has attracted most of the ministerial fire but it is also the organisation that is heard and believed around the world. It is believed because it has a reputation for telling the truth, even when truth is uncomfortable. It would be no service to Britain for the BBC to avoid discomfort and thereby lose credibility.'

When George Howard and I went to Milton Keynes on the Friday for the formal opening of our Open University Production Centre there by the Prince of Wales, Prince Charles made a series of pointed remarks about the need to back free speech which surprised and delighted us. And the first poll taken after *Panorama* seemed to vindicate our coverage of the Falklands. Eighty-one per cent felt that we should continue to pursue our traditional policy of reflecting the full range of opinion, though one in three felt there was too much information about the Argentine.

Meantime, the tension between the media and the Ministry of Defence continued unabated. Almost daily, Alan Protheroe would report some new asininity to me. In a *Listener* article written at the time he records the brief joy experienced by editors at a MoD briefing when they were told that a military photographer had been sent to Ascension Island to photograph the handover of Argentine prisoners of war. That was all the good news; the bad news was that the pictures would be brought back to the UK by an RAF VC-10 aircraft, thus ensuring further delay. When the editors pressed for reasons, it was finally admitted that the last time pictures were sent back by air from Ascension, they were impounded at Lyneham by HM Customs because they weren't accompanied by the correct documents!

Once the landings on the Falklands took place, our capacity to broadcast properly gradually improved. Brian Hanrahan, for BBC Television, had already coined the famous phrase about the Harriers on *Hermes*, 'I counted them all out and I counted them all back' (an elegant way of telling the truth without compromising the exigencies of military censorship). Robert Fox for BBC Radio also reported the recovery of the islands. Our troubles were not over, of course. There were often disagreements between the minders on the ground and the MoD in London which caused confusion and, at times, seemed to threaten danger. First, a pooled dispatch from Max Hastings reported intense bitterness amongst our troops at the San Carlos beach-head over a World Service report that the Parachute Regiment was 'due to hit Goose Green'.

Within a week of that story, a number of newspapers claimed that Colonel 'H' Jones, the CO of 2 Para, on the night before he was killed in the assault on Goose Green, had said that he would sue the BBC for manslaughter for suggesting that an attack on Goose Green was imminent. We looked into this immediately and established that the information was freely available in London from MoD and other sources. Two newspapers actually reported the recapture of Goose Green two days before it happened. And, anyway, the time-scale alleged by the reports did not fit the facts of the broadcasts. On top of which, Robert Fox, who had become very close to Colonel 'H' and was the only journalist with him the night before he died, categorically denied that the Colonel had ever uttered any threat to take action against the BBC, though he was furious with the MoD. But the tensions were there, nonetheless.

The day after the Argentine surrender, two journalists wrote absorbingly, I thought, though from very different standpoints about broadcast coverage of the Falklands War. In the *Daily Mail*, Herbert Kretzmer wrote: 'Television has been the indispensable messenger from the front. Its voices and pictures, sometimes long delayed, provided glimpses of burning ships, hillside funerals, exploding aircraft, troops on the march across misty landscapes. It was, in every sense, a shared national experience, unifying millions of strangers in a shifting mood of hope, sorrow and admiration. It was a time for staying home.'

And Chris Dunkley of the *Financial Times* had this to say: 'The fact remains that it is to television that one has turned to hear the latest about these matters. As a newspaperman for twenty years and a former reporter, I have watched with some sadness as television has taken over more surely and more thoroughly than ever that exciting area of immediacy that used to be the prerogative of Fleet Street.'

There had to be a post-mortem on the Ministry of Defence's handling of the media coverage which Alan Protheroe had described as 'close to disastrous'. In the event and in the calm of the aftermath, new arrangements were hammered out which should ensure that, if, unhappily, such an eventuality occurred again, broadcasters and the media generally will have a proper working relationship with the relevant military.

One final spasm occurred when the Prime Minister flew to visit the Falklands the following January. BBC Television News had a crew out there doing some follow-up stories, and we were tipped off to keep them there for a few days. The Prime Minister arrived, we covered her visit. It transpired that Bernard Ingham, the Prime Minister's Press Secretary, expected us to make our pictures available to ITN though there had been no previous indication that this was to be a 'pool' job. We thought this an unnecessary piece of charity. Alan Protheroe refused and violent telephone conversations followed between him and Ingham over a distance of eight thousand miles where things were said that I guess they now both regret.

At the time I happened to be in the West Indies visiting one of our overseas transmitters there, and went on to Ascension Island where we also have transmitters and where the BBC plays a big part in the administration of the island. The Prime Minister was due to pass through Ascension on her way home, and I prepared myself for a dressing-down, but my guardian angel allowed me to fly out just before she arrived from the Falklands. At all events, Alan's noisy exchange with Bernard Ingham, where threats were swapped and expletives freely used, became public because a radio ham overheard and recorded it. Soon afterwards, parts of that exchange figured in a Channel 4 programme about the BBC. So, even nine months later, the Falklands War was providing broadcasting material, as it did again with the very moving documentaries BBC Television produced about the Welsh Guardsman so badly burnt at Bluff Cove.

For the BBC, these were difficult weeks in terms of resolving the technical and logistical problems of keeping people informed about what was happening in the South Atlantic. Weeks, too, when the media, but particularly the BBC, were seen more clearly in the eyes of some politicians as an increasingly independent force. They were also weeks when that feeling about the BBC sowed seeds of enmity in the minds of some newspapers and politicians which would come to fruition at a later date.

8 Balance or Fairness? Ulster and the Miners' Strike

I read an extract from Tony Benn's diaries recently, headlined 'AT WAR WITH THE RIGHT-WING BBC', where he records how 'I shamed Hugh Greene with some of my thinking on local broadcasting and my desire to ease the BBC monopoly. I feel no sense of loyalty to him since the BBC is wildly right-wing.'

That sort of absurdity is something broadcasters must try to bear with fortitude, just as they must expect to read daily about the BBC being a nest of crypto-Communists. Right from the start, 'balance', or as I would prefer it, fairness, has been the engine of the BBC's journalistic activities. Clause Thirteen of the Licence requires that the Corporation should 'refrain at all times from broadcasting matters expressing the opinion of the Corporation on current affairs or matters of public policy'. The BBC cannot entertain an editorial opinion of its own. In a letter written by Lord Normanbrook as Chairman in the sixties, and reaffirmed by subsequent Boards at the time of Charter renewals, the BBC has continued to proclaim its duty to ensure a high editorial standard, and to produce programmes which 'so far as possible' do not offend against good taste or decency. There have also been several reaffirmations that the BBC will 'treat controversial subjects with due impartiality'.

These prescriptions deliver a clear message and one that all broadcasters in this country understand. Those who try to bend the rules, never mind break them, are soon exposed because broadcasting is such an open and public medium. I say that as roundly as I can, in the face of years of muttering about broadcasting organisations being in the grip of left-wing producer cadres.

There have been times when parliament, instinctively wary of the power of broadcasting, put obstacles in our way that made any kind of decent reporting almost impossible. When I joined the BBC, the bizarre 'fourteen-day rule' still prevailed. In an attempt to underwrite the supremacy of parliament, broadcasters were at that time forbidden to deal with any subject which might come before the House of Commons within the following fourteen days. Churchill himself had argued that it 'would be shocking to have debates in this House forestalled, time after time, by expressions of opinion of persons who had not the status or responsibility of MPs'. Since the parliamentary timetable has never been that exact, it meant that most subjects of importance never got any kind of airing, and the prohibition was eventually laughed out of existence and suspended indefinitely in July 1957.

But two major upheavals in our country – one still continuing after eighteen years, the other lasting only a year but dividing society, splitting village from village and causing feuds within individual families – tested our concepts of fairness to the limit and our audience's judgement of whether we were, indeed, being fair. The first is the question of Ulster; the second, the miners' strike of 1984–5.

I had an early personal introduction to the difficulties of broadcasting about Ulster when I was producing *Highlight* in the autumn of 1956. The very day the DG, Sir Ian Jacob, came to inspect us troops at Lime Grove, as I have described earlier, the IRA blew up one of the BBC's transmitters in Northern Ireland. As an organisation, the IRA had been more or less dormant for years. Their pre-war atrocities seemed a faint memory of the post-partition agony. So what were they up to blowing up things again, and particularly one of our transmitters?

Cynthia Judah knew a writer for films and broadcasting called H.A.L. (Harry) Craig. We talked to Harry on the phone and he gave a vivid account of how the movement still lived on in a twilight world, rejoicing, as he put it, in 'the hump on the back of Ireland'. And he was equally expressive on the air. I went out to dinner, pleased that perhaps we had shed some light on this odd event. When I got home, garbled messages from our Danish au-pair revealed that all hell had broken loose. Harry had stirred atavistic loathings among a few viewers but the Northern Ireland Government, and in particular the Prime Minister of the day, Lord Brookeborough, were very angry. There was much telephoning between the BBC and Stormont Castle over the weekend and Brookeborough appeared on *Panorama* on the following Monday 'to put the record straight'.

I learnt a further lesson on Ulster when we sent Alan Whicker, in 1959, to Northern Ireland to report for *Tonight*. The programme had filmed by then in most corners of the country and widely overseas. We had never yet set foot in that province of the United Kingdom. Alan's first story was about betting shops, already legal in Ulster but not yet on the mainland. In order to highlight the differences of the Province from the rest of the UK, he made reference, with pictures, to the RUC carrying guns, to the rich variety of sectarian graffiti offensive to Queen and Pope alike, to the differences in recruiting practices during the war. The film caused a storm. Although the differences were real, it seemed people did not care to be reminded of them.

The second Whicker report, about the widely-known gerry-mandering of housing allocation to the detriment of the republican population in Londonderry, caused an even bigger row. There was much anxiety at Broadcasting House and in BH Belfast. We looked at the other films with the closest scrutiny. There was one, I remember, about the Giant's Causeway where Alan was mildly critical of the catering arrangements in the café there. None of the other four saw the light of day. I vowed then we would never film again in Northern Ireland for *Tonight*.

But we did. In the early sixties, we took our courage in our hands, alerted our colleagues in Northern Ireland that we were on the way, and sent Trevor Philpott to see what he could make of it. Trevor was, as always, meticulous in research and execution. When the films were ready in rough-cut form, I insisted that the Head of Programmes for BBC Northern Ireland attend a pre-lunch viewing every day so that we could hear his comments and take appropriate action. Every day, poor Harry McMullen caught the 8.00 a.m. plane from Aldergrove (no easy shuttles then). There were many anguished cries and gasps in the viewing theatre but we worked our way through the films and all went out more or less as planned.

I knew from all this that our colleagues in Belfast were more sensitive about the Stormont Government than was common BBC practice with governments at Westminster. Indeed, Andrew Stewart, who was Controller there after the war, told me later that he had almost been treated as an unofficial member of the Northern Ireland Cabinet. There is a question to be answered one day as to how far the BBC – and Fleet Street, too, for that matter – was responsible for not informing the rest of the country of the conduct of political affairs in Northern Ireland in the fifties and sixties. At all events, the 'peace marches' of 1969, the introduction of the Army to secure the position of the Catholics and all that followed, were as much a shock to us in the BBC, I believe, as they were to the rest of the country. And as the tensions and the violence grew, with the IRA killings, Bloody Sunday, internment without trial, so the editorial responses became more complicated. We were already having to cope with our film crews being assaulted, our staff being abused and threatened by both sides of the divide, and that has gone on almost without change ever since. Our staff in Northern Ireland have behaved with great courage and total commitment for the past eighteen years, in the face of daily danger and difficulty.

The problems reared up. Should, for example, spokesmen for the

Provisional IRA be allowed access to the air? Charles Curran was the first Director General of the BBC to have to think through these complexities and, at a time when the Secretary of State for Northern Ireland was having talks, albeit secret, with the Provisionals. If they were kept off the air, you would be accused of taking a partial view of a complex political problem and, indeed, of possibly depriving the public of information which could prove vital. If you allowed them on the screen, you would be accused of giving succour to the enemies of the state and offering a free platform to murderers and thugs. Charles wrote of his own dilemma: 'The state authorities will undoubtedly say that to give such expression to physical dissent (i.e. bombing and murder) is to join in the attack on civil order in society. And yet the maintenance of civil order will depend on an understanding of the reasons for revolt and, presumably, on a rejection of those reasons.'

I remember Charles justifying to a wary News and Current Affairs meeting his giving of permission for David O'Connell, at that time widely held to be Chief of Staff of the IRA, to be interviewed about a threatened bombing campaign of the mainland. He felt sure, Charles said, that O'Connell meant what he said about this bombing campaign and people ought to be aware of the danger from the horse's mouth. It was Charles, though, who introduced the prescription, that still holds, that permission to conduct such interviews must be obtained from the Director General himself. He was cautious, and rightly. The very language you use can inflame and possibly lead to bloodshed. Our reporting came in for the most acute semantic study. 'The Army say', we would report; 'The IRA claim'.

The broadcasters' position was not made easier by the press suffering no such inhibitions. They freely quoted IRA spokesmen and interviewed whomsoever they pleased. They still do. The day following the Enniskillen Remembrance Day massacre, the *Independent* carried a long briefing by a Provisional IRA spokesman. The position of Sinn Fein as a political party adds a further twist to the rack. Although broadcasters for Radio Telefis Eireann were specific-ally forbidden from interviewing members of the IRA or Sinn Fein by Conor Cruise O'Brien's Act in the early 1970s (pressure continues from the broadcasting authorities to get the Irish Government to lift this ban), Sinn Fein has never been proscribed by the British Government. Moreover, it boasts an elected member of the UK parliament and a number of councillors who are regularly involved in broadcast discussion of local Ulster affairs.

At all events, we took our own decision to be cautious and pick our way a-tiptoe through this minefield. In such a highly charged and emotional situation, the broadcast picture or word carries a more potent message than the printed word. But others lashed us for what they saw as our unheroic, feeble approach to the Northern Ireland situation. I have mentioned the Annan Report quoting the distinguished American broadcaster Fred Friendly as being one outspoken critic of the BBC in this matter. Yet we were not that mealy-mouthed.

In late 1971, for example, we set about trying to mount a measured examination of the issues in Northern Ireland with specific interest in the future rather than the past; as the programme went forward in preparation, all the required consultative procedures were scrupulously followed, involving the Director General, the Chairman, the Board. Early warning came when the Prime Minister of Northern Ireland, Brian Faulkner, complained about the projected programme to Charles Curran. Reggie Maudling, who was then Home Secretary but was also responsible for Northern Ireland affairs, told Hill and Curran he thought the project 'potentially dangerous' and asked them to drop the idea. His protest was strong and after a press campaign against the BBC led by the *Daily Telegraph*, was reinforced by a letter sent to the press in which he said he believed the programme 'in the form in which it had been devised could do no good and could do serious harm'. He could, of course, have fallen back on the formal powers of veto which exist for the Government to use, and for the BBC to make public but he did not, contenting himself with thunderous objection. A precedent which was to have resonance some thirteen years later.

The programme's future took another tricky turn when all Stormont representatives pulled out. But, in the end, a comparatively obscure Unionist MP, Jack Maginnis, was persuaded to appear and the programme went ahead. It was generally held to be responsible to the point of dullness. As Lord Caradon, one of the three members of the 'tribunal' with Lord Devlin and Sir John Foster, rather charmingly said, 'We may have been dull, but not dangerous!'

It wasn't only Conservative Ministers who took issue with the BBC over Northern Ireland. Towards the end of 1979, the Board of Governors went to Belfast on one of their regular regional visits, in this case also to cast an eye over a newly opened studio block there. Afterwards, in the evening, there occurred the 'Second Battle of Culloden', as it was always known, because the bloodshed took place in the Culloden Hotel.

The Board entertained the Secretary of State, Roy Mason; the Commander of the Land Forces, Major-General David Young; the Chief Justice of Northern Ireland and the Chief Constable of the RUC, at that time Kenneth Newman. All was bonhomie over dinner. Afterwards, Michael Swann invited the Secretary of State to tell the Board how things were going from the broadcasting point of view.

101

Mason, we were told, came at them like an Exocet. He accused the BBC of disloyalty, of giving succour to the Queen's enemies, of being a propaganda outlet for the IRA. He was uncompromising. He reminded the Governors that the Charter and Licence were coming up for renewal and so was the licence fee, and that he had a hand in these matters. Nor was there any mitigating voice from the other guests. The Governors were shaken, but robust.

We were not feeble, either, when Ian Trethowan had to take the very difficult decision about an interview with the Irish National Liberation Army, a splinter group from the official IRA, who claimed to have murdered Airey Neave by blowing up his car outside the House of Commons. The organisation had not then been proscribed, though it soon was. Ian agreed to the recording of a hooded figure talking about Neave's murder and, later, to its transmission on the last night of the 1979 *Tonight* programme (the title had been revived briefly for the predecessor to *Newsnight*). It had, unfortunately, the feel of being rushed on to the air, almost as a final act of bravado before the programme's demise. Worse, Lady Neave had not been warned about its screening though the programme producers had tried to contact her. There was a big fuss and later Ian was sure he was wrong to have agreed to its transmission. The timing, so shortly after Airey Neave's murder, was not happy.

There were other moments of extreme sensitivity, even though our instructions about the interviewing of suspected terrorists included the Director General's personal permission to proceed as a first stage, and as a second stage to transmit. (A confusion in these arrangements contributed to some of the pain over the *Real Lives* episode later, which I discuss in Chapter 12.)

I have mentioned the Carrickmore incident. There was also an occasion of a different kind when Lucy Faulkner, National Governor for Northern Ireland for seven years, and somebody I greatly admire, nearly fell out with me when I was Managing Director of BBC Television. BBC-2 had produced a dramatised version of an event that took place at the time of the Easter Rising in 1916. The story involved the maltreatment of republican prisoners by a British officer, and the programme was due for transmission on the night when Bobby Sands, the hunger striker, seemed likely to die. Jimmy Hawthorne, the Northern Ireland Controller, phoned me to say Lucy was deeply anxious and felt we should withdraw the programme. He saw the obvious dangers of going ahead with transmission, but reminded me of the equal danger from the loyalist side if we cancelled it. I phoned Lucy. If Sands died, she said, and people were killed as a result, this programme might well lead to us having blood on our hands. It was a cruel dilemma. I felt we ought to risk transmission and rang her back to say so. She accepted the decision and prayed I would not be found wrong. Sands did die, but not that night.

The troubles in Ulster have tested us operationally and editorially to the limit. We have much experience there now, but as the *Real Lives* episode taught us again, Northern Ireland has always some new, devilish plot cooking with which to rack the broadcaster once again.

The miners' strike of 1984–5 subjected us to a different kind of examination. Firstly, it involved a massive BBC effort, not just from network television and radio reporters and crews, but also from many BBC local radio stations – Radio Sheffield, Radio Nottingham, Radio Humberside in particular – who themselves were the source of much of the news. Secondly, the hostility of much of Fleet Street towards the NUM, and especially its leadership, led in turn to hostility on the union's part towards all sections of the media. We came in for our fair share, as we came in for criticism from the public who, in the early part of the dispute, perceived an imbalance in our coverage, with Arthur Scargill, apparently, making too much of the running.

Mrs Thatcher told me at one point that, since she always listens to the *Today* programme in the morning, she used her husband, Denis, as a second line of defence during the miners' strike and asked him to stay in bed and keep a weather eye on *Breakfast Time*. When roars of rage emanated from the bedroom, she knew that Arthur Scargill was on television again!

But the concept of exact mathematical balance, which the BBC abandoned within individual programmes years ago because it leads to programme stultification, is not capable of pursuit if one party to the dispute hides its head in a plastic bag. Again, additional constraints in reporting this dispute arose from the very real risk of violence to reporters and camera crews and damage to equipment. Enough of that occurred for us to give priority to safety, which meant filming from behind police lines and was immediately taken as proof of partiality. Furthermore, what we broadcast often influenced the course of the strike. Early on, the BBC was seen by the union as an important channel of communication to its membership, just as later on the National Coal Board and the Government saw the importance of the media in trying to persuade the miners to abandon the strike. The strike also went on for an exhausting length of time, and was inevitably very costly for the broadcasters as well as everybody else.

Arthur Scargill's tactics as a media operator were a rich study. Within days of the beginning of the dispute, he said he was 'appalled' at the 'biased reporting' of a visit he made to Scotland. In fact, the union's viewpoint had been expressed on television by one of Mr

Scargill's colleagues, while he himself was busy turning down an invitation to appear on *Today*. And in all the interviews he gave, Arthur Scargill became increasingly adept at getting his own points across. Within the limits of common courtesy, all interviewers pressed him to answer the questions they thought viewers and listeners would wish to hear answered. He became extremely skilful at saying only what he wanted to say. And he tended to swamp all other union voices in a highly possessive way.

By contrast, the National Coal Board's posture seemed to fall into the pre- and post-Eaton phases, as one of my colleagues described it. Before Michael Eaton was thrust into the limelight, top-level Coal Board interviews were difficult to secure. Ian MacGregor did not like appearing himself and didn't much like others appearing in his stead. Once Michael Eaton arrived on the scene, contributions were readily available. In fact, he himself on more than one occasion rang *Newsnight* direct to offer an opinion.

Did we appear to be even-handed? Did we treat the police operations, massive as they were at times, properly?

We certainly dug deep into the issues and tried our best to reflect the views of miners, on strike or not, and of the wives, mothers and children. We talked to local shopkeepers, we talked about fund raising, about communal meals. We certainly did not feel guilty of Asa Briggs' statement about the BBC coverage of the 1926 General Strike: 'No attempt was made . . . to depict the realities of working class life, the sense of solidarity, struggle and occasional triumph which the strikers felt.'

And yet, the difficulties of achieving balance and fairness were thrown up in sharp relief. John Wilson, the Editor of News and Current Affairs for Radio, wrote a sober piece for us when it was all over:

The cruder notion of balance [he said at one point] took a hammering. An instance of what it amounted to was this. Mr Scargill made much news when he went to the Labour Party Conference while Mr MacGregor made no news when he did not go to the Conservative Party Conference. The Coal Board Chairman wasn't even at the CBI Conference. No news programme could ignore the stir caused by Mr Scargill in Blackpool. We certainly could not ignore it for the reason that Mr MacGregor, as we knew, would not be in Brighton to cause an equivalent balancing stir.

We had great problems, too, in attempting to tell the true story of the activities of the police during the strike. The violence at the

Orgreave coking works in the summer of 1984 provided enduring images of the dispute and caused considerable controversy about whether the BBC was attempting to adopt a position of neutrality between those who broke the law and those who were trying to maintain law and order. It has never been part of the BBC's position, obviously, to resist the edicts of the law: but when the police were turning back Kent miners at the Dartford Tunnel, setting up road blocks throughout the Nottinghamshire coalfield, and when the miners retaliated by cruising slowly along the MI and closed the Humber Bridge, these were events that had to be fully and properly reported. During November, the *Open Space* programme broadcast a piece which underlined the difficulties our crews and reporters faced when, for their own safety, they filmed from behind the police lines. This programme, put together by a group called Sheffield Police Watch who were sympathetic to the miners, filmed from behind the *picket* lines. It provided a sharp contrast to the pictures already seen of the Orgreave confrontation.

John Wilson also wrote illuminatingly about the violence problem. He said:

The strikers' argument was two-fold. About the first part we could do little. This was the claim that the very presence of the police – in great numbers, the riot gear, the drumming on the shields and the horses – was a threat and provocation. They said that a milder presence would have ensured milder behaviour by the pickets. It was not possible for us to test this claim. Only the police could do that. We certainly aired it in our programmes, national and local politicians spoke about it and we broadcast also the police response to it.

The other part of the argument was that once at a mass picket, the police often behaved very badly. (Particularly, it was claimed, the Metropolitan Police.) This is where we were bound by what we had seen ourselves. We reported what we saw the police do and they did not usually beat up pickets in our presence. They did not knock on doors at dawn when we were about. Because we can't be everywhere, we did not see them crashing across peaceful gardens and into quiet homes in search of troublemakers (as it was often said they did). The best we could do was to try and catch up with things after the event. Our news reports included the allegations and our feature reports evoked the atmosphere in villages where people felt victimised by the police.

Another charge against us was that we exaggerated the significance of the violence on the picket lines and grossly underplayed 'the issues'. We dealt with the issues exhaustively, if not conclusively.

About the rest we can be bold. The picketing was often on a large scale, the violence was often on a large scale, and these events were important. They mattered. They mattered because they happened and we did not have any other reason for reporting them.

John Wilson's paper wondered in conclusion whether, in this strike, the BBC was one of the losers, like the Coal Board, the NUM, the coal industry and the country.

It is an interesting fact that we received fewer complaints for our coverage of the miners' strike than we did for our coverage of the Falklands War. The explanation could be that the divisions created by the miners' strike were so strongly felt that lots of people could not or would not recognise neutrality. The vast silent majority may have regarded us as a fair reporter. Why then did even fewer speak out than normally do? It is certainly possible that we were not as good as we think we were. It could be that in our determination to be nobody's stooge, we disregarded decent doubts.

That is a proper explanation by a senior BBC journalist of the problems he had to cope with on a daily basis for more than a year, and of the underlying philosophical tensions the broadcaster must face. But these incidents are passing phases in the long-drawn-out discussion of balance and fairness. Were we unfair to the SDP and the Alliance in not giving them, as Dr Owen saw it, equivalence in our television news bulletins to the activities of the two main parties, even though in current affairs programmes the Alliance's views were tested almost nightly? We argued that news values should not be bent to satisfy party formulae, and especially party formulae based on votes cast in the country rather than the traditionally accepted pattern of seats won in the House of Commons. It was absolutely open to David Owen to contest that accepted pattern, as it was for him to take us to court which he duly did. We were trying, in a new situation, to be fair. He wanted the BBC to help him change the political mould and that is not part of our commitment.

But the attempt to be fair has thrown up problems and difficulties of a fundamental nature for the BBC. My story encompasses the development of those problems. When I joined the BBC, it was part of an establishment consensus that included, of course, the Labour Party and the TUC. The political parties defined the political and social debate and the permissible areas of controversy; the BBC, being the national instrument of broadcasting, went along with those definitions – including, for a time, the absurd fourteen-day rule. But

106

the arrival of ITV and a series of events thereafter – Suez, the anti-establishment revolution launched by *Look Back in Anger* and embracing CND, *Beyond the Fringe*, the Establishment Club – created a rift whereby the BBC became two things: a provider of radio and television programmes to the nation, which it has continued to do with great success and popularity, but also an independent institution which has increasingly attracted the hostility of the consensus to which it once belonged.

Suez and the BBC's attempt to tell the truth about the divisions within the country started the Tories' disaffection with the BBC. I vividly remember being a guest at a Bushmen Dinner – one of a regular series of occasions run by a Bush House club – where Charlie Hill, still a Government Minister, was the guest speaker shortly after Suez. His vitriolic attack on the BBC's handling of Suez was only matched by the fury it provoked among his normally peaceful audience. On *Tonight* we chose to interpret balance by being equally critical of both parties, instead of being equally uncritical. We identified with the viewers' interests and concerns, not the politicians'. We offered people a platform, but if often had a trap door in it.

And *That Was The Week That Was* distanced the BBC even further from the political establishment, particularly the Conservative Party, by its open mockery and total lack of deference. Labour, too, was to get a rude shock when it came into office; expecting a friendly BBC, it was appalled to find the BBC disseminating criticisms of its Government as much as it had done of the Tories. Hence the continuing rows with Harold Wilson, culminating in *Yesterday's Men*. By the 1974 election, 'the media' were perceived as an independent institution united by shared hostility to all politicians. And the increasing rancour and bitterness between Heath and Wilson made things worse: as Oliver Whitley put it, 'the nation divided puts the BBC on the rack'. Since 1979, a new factor has been brought into the equation: the Thatcherite philosophy of the market place can grant a tolerance, perhaps even a grudging respect, to those organs of the media which survive in a highly competitive market – however offensive No. 10 may find the *Guardian*, the *Observer* or the *Mirror*. Alone, the BBC can be held up to be subsidised by public money and licensed thereby to allow criticism of the Government to be voiced. No wonder we have had a few problems in the last years!

If my analysis is correct, it will need much wisdom from Government and from programme makers if they are to be brought closer together again, without the BBC returning to the neutral and negative role of the early 1950s. Yet the struggle to be fair is unequivocally bound up with the dedication to tell the truth.

I tried to express some element of that duty in a speech I gave in Glasgow in early 1983.

Dedicated to telling the truth the BBC is, come what may. Mr Begin first heard of the Beirut massacre, he says, from a BBC broadcast. When Alexander Solzhenitzyn came out of the Soviet Union, the first interview he granted was to a BBC man because he felt deeply grateful to the BBC for telling him what was going on in his own country. During the recent Falklands campaign, we received phone calls from Argentinian radio stations which, at least away from the microphone, doubted what they themselves were saying. Conversely, we showed Argentinian film which contradicted our own claims to have put the airfield at Port Stanley out of action, one of the few instances where the Argentinians came nearer the truth than we did.

Our country takes the BBC's dedication to truth-telling wholly for granted. You have only to look at the highly organised lying in the services of an ideology or a creed or a state which afflicts entire continents, to see how rare truth-telling is in broadcasting or, for that matter, what extraordinary efforts are being made by totalitarian régimes to prevent our undoctored broadcasts from reaching their own citizens.

9 THE NEW TECHNOLOGY

As I write in the late summer of 1987, the first British satellite to disseminate Direct Broadcasting by Satellite (DBS) should have been up in the skies for nearly a year. The launch date we all worked towards was September 1986. That it has not yet happened, and looks unlikely to happen for some time to come, is a matter of bitter disappointment to me and the BBC.

We started down the DBS road with high hopes back in 1980. An international conference had, as it were, carved up the skies rather as Spain and Portugal carved up the New World five hundred years ago. Each country was allocated a geo-stationary position for its DBS operations (that is to say, the satellite when launched would, due to the rotation of the earth, stay in the same place in space); with its geo-stationary position would go a 'footprint', the 'footprint' being the area that the satellite would cover, spilling far beyond national boundaries with the satellite power that was envisaged. Thus, the UK satellite, geo-stationary at thirty-two degrees west somewhere just off Brazil, would not only cover the United Kingdom with its footprint but large areas of Scandinavia, the Low Countries, France and West Germany. Equally, the Irish footprint would cover most of the UK. Those were the international arrangements.

The BBC applied to the Government for access to two of the possible five channels that went with every satellite allocation under the international regulations. We did that because we were keen to get involved in this technology, as we had always been throughout our history, not least because it must surely, one day, replace the transmitters that cover and sometimes despoil our countryside and become the new method of sending television and radio signals to everybody in the country. We also saw DBS as a new way of delivering quite different programme opportunities to an audience that would be making its selection on a new pattern, and we thought we could achieve that aim as well as anybody else. Moreover, we thought that in due time this new service might earn the BBC some additional money: not a lot, nothing that could come near replacing the licence fee, but additional money that might help to reduce the necessary increments in the licence fee which seemed to be a growing political worry. This satellite operation would, we were clear, be quite independent of the licence fee. It would be an additional service, paid for either by regular subscription or on a 'pay-per-view' basis. Exactly how, had yet to be resolved. But if you wanted it, it would be an extra commitment. If you didn't, you would continue to pay your licence fee and contribute to ITV through your supermarket visits, and enjoy the existing terrestrial channels.

But when in early March 1982 the then Home Secretary, Willie Whitelaw, announced that he was giving us the go-ahead for two DBS channels to operate by 1986, he underlined the Government's enthusiasm to get cracking in what he called 'an area of keen international competition'. He also said that independent television could move into the DBS area in the future and that the Government would soon have something to say about cable television. There was no doubt about the enthusiasm in Whitehall for the new technology.

Bill Cotton, our new Director of Development, and I had put down some markers on the key questions about what new programmes we would offer. I had stated publicly that these would be new services. There was no question of taking programmes off existing networks and moving them to satellite channels. We envisaged the first DBS channel carrying feature films, fresh from their first cinema showing and not subject to the 'terrestrial television' inhibition of having to wait three years for such films; plus a mixture of dramatic, orchestral and operatic productions not available to the existing channels, and 'live' events not, again, available to our networks. A whole golf tournament, for example, or a complete motor race. We talked then of the second channel as the 'Window on the World', featuring the best television from around the world. The Home Office believed this second channel should depend on a supplementary licence fee. I was clear that that was a wrong move. These new channels should be quite distinct from the licence fee. They should be an extra choice for extra subscription money.

Almost immediately, phase two of the new technology came upon us. This was the publication by a committee, known as the Information Technology Advisory Panel (ITAP for short) of a report to the Prime Minister on the possible development of cable television in Britain. Cable was already widespread in the USA, 'passing' something like thirty per cent of the homes there. But there were important circumstances in the USA differing from Britain. In the USA, the huge size of the country and the way television had spread meant that for many it was difficult to receive a clear picture from a normal transmitter mast. Cable, brought direct into your home from a nearby master transmitter, offered a clearly defined picture.

110

Moreover, the constant and brutal interruption of programmes by commercials on the American networks so incensed many viewers that they turned to subscriber-supported cable to escape the onslaught of the advertisements. In this country, ninety-nine per cent of the nation already had decent signals on three channels, with Channel 4 soon to offer a further choice; the BBC did not carry commercials and the IBA regulations for their showing on ITV were much tougher than in the States. The circumstances were markedly different.

But the ITAP Committee saw a new era, a second Industrial Revolution, whereby cable would not only bring new television choice to the home but also all the potential interactive devices – shopping, banking, all done through the cable system. They were sure that in order to attract people to invest in cable, it would have to be 'entertainment-led'. The viewers would have to be attracted by things they could not get on their available channels if they were to make themselves ready for the new revolution.

The Prime Minister was, by all accounts, fired by their enthusiasm. Kenneth Baker, then Minister for Information Technology at the Department of Trade and Industry, was aflame. Yet the Government, with cautious murmurings from the Home Office in its ear, was reminded that there were problems. Who should regulate all these cable activities? Should they be regulated at all? And if complete deregulation were allowed, might there not be unmentionable horrors released on the air with only the common law as the ultimate defence? There would have to be a committee.

On 22nd March, the Home Secretary set up an inquiry with these terms of reference:

To take as its frame of reference the Government's wish to secure the benefits for the United Kingdom which cable technology can offer and its willingness to consider an expansion of cable systems which would permit cable to carry a wide range of entertainment and other services (including when available services of direct broadcasting by satellite), but in a way consistent with the wider public interest, in particular, the safeguarding of public service broadcasting; to consider the questions affecting broadcasting policy which would arise from such an expansion including, in particular, the supervisory framework; and to make recommendations by 30th September, 1982.

The Government wanted cable to forge ahead. It wanted the inquiry completed in a hurry – six months, whereas the Annan Committee deliberated for two and a half years. It invited Lord Hunt, a former

Secretary of the Cabinet, to chair the inquiry and Sir Maurice Hodgson and Professor Ring to work with him. They called for evidence with despatch, and we bustled to accommodate them, as did many other bodies. Our position, reflected in our evidence to the Hunt Committee, was clear. We had no wish to be involved in cable, except possibly as a programme supplier. We were enthusiastic about DBS because it seemed to us a proper extension of public service broadcasting. DBS would be available to everybody in the UK if they wanted it, whereas we were sure cable would take years to cover fifty per cent of the population and would possibly leave the rest severely alone. We thought DBS would bring a genuine enrichment of choice and we doubted if cable would.

We phrased the argument quite strongly in our evidence to Hunt:

It has taken a sixty-year investment in skill and dedication to create the present system of public service broadcasting, which is universally acknowledged to be a public asset. It would take a much shorter time to erode the value of that national asset if the new cable services were permitted an operating philosophy made up of quick-kill methods of financial control, a cynical view of public taste and no concern for social side effects.

In particular, we warned about the possibility of cable operators going in for 'blockbuster' attractions, perhaps outbidding the BBC and ITV in key areas of sport or entertainment. It was difficult to avoid a sense of special pleading, but we were genuinely concerned. If a cable operator bought up, say, the FA Cup Final or the Olympics, how would the normal viewers feel if those events disappeared on to a cable system which they almost certainly could not receive anyway? Access, we pointed out, would be determined by economic status. 'If cable becomes symbolic of what Mayfair can have but Brixton cannot, what Metropolitan Man may enjoy but Rural Man is denied, then one more social tension will be generated in an uneasy age.'

It was said, of course, that we were Luddite, but we weren't. It needed careful thought and the Hunt Committee didn't have much time.

Meantime, we were set on getting our BBC DBS channels under way. The Government had stipulated that the satellite must be British-made, and to that end, a consortium of GEC, British Aerospace and BT was formed, calling itself UNISAT. Very early on in our negotiations with the new consortium, the price of the satellite became a matter of dispute between us. It remains to this day a matter of prolonged and continuing litigation.

112

Eventually, on 30th July 1982, a meeting was held in Kenneth Baker's room in the Department of Trade and Industry. Kenneth was, as always, debonair and bullying by turn. He wanted DBS to go ahead soon as part of 'the information technology-led industrial revolution'. But the Government intended to have no financial involvement, and he made that very clear. It was essentially an arm-twisting session to urge the project on. Speed, he said, was of the essence.

But already another, and this time technical, hazard had emerged. It was to do with the technical standard of the new Direct Broadcasting by Satellite. Long years ago, different parts of the world adopted different technical standards (and sometimes different numbers of lines) as they developed television. The Americans and the Japanese (orchestrated by the Americans) work off a standard called NTSC; most of Europe adopted a German system called PAL; a strange alliance (led by de Gaulle) of the French and the Russians took a system called SECAM. None of them was complementary; converters had to be created to enable conversion of standard. If possible, it was clearly paramount that we should all, particularly in Europe, share a common DBS standard. But should it be the PAL system, on which most West European television functions, or should there be a new standard for the new beast?

The Government asked Sir Anthony Part, a retired civil servant, to chair a group to pronounce on this matter. The Part Committee chose a new system, invented by the IBA engineers and known as C-MAC. But no precise specification yet existed for C-MAC and it was to be many months before one did. What of the rest of Europe? Would they adopt this system as the universal one? What, in particular, of the French? They had gone their own way, together with the Russians, in terrestrial television with the SECAM system. Would they accept a British invention as the perfect answer? Nothing daunted, Sir Anthony Part stumped his way round Europe on a journey of preaching and proselytisation in 1983 with our own Director of Engineering, Bryce McCrirrick, accompanying him. There was no general agreement. There *was* agreement months later when the European Broadcasting Union adopted C-MAC; but by then the scenario had changed dramatically and, anyway, the French had produced a refinement of their own called D2-MAC!

The Hunt Committee duly reported to the Home Secretary by the end of September 1982, and their findings were published shortly afterwards. To nobody's great surprise, they supported the introduction of cable. 'It is,' they said, 'all about widening the viewer's choice. It should be innovative, experimental and sensitive to local feeling.'

113

It must also, they said, 'operate within certain, albeit liberal, ground rules'.

We thought it sensible that there should be a cable authority to award the franchises and monitor the performance, and we believed it was in the public interest that pay-per-view should not immediately be admitted as a means of payment for individual programmes. That protected the licence-paying viewer, at any rate for a while, as most certainly did the committee's recommendations that cable operators should not be allowed to obtain exclusive rights to national sporting events.

Then, with everybody else, we joined in the Great Cable Debate. On the one side were ranged those who enjoined us to heed Arthur Hugh Clough's injunction, 'But westward, look, the land is bright'. They waxed lyrical about the growth of cable in America, they compared the more than twenty channels available on cable in Manhattan to, as they saw it, the pathetic summer offerings of our four channels. They talked of freedom and compared the strict regulation of television unfavourably with the freedom of the publishing world of books. Against them spoke the anxious and sometimes querulous voices of those who feared the destruction of public service broadcasting, others who foresaw a tidal wave of pornography.

In December, an information technology conference was held under Kenneth Baker's auspices at the Barbican to mark the end of 'Information Technology Year'. The Prime Minister opened the conference with a firm personal commitment to encourage its expansion. 'We are determined,' she said, 'to encourage cable systems, not just for more entertainment but eventually for a huge range of two-way services.' I spoke at that conference myself. I noted that there had been 'much talk in the Commons the other day about the BBC having led the counter-attack on cable. That is nonsense. I have said time and again through the summer and autumn that the BBC, which has been in the forefront of new technology from its inception, welcomed and looked forward to the arrival of broadband cable in partnership with DBS.'

But my main theme was the notion of 'widening choice'.

It is very important that this expression be rigorously examined. If in the United Kingdom, as a result of cable expansion and satellite transmission, we go from four national television networks to, say, eight plus dozens of localised cable channels, there would be no widening of viewer choice if all these outlets transmitted the same or different episodes of *Dallas*. I am not using an absurd example. Try switching from channel to channel in the United States and make up your own mind whether the fare being offered there is as varied and spread over half as many programme areas as our four national television channels here in Britain at present provide . . . You can widen viewer choice over four networks and narrow choice over forty.

In the event, the growth of cable in Britain has been painfully slow and has not, in my judgement, led to any real widening of choice, for the simple reason that there are not enough good programmes to go round and no cable operator is going to start *making* any programmes until he is assured of being able to run a reasonably profitable business in the first place.

As the end of 1982 arrived, I could look back on a bumpy six months – the Falklands War, followed by DBS almost every hour of the working day. I got a nice Christmas note from George Howard: 'You've made a splendid start,' he wrote, '(I hope that doesn't sound patronising!) and I'm sure the next seven months [until his retirement] will go along as robustly and enjoyably.'

In February 1983 the Governors agreed that we should send the Home Office our financial projections for DBS, with a view to increasing our borrowing powers. It was agreed between us that the DBS operation was not in any way to be a burden on the licence fee, but must be financed by borrowing from the bank, as would be necessary for any other commercial venture. One had to recognise, however, that *in extremis* our collateral consisted of the plant, the buildings and the licence fee. We were all well aware that the figures for satellite broadcasting were going to be big. Quite apart from the bugbear of the C-MAC standard, our best estimates (and later-comers did not find much cause to dispute them) indicated losses of around £350 million in the first years, with profitability occurring possibly in Year Six. Yet we were sure that this was a new method of broadcasting in which we should involve ourselves, provided the conditions were right.

There was, however, still no confirmation by the Government of the C-MAC position and until there was such a confirmation, no manufacturer would hazard a price for a DBS set, never mind start thinking about production. But I was sure that unless, say, 250,000 sets were *ready* in the market place by September 1986 at a price people could afford, we would be broadcasting to nobody but sheep.

The air was thick with gossip, but there was no movement. At a long meeting in August, the Governors went over the ground with us again. There was talk of involving commercial partners, but we did not think the time was ripe. There was talk of a formal approach to

115

the IBA or ITCA for co-operation (I had already had an informal talk with John Whitney, the Director General of the IBA) but it was felt that that would fundamentally alter the BBC's position. We issued a public statement that the BBC continued to think DBS was something the BBC should undertake 'under proper conditions'.

On 19th August we were back again in Kenneth Baker's office, this time with our new Chairman, Stuart Young, who had steeped himself in the DBS background. Stuart put to the Minister in the strongest terms the two cardinal points: the need for 250,000 sets to be ready in the market place when the satellite flew, and if the standard was to be C-MAC, then cable operators 'must carry' in that standard. Otherwise, once again, we would have been isolated technically. Kenneth gave no commitment, but we registered our point. Quite by chance, the day before this meeting, I thought I saw the first chink of light. At one of a regular series of lunches that I gave for politicians, civil servants and industrialists, I entertained Peter Laister, the Managing Director of Thorn/EMI, soon to become its Chairman as well. We touched on DBS and its problems and he was very sceptical about its future, though towards the end of the lunch he seemed a little more enthusiastic. Now, if we could interest Thorn/EMI, the biggest set manufacturer in the country, in some form of partnership, then at a stroke we might crack the set problem.

Over the next two or three months, the situation developed at great speed. Laister himself seemed to show growing enthusiasm for the project, though some of those around him were markedly less keen. We ourselves were actively discussing the siting of the DBS HQ alongside our new studios in Newcastle: things were moving apace. There were meetings at the Home Office where we pressed the Government again for a universal technical standard, but also asked now that they wait till Thorn and we had settled on PAL or C-MAC; meetings with the IBA who were now keen to be involved; further meetings with Thorn to encourage their interest; meetings, of course, of our own Governors where Stuart Young and I regularly brought them up to date.

Late in October, a further complication arose. The IBA were objecting to Thorn's possible association with the BBC because Thorn had a shareholding in Thames Television. Laister and I saw the Home Secretary, Leon Brittan, independently on 14th November. We went over the ground fully and I asked Leon Brittan if he could persuade the IBA not to complicate the issue with Thorn. The crucial meeting took place on 11th December at Thorn House. We thought it so important that the Chairman, the Vice-Chairman (Rees-Mogg) and all the senior management involved in DBS were present. Laister told us that Thorn had decided they did not want to enter into a partnership: they felt it was too high a risk. But they remained interested in some commercial form of DBS, if it could be worked out.

In fact, we spent another nine months working first with the IBA, then with the ITCA (the ITV Companies' Association) and later, at the Government's insistence, with the so-called 'Club of 21', which included outside interests to avoid the political embarrassment of the broadcasting duopoly being extended to the skies. The Club, too, after further study, concluded that DBS as planned was not a viable business. Later still, the IBA was authorised to offer franchises for future DBS operations. In the meantime, the Murdoch Sky Channel operation, with low-powered satellite feeds to cable heads, had come into being, and at the beginning of 1987 some of the ITCA companies started up the Super Channel service of the 'best of British broadcasting' for European cable heads, with the BBC involved as a programme supplier. The new technology is with us in a variety of forms. But we failed with the 'big one' – the first DBS public service in Britain.

Looking back, the long drawn-out discussions caused great anxiety within the BBC. Both the Governors and the Management were rightly worried about the possible financial damage to the heartland of the BBC operations. Nobody had any experience of this kind of venture; judgements about satellite and programme costs were obviously important, but expectations about the manufacture, delivery and sales of receivers were critical. At times we thought we could persuade the Department of Trade and Industry to go in for a pump-priming exercise to get the making of the sets started. They were, after all, doing such things throughout the rest of the economy. But the Government's philosophy was clear and undeviating. They had made the opportunities possible within the international law agreements. It was up to the BBC, or anybody else, to pick up the baton and run with it, or not. They would not put one penny of public money towards this kind of venture which they saw as purely commercial. That the French and the Germans were backing DBS as a nationally funded enterprise moved them not at all. This was a new medium that would be funded by consumer participation, or not at all. They did not like the thought that it might fail, but they were not to be harried into a change of policy by the prospect of failure.

The DBS argument, protracted as it was, was one of the few things that gave me sleepless nights in my time as Director General. Indeed, I think the very real prospect of bringing the BBC to the brink of bankruptcy induced attacks of asthma which I had not experienced since a favourite Siamese cat introduced me to it seventeen years earlier. For a while, I was quite ill. At times, I have wished (like Home Office officials frequently did) that we had never heard of DBS. I still believe we were bound to offer ourselves as leaders in a difficult enterprise. But it was certainly one of the chief failures in my time as Director General of the BBC.

10 THE BBC AND FLEET STREET

The relationship between the BBC and Fleet Street has always been ambivalent. The newspapers have battened on broadcasting – its programme schedules, its stars, its rows – from the earliest days; and in these latter years, papers like the *Sun* or the *Star* would, seemingly, not be able to publish at all unless they had the latest exploits of some *EastEnders* performer to report, or the fictitious lives of the fictitious characters before the serial ever began to fill their columns

Television and its people, just as much as pop stars, are daily grist to the tabloid mill. And if you go into any Fleet Street (or now Wapping) office in the early evening, the journalists are glued to their radios or television screens. That is where they get their news from, as do most of the population; much more than from the established news agencies. Conversely, their dependence on the speed of the electronic media breeds jealousy and, among their masters, dreams of endless expansion. The Murdochs and Maxwells have a long history behind them of involvement in the wider media field and daily give evidence of their intention of expanding the frontiers of their empires.

On the day after my appointment as DG, I had quite a friendly press. I was the first professional producer, they noted, to become Director General of the BBC. I happened to know all the television reporters well from my time at the Television Centre. And even when we launched breakfast television just before I left the Television Service, those who saw that as a further piece of foolhardy BBC expansionism wrote in guarded terms. That reasonably happy relationship with the press seemed to change with the Falklands War. The Murdoch papers, but others as well, fell upon the BBC for what they called our lack of patriotism, as I have recorded. Nor did our involvement in DBS improve the relationship with Fleet Street. Many newspapers were committed to the development of cable and because we asked questions about its future possibilities, we were severely attacked. By putting ourselves forward as the pioneers of satellite technology and, therefore, as potential adversaries, we appeared, in the eyes of the press, to compound the felony.

There was a lull before the storm broke about us. But we were beginning to go through a period of difficulty which the press would not catch up with for a while. The Television Service's audience figures were poorer than they had been for years. We had dropped from what we all thought a reasonable balance of around 50:50 to a ratio of 58:42 against us. This was close to what I had always believed could be a real danger mark for the BBC. A downward slide of that kind contains its own momentum, and if ever there came a time when half a dozen people in a pub had not seen BBC programmes for days or weeks, then the whole fabric of the BBC's relationship with its audience and its right to the licence fee would, I thought, be in peril.

There were many reasons for what was happening. Channel 4 had arrived and, though it had no hope yet of picking up the ten per cent of the audience that Jeremy Isaacs, its Chief Executive, aspired to, it was new and it was different. Again ITV, clobbered for years on the popular viewing night of Saturday, had settled for a scheduling pattern of game shows and had given up any pretension to varied entertainment. The consequent loss of two or three ratings points at the weekend can have a troubling effect on the overall balance. For years, of course, people had wondered why the BBC should concern itself with competing for the audience's attention. Reith himself at the very beginning recognised the importance of 'entertainment' in broadcasting – with information and education it was one leg of the tripod on which he established the BBC. We knew that we were uniquely privileged in the international broadcasting world in having been able to build a strong programme base, particularly rich in popular drama and light entertainment, before the arrival of commercial competition; we were privileged, too, in the existence of the licence fee which allowed us, even in the new circumstance of commercial opposition, to adapt the principles of public service broadcasting to the new times and yet to continue to take risks, to try out new programme formats in ways that commercial broadcasting normally avoids. We learnt, too, the tricks of the 'ratings game'; how to support one winning programme with another, how to 'hammock' a less appealing programme between two successful ones. Our financial position made it possible for us to write off an evening for some special purpose, whereas that was difficult for the commercial companies for fear of offending the advertisers; equally, we knew that it was just as important to appeal to the mass of the audience as it was to serve the legitimate interests of minorities. So, if it seemed wise to strengthen, for example, the offerings on a Saturday night with better comedy, light entertainment and popular drama, then we thought it essential for the BBC's relationship with its own public that it should do so.

We had orchestrated this approach with some skill for a number of years. Suddenly, it seemed to be going wrong. I had the feeling, too, that the management of the Television Service was in disharmony. Aubrey Singer was still Managing Director, Brian Wenham had moved from running BBC-2 to become Director of Programmes when Bill Cotton went to concentrate on DBS. I had promoted Mike Checkland to be Director of Resources, Television – a new job and one with his background in planning and accountancy that was tailor-made for him. But somehow, the chemistry was wrong.

I wondered, over the Christmas break in 1983, how to resolve these difficulties. It seemed to me that Aubrey was spending too much time trying to become a feature film mogul and not enough being in close touch with the running of the Television Service. I began to feel, too, that both Brian Wenham and Mike Checkland would flourish better under a new boss. I also believed that Alan Hart, who had done a three-year stint in charge of BBC-1 (which is certainly enough time in that most demanding of jobs) should be replaced quite soon. Early in January 1984, on the way home from the Wiltshire shoot we both enjoyed, I talked to Aubrey about possible early retirement. Aubrey was not happy but could see there might be possibilities for him to develop in the field of independent production. I discussed this with Stuart and the Board. These changes were finally agreed in February, with Bill Cotton becoming the new Managing Director of Television.

January 1984 was the month the press began to turn on us, in a campaign sustained for eighteen months or more and, I believe, unprecedented in the history of the BBC. The spark that started the fire was a mini-series called *The Thorn Birds* based on Colleen McCullough's book, which Bill Cotton, as Controller of BBC-1, had bought a couple of years earlier on the annual winter buying trip to Los Angeles. It was no better, but certainly no worse, than many other American 'mini-series': their word for what we call a serial. We bought these American mini-series, as we have over the years bought their series like *Dallas* or *Dynasty* or *MASH*, because they brought a new ingredient to our schedules, being made in a different way from our own programmes. We bought them too, let me say without shame, because they were cheap. The American producers in Hollywood had virtually covered their production costs with their US network sales. Overseas profits were gravy to them. Thus, these programmes came to us, often having cost $1 million an hour or more, for a tenth of what our own drama cost us.

So we had bought *The Thorn Birds*, which duly won a considerable audience, but we made the great mistake of running it at the same time as Granada's adaptation of Paul Scott's *The Raj Quartet*, which they called, from the title of one of the books, *Jewel in the Crown*. It was as splendid a piece of work as their adaptation of *Brideshead Revisited* had been a few years earlier. For us, the comparison brought down the wrath of the Eumenides in the shape of one Max Hastings.

Max, the son of my old friend and *Tonight* colleague, Macdonald Hastings, is a big, rangy person with large spectacles and a penchant, like his father, for field sports and the country life. He is, at the time of writing, Editor of the *Daily Telegraph*. I gave Max his first job. He refused to go to university and instead came, at the age of eighteen, to work with us on *The Great War* series. He had, thereafter, done time on *24 Hours*, had reverted to Fleet Street, had made a considerable name for himself as a columnist, and a more famous name wearing his para boots in the Falklands War.

In mid-January 1984, Max let his polemical pen loose on the BBC. The *Standard* published a piece by him, arising out of the *Thorn Birds* controversy, entitled 'Who Will Halt the Runaway Beeb?' He noted that 'on two Mondays running the prestige current affairs *Panorama* was displaced to make way for one of the most paltry, tawdry imported soap operas that any television channel has ever had the contempt to inflict on the viewing public [I have to record that it was watched by fifteen million people] . . . on ITV Granada's *Jewel in the Crown* sweeps all before it [It was watched by nine million people].' The tone of the piece was full of hyperbole, but, rising to his theme: 'Never,' he wrote, 'has the leadership of the BBC seemed more pathetically inadequate, bankrupt of ideas, lost for a course.' I was described as 'the hapless Director General', Brian Wenham lumped in with me as 'the graceless Controller [*sic*] of Programmes'. My first reaction was fury; my second that Max must be auditioning for some job and showing he could wield a purple pen with the best of them.

Three weeks later Max returned to the attack. He pointed out how many good people we had lost, though he did not have the grace to record that some of them had left twenty, even thirty, years earlier for perfectly good reasons, like wanting more money; he grudgingly admitted that we still made some good programmes (a month later the BBC won eleven out of the fifteen British Academy of Film and Television Arts Awards for the previous year's productions); he described me as 'cursed by shyness in his human relations, much recent poor health, and a talent for executing rather than innovating'. As I said in a talk to our radio staff in Broadcasting House, it was true, as they could probably hear, that I had had a bad cold. He finished up with a piece of rodomontade about a permanent slide affecting the BBC if we did not follow a decent Thatcherite policy of severe cutbacks, particularly in local radio.

122

We seemed to be in for a difficult time with the press. Little did we know what The Thunderer was dreaming up for us. In the meantime, the management changes I had initiated in January 1984 now needed final resolution. The licence fee was due for renewal at the end of March 1985. I felt it time to ask our Director of Finance, Paul Hughes, who had been twelve years in that office and seen many licence fee negotiations, to retire. I wanted his deputy, Geoff Buck, a wonderfully quirky individual who thought anything less than a ten-hour meeting a passing interlude, to handle the coming discussions. And Bill Cotton and Brian Wenham had been talking to Michael Grade about taking over BBC-1 from Alan Hart. Michael, a younger member of the famous Grade family, had left being Director of Programmes at London Weekend Television (where, it must be said, I had had some harsh things to say when he tried to engineer an ITV monopoly of the Football League contracts) and was now working most successfully with his wife, Sarah, as producers in Los Angeles. Michael came to London in April and we all had dinner together. I had doubts about his fitting into the BBC – he seemed to me a natural bird of passage – and he had problems about returning to this country. But he resolved his anxieties in the late spring and arranged to join us in September. Geoff Buck duly became Director of Finance in April. Everything seemed to be falling into place.

But even with the holiday season starting and the Proms about to fill the Albert Hall again, the DBS negotiations with our new partners of the Club of 21 continued to preoccupy us. In July we were asked to go to the Home Office to receive the first salvo over the coming licence fee negotiations. We were soon to hear from the Prime Minister herself what she thought about our finances. Her relationship with the BBC was always refreshing, as evidenced by a dinner she attended with the Board of Governors and the Board of Management in the early summer of 1983. She cheerfully accused us of insanity over our reporting of the disembarkation of troops from the *QE2* in the Falklands, quoting as a parallel what she described as American television losing the Vietnam War, and roundly denounced the Governors for dereliction of duty. Later, in further conversation, she announced: 'By the grace of God, we had the wisdom to elect a Polish Pope.' 'I did not know,' murmured William Rees-Mogg, 'that she was now a Cardinal.'

At the Home Office, Leon Brittan spelt out the Government's philosophy about the licence fee. There would be great difficulties with his colleagues, he said, when it came up for renewal in the spring. 'I want an independent value-for-money inquiry into the BBC,' he said. We pointed out that we already had rolling activity reviews going on, which in a seven-year period would take in every department in the Corporation, with independent assessors involved. That was not good enough. He must, he said, 'have a bit of paper in my hand when I stand up in the House and announce the licence fee increase'. Stuart and I discussed it with the Board. It was tiresome, but we had nothing to be ashamed of. So we commissioned Peat Marwick Mitchell, the international firm of accountants who had been involved with the BBC on a previous occasion, and geared ourselves for another six months of intensive senior management involvement.

When a number of us met Mrs Thatcher in the autumn of 1984 for lunch at No. 10, we got a vivid picture of her own views about the licence fee. The occasion was within a few days of the Conservative Party Conference in Brighton where she so nearly lost her life at the hands of the IRA, as others did. We thought she would wish to cancel the lunch, presuming she would still be in shock; but she did not cancel it and spoke movingly of the bomb and its effect on her and her immediate colleagues. She was, I remember, particularly disturbed after the explosion to discover that her husband was wearing a pyjama top and bottom that didn't match: 'It wasn't even a mix-match!' she said.

As to the licence fee, if it rose in due course to a figure of £100, she thought that would be a political impossibility. 'Why don't you take a little advertising,' she said. 'A minute or two, on the hour or whatever.' I explained that I thought the BBC taking advertising would have a devastating effect on other parts of the media, because if we had to we would certainly raise the money; and that taking a little would only lead in time to taking more. 'Just the sort of arguments,' she cried, 'that were used when we introduced ITV.' I demurred, saying the case was quite different, but she was not to be dissuaded. Bernard Ingham, the PM's Press Secretary, wrote a note afterwards saying that he thought it had been a very good occasion, though he pointed out that the media, and especially broadcasters 'are not the Prime Minister's natural habitat'. It was, sadly, the last such occasion in my time. Though we proffered several invitations, they were not taken up.

Throughout the summer of 1984, we worked on the financial projections for the licence fee increase, while the accountants from Peat Marwick Mitchell beavered away at their value-for-money investigations. We were reasonably sure from what Ministers and civil servants had told us that the Government was intent again on a three-year settlement, something that George Howard and Ian Trethowan had successfully argued for and so broken away from the annual negotiations of the 1970s that had bedevilled the BBC. There had only been eight licence fee increases in our history, but five of them had occurred, because of inflation, in the eight years between 1976 and 1984 and that had caused the licence fee to incur sharp political overtones.

Yet it seemed to us to continue to be one of the best bargains available in Britain. For £46 or 12½p a day, you could listen to four national radio networks, to local radio in nearly thirty towns in England and to special services in Scotland, Wales and Northern Ireland, and watch our two colour television networks. Of that £46 licence fee, £35 went towards the cost of television. That meant *2p per viewing hour per average viewer*. That was less than the price of a cigarette and less than the petrol needed to drive one mile. And if you were a *Daily Telegraph* or *Times* reader, the daily cost of each paper was roughly equal to the cost of viewing *ten hours* of BBC television.

These were all telling arguments. But we knew we had a battle on our hands. ITV is free, they said, you don't have to pay for it if you don't watch it, whereas you have to pay for the BBC to operate a set. Of course, ITV is not free. We all pay towards the £1 billion plus it costs every time we go to the supermarket, but it is a strong psychological argument. Then, many politicians dislike what they see as a regressive tax levied on rich and poor alike, bearing, in their view, particularly heavily on old-age pensioners. It was, they claimed, an intolerable burden. We knew it was not and research we later carried out for the Peacock Committee confirmed we were right. Eighty per cent of the population find no difficulty in paying the licence fee. The twenty per cent who do find difficulty are the same people who are in trouble paying their rent, their transport and many other things. Because it was going to be a battle, I was sure we should conduct it in public. We had a perfectly good case and we should explain that case fully to the viewers and listeners. We discussed this approach with the Board and in the autumn we decided that we would go public just before Christmas, even though the whispers from the Home Office were that Government would frown on a public discussion.

Stuart, Geoff Buck and I launched the campaign for the licence fee increase from £46 to £65 at a press conference in December with the slogan, 'The Best Bargain in Britain'. Coincidentally, at a lobby briefing at No. 10 Bernard Ingham was asked about the licence fee as our remarks came up on Ceefax, and let it be known that the Prime Minister was in favour of the BBC taking advertising. The press naturally picked this one up and ran with it. 'Thatcher favours some ads on BBC' said the *Telegraph* the following morning. Others were more predictable. 'BBC blasted over bid for £65 licence' shouted the *Express*, and in an unusually long leader, the *Express*'s advice to Government was stern: 'Ministers should know what their answer should be: NO!' It concluded, 'Attached to the bloated, overfed body of the BBC, a begging bowl is offensive. It is time Aunty's pathetic pantomime was stopped. Now is the time to stop it.'

I had some weeks earlier had a passage of arms with the *Express* when they kindly gave me space to respond to an attack they had made on the licence fee. At that time, I wrote, 'I am tempted to ask why the *Daily Express* at 18p a day is so expensive. Here's the BBC on air virtually round the clock, three hundred and sixty-five days a year, with all its services, at a cost of £46 a year. While the *Express* (which doesn't publish on Sundays, Good Friday or Christmas Day) costs over £55 a year . . .' But such arguments cut little ice. We were the big spenders, out of control. We should take advertising like all other sensible commercial people.

In the New Year, Stuart, Geoff Buck and I set off round the country to try and spread the message. Stuart was at his very best in these encounters. Although he tired more quickly than before his illness and was in some pain, he was a brilliant accountant and relished the arguments surrounding the licence fee. Moreover, by his own admission, when he became a Governor, he expected to find the BBC inefficient and not cost effective. What he had seen with his own eyes convinced him that we were an extremely efficient broadcasting operation. And if ever he thought advertising was a financial panacea for the BBC, he had changed his mind about that too. He was now a committed advocate of the licence fee and argued the case with fluency and passion. Geoff Buck, too, exposed for the first time in his life to the glare of publicity, began to enjoy the jousts. Nobody could easily beat him.

With two of the best accountants the BBC could boast, I like to think we were quite a formidable team. We gave press conferences and did television and radio interviews up and down the country, and I began to feel that we were getting our case across. Certainly, the papers outside London responded more favourably than Fleet Street had. The *Glasgow Herald*, while chastising us for 'spreading their cash too widely' said, 'If the BBC needs a colour licence of £65 to provide the occasional treasure among the trash, it should be given the money.' And the *Birmingham Post* echoed those sentiments: 'It is surely preferable that the BBC, one of the last bastions of truly independent broadcasting, should be allowed to retain its great tradition.'

Just before Christmas 1984, Peat Marwick Mitchell finished the first draft of their report, though it required further revision in the New Year. We published the main report in March. Though it identified possible savings of between one and two per cent, it seemed to us to give us a clean bill of health and we said so. It was not the easiest document to assimilate at a glance and at the press conference we held to publish it, I could soon see the eyes of the reporters present glaze over with incomprehension. They had come presumably smelling blood (or their editors had). There seemed no blood to find. And the press the next day was pretty good, apart from *The Times* reporter who had found himself unable to print a good word about the BBC for many weeks past. He pursued the PMM staff who had worked on the report and triumphantly quoted one of them as saying the BBC 'had given the wrong interpretation'. We later got a letter from PMM to confirm that we had not. But, to our surprise, at a meeting at the Home Office that same day, Leon Brittan told us with, I thought, some pleasure that he found the PMM report critical of the BBC. In the same breath, he also assured us there was no question of the BBC being invited to consider taking advertising at this stage.

As we were about to set out on our journeys round Britain to proclaim the virtues of the licence fee, *The Times* uttered. On 14th January, 1985 it wrote the first of three consecutive leaders – something it had not done since the Abdication of King Edward VIII in 1936. Others were to follow, but this was clearly a momentous occasion. The first salvo began thus:

> Tomorrow the Labour MP, Mr Joe Ashton, launches a Bill calling for the BBC to take advertising. Last month, on the very day that the BBC began its campaign for a forty-one per cent increase in its licence fee, the Prime Minister let it be known that she too favoured BBC advertising. The BBC is today accused, with varying degrees of fairness, of inefficiency, unaccountability, self-aggrandisement, feather-bedding its employees – everything from impoliteness to John Selwyn Gummer to failing to make *Jewel in the Crown*. Are the critics justified? In their main principles: yes . . . The BBC should not survive this parliament at its present size, in its present form and with its present terms of reference intact.

We were then told that we were not doing well enough in audience terms to justify the licence fee; that we had expanded '*pari passu*' to take in local radio, a new television channel (a reference to BBC-2 which came into being twenty years earlier) and breakfast television; that the new technology extending consumer choice would make it still harder for us; and that, anyway, the political climate had changed and the existence of the duopoly had to be justified. The second of its tablets meandered round the question of advertising support 'to generate the revenue to pay for many programmes'. It had some sharp things to say about what it saw as the broadcasters' self-serving arguments about the maintenance of programme standards. 'Suppose,' it argued, 'it were proposed that all cornflakes boxes have printed upon them the works of Shakespeare. Would that mean we had the highest quality cornflakes boxes in the world, or would it mean we were rather foolish? We need a more open – less monolithic – system of broadcasting in which customers can choose what qualities they want from their television screens and radio sets.'

The resolution of these long and rambling dissertations came in the last deliverance. 'The Government should concede no increase in the licence fee,' trumpeted *The Times*. 'It should consider quickly the establishment of a new broadcasting commission to auction franchises that are currently held by the BBC.' A new quango to flog off the BBC? Well!

The message was clear, though the language was cloudy. This kind of rhetoric, particularly as we were now deeply involved in the argument about the licence fee increase, called for as tart a response as we could engineer. I asked for space in *The Times* and got it in February. To be fair, they only altered the odd word. I wrote:

Anyone coming fresh to British broadcasting and reading the press on the subject might tend to believe he or she had arrived just in time to attend the funeral of public service broadcasting. They might also believe from their reading that there are two kinds of broadcasting – popular broadcasting vainly and wrongly attempted, if not usurped, by the BBC, and minority broadcasting which a properly amputated BBC might as well continue to engage in, since there is no money to be made in it.

While warmly welcoming the Granada successes of *Brideshead Revisited* and *Jewel in the Crown*, I catalogued the kind of serials we had broadcast in the same period: *The Living Planet*, surely one of the best natural history series ever made (apart, of course, from *Life on Earth* four years earlier). We won many awards for the two Le Carré adaptations, *Tinker, Tailor* and *Smiley's People*, and for the *Barchester Chronicles* and *The Boys from the Blackstuff*. We had produced a string of other excellent serials, classic and contemporary.

I was, frankly, fed up that some twenty hours of work, however good, should be held as proof of failure against some two hundred hours of work, no less distinguished, over the same period. I went on:

Only a bigoted partisan could conceivably claim *all* broadcasting virtue for the BBC. But individual programmes or series are one thing. The vital work of six orchestras all over the country, the depth of the BBC's educational commitment, the hundreds of radio and television plays we broadcast each year stimulating creative writing at every level – complete services with their balance, peaks, troughs, with their required universality of reach – who has ever dreamt of challenging the BBC on the broad ground?

But we had taken a drubbing and some of the mud stuck. I confess I was so incensed by the behaviour of *The Times* (and must concede that few voices, for whatever reasons, responded on our behalf though there was much dark talk of suppression in *The Times'* correspondence column) that speaking at the end of January to the Radio and Television Industries Club lunch, I decided to cut loose. Stephen Hearst, my Special Assistant, had drafted the speech and phrased the point beautifully:

> The three recent leaders in *The Times*, culminating in the splendid idea that the licence fee should not be increased and that the BBC franchises should be put up for public auction, have freed me from one or two inhibitions. Who, I would like to ask, is more likely to serve the public interest – a broadcasting organisation which is considered the world over as the leading producer of quality programmes, or *The Times* whose recommendations, if acted upon, would have the practical effect of enabling its owner, Mr Rupert Murdoch, to acquire some of the most valuable broadcasting action in the United Kingdom?

This speech, I am happy to relate, got me into trouble. The Independent Directors of *The Times*, an august body established when Lord Thomson bought it to protect its editorial independence, wrote to me through an old friend, Hugh Trevor-Roper (Lord Dacre of Glanton) telling me that the editor, Charlie Douglas-Home, had complained to them that I had implied Murdochian interference. What evidence, they asked loftily, had I for making such suggestions? None, I replied. I did not work for *The Times* and so had no knowledge of what goes on there. But, I added, it seemed a reasonable supposition and it is what many other people think. I was then treated to a pompous piece in *The Times* explaining to the world that I had admitted having no evidence for this scurrilous suggestion. Some time later, before his tragically early death, Charlie Douglas-Home came to lunch at Broadcasting House, and I asked him about the editorials. Nothing to do with Murdoch, he said. A 'collegiate' decision inside the paper on a topic of proper national interest. Fair enough. Yet, a year later, at the 1985 Royal Television Society Conference in Cambridge, there was Murdoch interviewed by

129

Alastair Burnet on film in New York arguing that the BBC 'should be privatised'. The 'collegiate' decision was not, obviously, out of tune with its master's voice.

Now we waited for the Home Secretary to deliver his judgement. Alarm bells rang in a small way when a senior civil servant, at a party in Broadcasting House, was overheard to say, '£65? You've got your figures the wrong way round!' On 26th March, we went back to the Home Office for the deliverance. Leon Brittan first told us that there was to be a committee of inquiry into the BBC's finances (after six months of Peat Marwick?) and spelt out its terms of reference. At least it was to include the possible impact of advertising on ITV, ILR and the press. He showed us the composition of the committee and though we could immediately see Professor Peacock, the Chairman, and Sam Brittan, his brother, of the *Financial Times* as free marketeers, the other members suggested offered an interesting mix. They would, he said, be expected to report to him by the following summer, July 1986.

Then he turned to the licence fee increase. It would, he said, be £58 not the £65 we had wished for. He reminded us of the pressures on him to agree no increase at all. It would last, he said, for two years anyway, because that would encompass the resolution of the Peacock Report. He explained how he arrived at the figure of £58. He had lopped off all the developments we had put forward – enrichment of television drama, introduction of daytime television, completion of the English local radio chain – and that reduced the total figure to just under £60. Then, whereas PMM had identified potential savings of around £20 million, he cheerfully encouraged us to do better than that. Save £65 million, he said, and that gives me my round figure of £58.

I left Queen Anne's Gate knowing that we had real financial trouble in front of us, and big decisions to take. On top of which we now faced another twelve months of scrutiny by another committee. Peacock was about to take to the air.

11 THE CLOUDS GATHER

It was not just the clamour in the press that made for uneasiness during the spring of 1985. The management changes in the Television Service had ruffled the surface of the place, but there were other major initiatives which were taxing the nerve of both Governors and BBC management.

There was, firstly, the matter of The Langham. The BBC had bought this listed building, the first Victorian hotel to be built in London, just after the war, and over the years it had been converted and re-converted for office use. It stands, massive and forbidding, on a prime site opposite Broadcasting House and All Souls' Church, just at the point where Nash's ceremonial route kinks to the left to debouch into Portland Place. For a good many years, the BBC had conducted an internal debate about how and where its operations should be housed in the future. Broadcasting House, built in the early 1930s, was hopelessly out of date as a modern broadcasting centre. It needed several million pounds spent on it every year just to keep it in some kind of operational mode. And even then, drama productions had to be stopped to avoid the noise of the tube trains passing by underneath, and our working lives were constantly made miserable by the whine of drills and the pounding of hammers renovating the building. There was another important factor. The BBC owned the freehold of Broadcasting House, of the extension to BH built in the 1960s, and of The Langham. The rest of the Radio Directorate and other staff were spread through more than twenty rented properties in what we called the 'W1 village', with expensive rentals requiring constant renewal.

More than fifteen years ago, there was talk of moving the whole operation out to the White City area, alongside the Television Centre. This was known somewhat whimsically as the 'Albino' project. But the industrial troubles of the late 1970s buried that idea. There was apprehension that moving another five thousand-odd people out to W12 might exacerbate an already delicate industrial relations situation. But something had to be done. Soldiering on in a decaying Broadcasting House and expensively rented property was no longer an option.

George Howard, owner of the magnificent Vanbrugh-designed Castle Howard in Yorkshire, was keen to mark his chairmanship by initiating an equally magnificent building for the BBC. And so it came about that we set up an architectural competition for the rebuilding of The Langham to provide the Radio Directorate with modern facilities and to rehouse all those presently situated in the rented accommodation of the W1 village. A shortlist of three architects was prepared, and each of the three appeared to deliver a presentation before the Governors. There was no doubt in my mind that Norman Foster, a leading British architect then busily involved in the construction of a Hong Kong bank which had been called 'the most expensive building in the world', was our man. Norman captured the imagination of everybody in the room with his enthusiasm, his vision of a building that was full of light and perspective, and one that would positively enhance Nash's processional way and his elegant church opposite. We nominated Foster as the architect to rebuild The Langham.

There were early anxieties about the cost of the venture. The licence fee negotiations were still more than two years away, but we were talking of a building costing £100 million and more, and the whole process would inevitably be conducted in the full glare of publicity. There was bound to be a public inquiry before we would get planning permission to demolish The Langham, and opposition from conservation groups such as the Victorian Society. There were bound to be political voices raised to question whether it was a proper thing for the BBC to invest so heavily in a new building when many MPs themselves were forced to work in fairly squalid conditions. But the die was cast, and Foster and his partners, backed up by a formidable battery of specialist consultants, flung themselves into the task of interviewing all departmental heads, studying every aspect of the radio operation, of planning and designing. Dick Francis, the Managing Director of Radio, was rightly fired with enthusiasm for the new project. It became his baby. Control groups were set up. Gradually, early models began to emerge for the Governors to see. The work moved ahead apace.

But the doubts and the worries continued. In October 1983 the Elstree studios came on the market, since the new Central Television company was moving its entire operation to the Midlands. There were good studios, there were all the concomitant operational facilities, there was ample office space for future development such as daytime television, there was also a large lot with the potential for a permanent set for the twice-weekly serial that we were planning, and which was to become *EastEnders*. After some hesitation, we bought Elstree. But as Norman Foster's work neared completion – he had worked his way through more than forty developments of the building and the final model held to me the promise of a very fine building - and we prepared to go for planning permission, the unease amongst the Governors was palpable.

In October 1984, David Holmes, the Secretary, passed on to me the substance of a conversation he had had with William Rees-Mogg. Rees-Mogg, he reported, was turning against The Langham project. If that was the case, other Governors would be likely to follow suit. At a meeting in early 1985, the Governors once again winced when the detailed costs of Foster's consultancy fees were exposed to them. By then, another option had opened up. The White City greyhound track site was on the market. Stuart himself undertook the negotiations to buy it and by June, the Board confirmed the purchase of the White City site, and The Langham development was aborted. This change of tack caused, naturally, pain to Foster and much upset among the radio people, and particularly to Dick Francis, who did not fancy a move to west London. But a year later The Langham was sold to Ladbroke's for development as a hotel. The new radio centre and the new home for the staff of the W1 village was to be in W12.

There followed a series of incidents that gravely disturbed the working relationship between the Board and the management. Some of them were quite trivial in themselves, others less so. Together they began to look almost like a case law of management failure.

First, there was the *Dr Who* row. Michael Grade had decided that this long-running sci-fi serial (it had been on the air without a break since Sydney Newman started it twenty years earlier) needed a rest to allow for a rethink and refurbishment. He decided to take it off for a while, and provoked a furious response from *Dr Who* fans, of whom there are a great many the world over. The Governors found the BBC under attack for something of which they had no advance warning.

In March, it was the case of Dr Gee that infuriated them. Dr Gee had brought a libel action against the BBC over an edition of *That's Life*. The case had been in court for many weeks with Dr Gee himself still giving evidence in the witness box. He had a panel of expert witnesses to follow, and we had our own panel to follow them. Another factor was that the judge had dismissed the jury. In February, the BBC's counsel came, surrounded by juniors, to tell me personally that the case could go on for months yet, with costs rising to astronomical figures. The Governors were horrified and clearly thought we had bungled. They were particularly sharp because Rees-Mogg had previously been critical of the way we handled our libel actions and had called for quarterly reports to the Governors of our legal processes. I decided we must settle, but at great cost to the BBC.

The Governors were embarrassed, too, by the ludicrous developments that followed Thames Television's raiding of *Dallas* from the BBC, when the IBA had tried to strong-arm Thames into giving the American serial back to us. The day after the Board meeting when Dr Gee was discussed, I had lunch with Stuart and William Rees-Mogg and they explained the Board's sensitivities and how some of the newer Governors were finding relationships with the management uneasy. I thought the lunch a useful occasion because it seemed to clear the air.

But when I got back from an Easter fishing holiday in Scotland, the Governors finally exploded. David Holmes had had the elegant idea that the Board should meet at Elstree, our recent acquisition, and that they should see the new set for *EastEnders* and lunch with the cast. *EastEnders*, soon to become a runaway success, was the outcome of a long-standing wish of ours to revive the twice-weekly serial. Back in the 1960s, first *Compact* and then *The Newcomers* and *United* had done reasonable business for BBC Television, but somehow the will had faded and *Coronation Street* had been left for many years, together with *Crossroads*, to ride this field on their own. Alan Hart worked hard on the concept when he was Controller of BBC-1 with Jonathan Powell, Head of Series and Serials, and it was they, with Julia Smith, who had done excellent work on *Angels*, who brought about *EastEnders*. The purchase of Elstree made it possible for the whole operation, including the building of Albert Square, to be located there. But when the Governors got to Elstree, they were in angry mood on two counts. Firstly, they had not known (nor had I) that the Head of Religious Programmes in Television had decided not to carry the Pope's Easter Message – 'Urbi et Orbi'. This was the first time, I think, since it was made available through the Eurovision network that the BBC had not carried it. It was argued that the cost was high and the audience tiny. But the Board was cross and William Rees-Mogg, as a devout Catholic, was especially incensed.

Worse, early on the Wednesday morning preceding the Governors' normal Thursday meeting, BBC Television had, quite unscrupulously in my opinion, transmitted on *Breakfast Time* an interview given by Princess Michael of Kent to TV-am about her father and the publicity then surrounding his activities. The BBC had approached TV-am asking for normal 'news access', which amounts by custom and practice to around two minutes' worth, and were refused. *Breakfast Time* then simply recorded the entire interview off-air and ran it at full length, even removing the TV-am label.

When, on the Wednesday morning, as I prepared to attend a meeting of the General Advisory Council, Alan Protheroe told me about the incident, I was quite amused, less so when the full implications sank in. Alan was immediately called to court to deal with an injunction pressed upon us by TV-am and I had no chance of further contact with him till the next morning.

When the Governors emerged grim-faced from their private sessions, Stuart left me in no doubt that there was trouble afoot. They demanded to know who had made the decision. I did not know, nor did Alan. He sat in the meeting, white and tense, while I tried to assuage their anger. They insisted on issuing a statement that the Governors would get to the bottom of the whole affair. After a difficult lunch, I called in the editors involved, and we established who had taken the final decision. The Governors never did get to see the set of *EastEnders* or meet the cast. It soon emerged that Michael Shea, the Queen's Press Secretary, had clearly told the BBC that they had news access to the interview, as is normal in these matters. But *Breakfast Time*'s piratical intervention left us all exposed. The resulting legal contest has only recently been settled.

I thought it would be an emollient move to invite Stuart to join the Board of Management for lunch the following Monday after our regular weekly meeting. He had warned me the Governors were ganging up against Alan Protheroe and the lunch went badly. Stuart was abrasive, and Alan responded too sharply. It was, I noted in my diary, 'a bad time'. The following day, Stuart was again hostile about Alan and I should have sensed what was coming.

The next day – 1st May – the Governors held an unusual private meeting at 4.00 p.m. before the more orthodox Board of Finance meeting. David Holmes told me they would like me to join them for supper; on my own, apart from him, which was odd. Normally the other Directors at the Finance meeting were free to come to supper. For more than two hours, the Governors explained to me that they had lost confidence in Alan Protheroe in his present roles. (Alan, a native of St David's, was known to all in the BBC as 'The Colonel' because of his rank in the Territorial Army. Starting with the *Glamorgan Gazette*, he had worked his way through BBC Wales from reporter to Editor of News and Current Affairs and through Television News to being its Editor. His journalism was very soundly based. Short, chain-smoking, highly strung, bleeper always in action, he would occasionally go 'over the top'; but he is not alone in that in the land. Though he was unfailingly courteous to the Governors, I sensed that the rapport between them was never strong.) There was, they said, no lack of regard for his professionalism, dedication and commitment. But they indicated that they were too troubled by his occasional, and repeated, displays of erratic emotion to allow him to continue with his present responsibilities. The whole Board wished him to be placed in another role which would suit his particular strengths. I was flabbergasted. I argued strongly against the proposition, but agreed that I would give thought to what they had said and come back in a few weeks' time with ideas.

We had been in discussion for nearly three hours when Stuart produced their next surprise. They wanted me to understand – while in no way, they said, criticising my performance as Director General – that the task of directing and following through the use of resources by the Corporation was, in the context of 1985 and beyond, too great a task for any Director General on his own. They wanted a Deputy Director General to undertake that role and they wanted Michael Checkland to be that person. (Echoes of a time when the Board tried to press a deputy on Charles Curran; at that time, to underpin him editorially.) I said I did not believe there was such a need; I had personally put Michael Checkland in charge of the Television Service's Planning and Resource Management because that was where three-quarters of the BBC's money was spent. I saw no need for such a change, but I would also give that proposition further thought.

Well, I thought, we can see where the wind is blowing. As we broke up around 11.00 p.m., I took small comfort from the kind of things they had said, as expressed in David Holmes's minute: 'The Board, on several occasions throughout the evening, declared its whole-hearted confidence in the Director General personally. It wished no heads to roll. It wished changes to take place calmly and rationally.'

I was very angry. It seemed to me that the Board was rattled in a way that it had no need to be and was taking it out on Alan quite unfairly. They should turn on me, if anybody. I detected Rees-Mogg's hand again; he seldom had anything good to say about Alan, who had worked for the BBC with fanatical devotion. We all knew Alan went over the top occasionally: was emotion supposed to be a commodity banned from the BBC? The following morning's Board meeting was orderly, but Alan refused to lunch with the Governors. I sent him a note saying he must come, and come he did. Later in the afternoon, I told him the full tenor of what had been said over the previous night's supper. He must give up the Information Division. I was confident, otherwise, that he could continue to carry out the rest of his duties. This time he had every cause for emotion. It was a sad meeting. That evening, there was a reception in the BBC's rather grand Council Chamber, where the portraits of Reith and other former DGs, like so many Doges, stare down upon you from the walls. The occasion was the publication of yet another of Asa Briggs'

136

histories of the BBC – a short version this time. Sir Ian Jacob was there, Sir Hugh Greene was there. It should have been a very pleasant evening. It had, nevertheless, been a very bad day.

Time to reflect came immediately because Sheila and I set off within forty-eight hours on an invited visit to the Cyprus Broadcasting Corporation and to the Greek broadcasting authorities. As we set eyes on the wonders of Delphi and the Acropolis for the first time – strange that I, who had spent more than ten years of my life studying classical Greek had never yet set foot on the Greek mainland – there was time to try and think through a clear crisis of confidence between the Governors and ourselves. There had been a good deal of grumbling when I nominated Alan as my deputy, after Aubrey Singer retired – both Dick Francis and Douglas Muggeridge, the Managing Director of External Broadcasting, had been unhappy; how would my fellow directors respond to Mike Checkland, however brilliant an accountant he was, deputising for me in everything, including programme matters of which he had no immediate knowledge? As against that, I knew we had to make quick moves to deal with the shortfall on the licence fee. It was probably true that, with Peacock and a host of other things to deal with, I could benefit from somebody as sure-footed as Mike to stand beside me. Mike, a 'Brummie' by origin, is an expert accountant. Short and wiry, he had joined the BBC from Thorn and quickly graduated to become Chief Accountant of the Television Service in Huw Wheldon's time. I had negotiated to bring him back to the Television Centre as Controller of Planning and Resource Management; his time in that job and then as Director of Resources for Television had given him a unique understanding of managing resources in the pursuit of good programme making. I could see he could be a great support to me over the next few years.

We planned to have a couple of days off in Venice on the way home after saying goodbye to our Greek hosts, who were in the throes of a general election and, therefore, somewhat distracted. Sunday in Venice was perfect. I woke early on the Monday morning with a raging fever and a very sore throat. We spent most of the day re-arranging flights to get home; and when we got to London, I headed for bed. On the Wednesday, the day before the next Governors' meeting, Alan Protheroe came to the house in the afternoon. He was very anxious about the Governors: 'We are heading for a crisis,' he said. And later in the evening, Stuart came round for a chat. He was very friendly. I said I was happy at the idea of Mike Checkland as my deputy but had not yet spoken to him. I hoped to be able to talk to the Governors about it in the morning.

I was still running a temperature when I went to the Board meeting. Nor had I had the chance of speaking privately to Michael

Checkland. So when Stuart called on me to speak, and I said I wasn't ready, he looked affronted. The following day, he and I had a rowdy meeting. He read me a letter he had written to me which I found deeply offensive and promptly tore up when I got back to my office. It included phrases like 'we wish to show you every consideration but things cannot go on as they are.' I told him I would ring the Governors individually the following week and discuss my thoughts with them. Which I duly did. My diary records, 'There was much talk at the meeting with Stuart about credibility. I thought he was crackers.'

A short period of calm ensued as Stuart flew off on a formal visit to Egypt, Israel and Saudi Arabia, the latter a genuine diplomatic coup for one so closely identified with Jewish causes in Britain and also with Israel. These alarms and excursions apart, we had urgent business to pursue. The licence fee settlement had left us with no possibilities of any development. Indeed, it left us with a clear need to cut back our activities, to encompass the £65 million-worth of savings that Leon Brittan had thrown at us to be found over the three-year period. We could probably muddle through again, as we had done many times before. The payment of the licence fee is channelled through the Home Office on a regular system, based on forward projections of the number of licences, colour, in particular, they think the public will subscribe to. There was always the possibility that the Home Office's forward estimates of licence fee take-up would prove to be pessimistic and we might turn out to be a little better off. Equally, the converse was possible. Some of us felt that we had had enough of this survival by the 'skin of your teeth' mentality. Surely, now was the moment when the public and the staff would understand that we wanted to improve the services we offered them and that we would need to take radical measures to ensure we could make such improvements. It was no time for laborious committees, taking months to plough through their terms of reference and report to a management who might by then have lost interest in why they were ever set up. It seemed a time for swift action, not least because we would be immersed in the Peacock preparations and discussions within a matter of weeks.

So I decided to ask a very small group of senior managers, whose combined BBC expertise totalled over a hundred years, to undertake a lightning investigation into the way forward and report back to me within a month. They were known formally as 'The Director General's Study Group', more commonly as 'The Gang of Four', or 'Black Spot'. Geoff Buck, our newly appointed Director of Finance, was the leader; with him Michael Checkland, the newly appointed Deputy Director General; Geraint Stanley Jones, then Controller of BBC Wales and soon to become Director of Public Affairs and later

138

Managing Director of Regions; and David Hatch, at that time Controller of Radio 4, later to be Director of Programmes and now Managing Director of BBC Radio.

What they came up with was the distillation of their combined experience, but checked against interviews with some two hundred managers in BBC centres all over the country. They advocated restoring the programme developments that had collapsed with the licence fee settlement – enriched television drama, daytime television, completion of the English local radio chain, strengthening of regional television news – but also more contentious propositions: more independent production opportunities in television and radio, examination of the costs of in-house catering, cleaning and security and building maintenance by comparison with tendering by outside contractors. They argued, too, for a severe retrenchment in Engineering Division's provision of specialist equipment. More buying off the shelf and a departure from the 'Rolls-Royce' approach. To pay for the programme developments, they argued for a severe slimming down of 'the corporate belly' – not an attractive phrase but a vivid one – and the transfer of the money saved to the editorial heart.

It was a tough document. We spent a weekend in July with the Governors at a conference hotel in Hampshire thrashing out every detail, and there was much pain. The Director of Engineering, Bryce McCrirrick, argued fiercely against the shredding of some of his departments where the study group thought the same results could be achieved out of house. The Managing Director of Radio, Dick Francis, fought a characteristically stubborn rearguard action against their plans for restructuring the English regions which would involve local radio being responsible to regional heads of broadcasting rather than to the local radio management in London.

At the end of our deliberations, we had a concrete plan which I could hand to Michael Checkland for implementation. And, give or take the odd wrinkle which had to be ironed out, the greater part of the £32 million the group identified as possible savings has now been diverted to the air or the screen where we wanted to see it spent. I wrote in our own magazine, *Ariel*, at the time: 'We've certainly yanked hard on the tiller to change direction in the 1990s and beyond. I can't tell any more than anyone else what the effect of cable and satellite and media developments in general are going to be over the next fifteen years, but I would bet the BBC will be something like we see it in this plan in fifteen years' time.'

We left our Hampshire retreat tired after a long weekend and a difficult, tense spring. We had an agreed plan for the future and we seemed to have a better working relationship between the two boards. That was to be tested almost to destruction within a month.

12 REAL LIVES

It was a glorious summer's evening in Helsinki. Sheila and I had flown in that morning from up country after a few days' rainbow trout fishing. We lunched with the Finnish Director General, toured their television studios and now we were boarding the huge night steamer bound for Stockholm and the rest of our holiday in Sweden.

The ship was packed with people. We found our cabin and at 5.45 p.m. I heard my name called over the Tannoy. Would I go to the Purser's Office? It was the Finnish television people on the phone; would I ring my office in London urgently? The ship was due to sail in fifteen minutes' time. I had got rid of all my Finnish money and, anyway, the phone booths were full. As soon as we sailed, I went to the radio phone operator and rang London.

Ros, my Personal Assistant, said: 'Alasdair, there's a big problem. I'll get Mike Checkland for you.'

This was Mike Checkland's first occasion deputising for me since he had been appointed Deputy Director General. I could not imagine what the difficulty might be. Mike came on the phone.

'Have you heard of Martin McGuinness?' he asked.

'Yes,' I said. McGuinness had been named as a leading figure in the IRA for many years.

'Do you know about a programme involving Martin McGuinness?'

'No,' I said.

He then explained that the *Sunday Times* had run a story about a programme involving Martin McGuinness; that one of their reporters, at a press occasion in Washington where Mrs Thatcher was present, had asked the Prime Minister a hypothetical question about her reaction if she learned that a British television company (not naming the BBC) was going to interview a leading member of the IRA. Mrs Thatcher, Mike told me, had spoken in the strongest terms. He went on to tell me that the Home Secretary had written to the Chairman invoking considerations of security and asking that the Board should refuse to show the programme even if it were hostile to terrorism. A special meeting of the Board had been convened, he told me, for the following day to consider what to do.

I asked if the meeting could be postponed to give me time to get home. Mike said that was impossible; the Governors had already been alerted. Nor could the programme be deferred, because it was already billed in *Radio Times*. The entire Board of Management, he told me, had seen the film that morning and had agreed that with a carefully phrased introduction, some minor changes and a discussion afterwards about the nature of terrorism in modern times, it was transmittable.

'What do I do,' he asked, 'if the Governors insist on seeing the film?'

'You must remind them,' I said, 'that there is no tradition of this in the BBC. It hasn't happened for many years and it should not happen. They should avoid it if at all possible. If, in the end, they insist, they do, of course, have the right.'

I was dismayed. Given the background of the past few months, who could imagine what might happen now? We were not due to dock in Stockholm till 9.00 a.m.; the Board meeting was due to start in London at 11.00 a.m. There were no planes I could catch back to London till the afternoon. I had to sweat it out. We had a very uneasy dinner on board and I do not remember that the motion of the boat induced much sleep.

I had told Mike Checkland I would ring at lunchtime (British time) and when I did, he said they were in the middle of a lunch adjournment. He told me the Governors had anguished over viewing the programme, but had decided they must see it if they were to give the Home Secretary a measured response. He said he thought things were going badly. Later in the afternoon we spoke again and he told me the Governors had decided against transmission. I asked to speak to the Chairman and told him I thought this was a disastrous move.

'I'm sorry,' Stuart said. 'But anyway, it was a lousy programme.'

'Oh?'

'Yes. It made them out to be nice guys, bouncing babies on their knees. A few of your Board of Management colleagues have been making some unfortunate remarks and I think this is a time for unity, Alasdair.'

In further conversation with Mike Checkland and Bill Cotton, I said I would come home straight away. Both of them thought that a pointless move, since the Governors had now gone their several ways for their summer break.

The next three days were a misery. I could see that the climate of opinion after the American networks' coverage of the recent TWA hijack by Arab terrorists at Beirut in June had become heated; the Prime Minister's remarks to the American Bar Association's convention in London when she spoke sharply about 'starving the terrorists of the oxygen of publicity on which they depend' might have affected the Board's thinking. I did not then know that Leon Brittan had used the same phrase in his letter to the Chairman. Moreover, a formal letter from the BBC's sponsoring Minister (the Home Secretary) asking that a programme should not be shown (even though he had not, of course, seen it and could have used his powers to ban it, if he so wished) could not easily be shrugged off. Yet my colleagues in the management had seen it, had judged it transmittable and had been overruled. The proportions of the crisis were stark enough.

We flew home on the Saturday and that evening I saw a cassette of the programme. I had been told that some Governors thought it was 'soft on terrorism' because it adopted a documentary, not a hard current affairs, approach. I could not share that view. As I told the Board of Management the following Monday, I took a more relaxed view of the film than they had apparently done; but then they had viewed it in a very heightened atmosphere the previous week. From conversations over the weekend and on the Monday, I got further information about the way things had gone at the Governors' meeting. I learnt about the telephone call from the Home Office revealing the Home Secretary's message about the programme which he was issuing to the press; about Stuart's insistence that the message should be sent to him in letter form and about its delivery on the Monday evening, containing the emotive statement that 'Even if the programme and any surrounding material were, as a whole, to present terrorist organisations in a wholly unfavourable light, I would still ask you not to permit it to be broadcast.' I learnt how the Governors had been greatly torn over the need to see the film, after Mike Checkland had conceded that there had been 'a technical foul' over the procedure of referral upwards: not, in my opinion, a critical failure because the Controller of Northern Ireland, Jimmy Hawthorne, and his staff had been fully consulted throughout. But the relevant BBC document does state that 'Interviews with individuals who are thought to be closely associated with a terrorist organisation may not be sought or transmitted – two separate stages – without the prior permission of DG.' That had not occurred. The programme had been mentioned casually to Alan Protheroe, who asked: 'Does Jimmy Hawthorne know about it?' and when reassured that he did, gave it no further thought.

I learnt how the Governors, with Rees-Mogg providing a strong lead, had decided that they must see the programme. How they had viewed it in concert (you should always see contentious programmes on your own, in my judgement), how their catches of breath and shared angry glances indicated general disapproval. How Rees-Mogg, clearly believing in conspiracy because of Jimmy Hawthorne not having told his National Governor, Lucy Faulkner, about the programme (she was then within hours of retirement, but might well have expected to know something of the programme at an earlier date), had proclaimed it 'totally unacceptable'; how others, catching the mood, had cried, 'No show' or 'I hate it, I hate it'. It had, by all accounts, been a thoroughly obnoxious occasion.

I also learnt how Jimmy Hawthorne had been bent on resignation but had been brought back from the brink by a phone call from Stuart, who had gone north to a golf tournament in Scotland.

After the Board of Management on Monday morning (5th August), I decided to ask the Chairman to join a number of us for lunch to see if we could find some way out of this mess. I asked him if he would agree that I should contact as many Governors as I could get hold of and read to them a statement we had drafted which indicated that we would explain the context of the film and probably hold a discussion afterwards – very much what the Board of Management had suggested at the last Governors' meeting. Stuart seemed tired and listless. I am sure he was often in greater pain than he would admit. He said he had no objections. Out of the seven Governors I managed to contact that afternoon, five thought this was a reasonable way forward. Two – William Rees-Mogg and Daphne Park – did not. William stated that the Board had taken a decision and must stand by it; otherwise, there must be a further meeting of the Governors to consider my proposal formally. Daphne Park was no less adamant: it was, she said, 'a Hitler loved dogs' programme and there would certainly have to be another Board meeting before any change of mind could be contemplated. The Board duly reconvened for the following (Tuesday) morning.

When we met in the morning, I had in front of me copies of the statement we had prepared about the need to transmit the programme. This to me was the heart of the matter and I was sure the statement must be issued that day, although it would probably not affect the strike the National Union of Journalists had already called for the following day – Wednesday, 7th August. But overnight Stuart, who looked really tired, had prepared a long statement about the Board's constitutional position which, at an early hour, David Holmes, the Secretary, was recasting for gubernatorial study. Stuart wanted this paper read and fully discussed, he said. 'The programme is not important,' I recorded him saying in my diary. Much to my indignation, some two hours were spent on a tedious, line-by-line discussion of this document. I pressed them to consider what I had to say about the programme and they touched on it for ten minutes before Stuart had to leave to host a lunch for Norman Tebbit. Oddly, he called on John Boyd to speak because, I presume, he was sitting furthest away on the right. John had not been at the previous meeting, he had not even seen the programme; but that did not inhibit him from banging the table, demanding that the Governors stick by their original decision and be seen to govern. On which unhappy note, they broke up for lunch.

My Board of Management colleagues, meanwhile, were waiting in an office downstairs. Stuart had asked if I would like them all to be present; but I felt that I was the only one, having missed the previous week's episode, who carried no baggage from that meeting and so might achieve something on my own. When we sat down again after an uneasy lunch, William Rees-Mogg and Daphne Park spoke strongly against any change of stance and the others were not disposed to shift either. The journalists' strike the following day was another reason, as they saw it, for not being pushed around. I reminded them that, as Editor-in-Chief of the BBC, I was giving them my carefully thought-out advice which they had lacked, and complained about lacking, the previous week. If they rejected that, they would provoke a situation of great constitutional difficulty. Yes, they said, you are the Editor-in-Chief; but we are the Board, we are the BBC, and we see no reason to move from our position. We argued for a while, but got no further; except that I insisted I must take a public stance in the matter and I must be clear what they were saying.

'Are you saying that this programme is never to go out?'

'No,' they said, 'not never.'

'Can it go out this autumn?' (As I had said it would in my draft statement.)

The autumn, William Rees-Mogg thought, was too early. He said: 'Not now. Never is too definitive a word to use. But not the autumn.'

On that fractious note, we parted. I had no authority to say when the programme could go out. I was in despair. Stuart said to me later in the day: 'Whatever hits the fan, I won't resign. I hope you won't either.' Alwyn Roberts, the National Governor for Wales and the only Governor to argue at the first meeting for the programme to be shown, came and had a drink with me in my office. We were both shattered.

Resignation seemed the only way out. On the other hand, I felt people in the BBC would rightly expect me to sort out this hideous situation.

The following day, 7th August, the NUJ strike was solid. Even the External Services people at Bush House came out. The reaction from America and the Western world generally was one of dismay. The only joke of the week was that the Russian jammers gave up their monitoring because the External Services were broadcasting no news, until we happened to broadcast what they thought was a 'dissident' opera and the jammers had to leap into action again. In Belfast, the striking journalists added a wry note by playing a video of the *Real Lives* programme in the street outside Broadcasting House.

I went to the Television Centre and spoke to the senior staff attending the weekly programme review there, in an attempt to keep morale on some kind of keel. The Governors' statement, reaffirming their constitutional position, was all over the newspapers. There was nothing I could say about the timing of the programme's transmission; only that I was determined it would go out. I said the same to the senior Radio management in Dick Francis's office, having asked Brian Wenham to start drafting a statement of the management position. Stuart, William Rees-Mogg, Alan Protheroe, David Holmes and I lunched together before going to the Home Office to see the Home Secretary, as Stuart had requested. Stuart was robust in his criticism of the Home Secretary's letter to the Board. Brittan was equally firm. It was, he said, entirely the BBC's responsibility what programme it did or did not put out, but it was no less his right to make representations. 'I am,' he said, unconvincingly, I thought, 'just like any other private citizen and so at liberty to make representations to the BBC.' We told the press waiting on the doorstep of the Home Office that we had had a frank discussion with the Home Secretary and that later on in the evening, I would make a statement.

Back at Broadcasting House, the Board of Management and I considered the draft statement that Brian Wenham had produced and finalised it. I sent a copy to the Chairman. I give the text below in full because I think it is worthy of reproduction.

Last Tuesday the Chairman of the BBC Board of Governors issued a full statement on the position concerning the *Real Lives* documentary – *At the Edge of the Union*. The facts as stated there are correct.

Other Governors have also made their views known – in formal interview, in off-the-record briefings, or in pavement remarks.

It is now time for the staff to hear my views and those of the BBC Board of Management.

As the Chairman said in his statement, the day-to-day management of the Corporation is devolved to the Director General, whom the Board appoints and who is Editor-in-Chief, and through him to the Board of Management.

The Board of Management regrets that the Governors could not accept the clear warnings that were given to them, at the meeting on 30th July, on the effect their decisions would have on the BBC's perceived independence at home and abroad and on the morale and confidence of staff in the domestic and external services.

My Board of Management and I now wish to make clear what we require of those who work for and sustain the BBC. In all programme matters we all seek the truth in a forthright and an even-handed manner. That is the BBC tradition. It transcends and overrides the particular views of any individual member of staff. It transcends any external pressures. It transcends the attitudes of any Board of Management or any Board of Governors.

In the matter of Northern Ireland, the BBC has not and will not provide unchallenged opportunities for the advocacy of terrorism. We will continue to follow the policy laid down by my two immediate predecessors – Sir Charles Curran and Sir Ian Trethowan – and by myself. That policy extends to the exploration and explanation of the views and motives of those who avow terrorist activity – and their associates. It includes, on occasion, the use of broadcast interviews. The Chairman and I reaffirmed to the Home Secretary that the policy remains unchanged.

As to the preparation of *Real Lives*, I endorse the views of my colleagues on the Board of Management that the intention of the programme was proper and that those involved in the making of the programme behaved scrupulously in the discharge of their duty. There was, however, a failure to observe the guidelines at the highest level.

I share the view of my colleagues on the Board of Management that additions can and should be made to the film before transmission – for the purpose of greater clarity and without impairing the integrity of the programme. I am asking the departmental head, Will Wyatt and the producer, Paul Hamaan, to undertake that work and to show the expanded film to me.

I shall then be able to come to a decision concerning the transmission of the film and convey it to the Governors.

At 9.00 p.m. that evening, I called a press conference to explain what we had said to the Home Secretary about his letter and how we hoped to proceed with the programme. I was, of course, in the miserable position of being unable to say when the programme would go out, a state of affairs that my own staff also found deeply unconvincing. The following morning I went on the *Today* programme and then on *Breakfast Time* to elaborate. Twice Stuart phoned to complain about nuances of delivery, though I did my best to explain the Governors' rights and position.

When I returned to Broadcasting House, David Holmes told me that the Chairman was beside himself with rage, having seen a copy of our statement and because some Governors had telephoned after hearing and seeing me to complain that my broadcasts were disloyal to them. I called Board of Management together and suggested Stuart join us at 11.15 a.m. He came in, white, but controlled. He accused us of disloyalty, of lying, of cowardice in not accepting the blame for having put the Governors in such a quandary in the first place. When he had had his say, I pointed out that it was the Board who had taken the wrong decision, and that we said openly in our statement (which was now issued to the press) that there had been a failure in the referral process, even though I did not regard it as very important. I assured him that, one way or another, this programme was going to be shown at some point in time. I then spoke to the radio staff and on the ring main round the BBC generally. Later, I saw Stuart, who seemed drained of life, before he went off on holiday to France. I was left to chew the cud and think over a way of resolving the impasse.

Not that I had much time to chew the cud. Ten days later the *Observer* broke a story that MI5 had been vetting BBC staff for years, and that we had an MI5 officer sitting in BH. We had indeed Brigadier (retired) Ronnie Stonham sitting in BH and he was involved in the vetting process; he was not working for MI5. But there was no denying that we had submitted many of our staff, especially in the news and current affairs field, to 'vetting' ever since the war. As a departmental head in television, I had first run into what seemed to me a distasteful procedure where the infamous 'Christmas trees' were stuck on personal files to alert personnel officers to potential problem characters. I had myself undergone the procedure when I rejoined the BBC in 1967; the gentleman who came to see me was, I remember, electrified by the news that I had been in East Germany and Czechoslovakia for a few days on business, and my barrister neighbour was duly subjected to close cross-examination about my background. I had, to be truthful, forgotten all about the procedure; though I very soon found out that our people in Bush House positively wanted to be vetted for fear that the KGB would try to infiltrate the vernacular departments. But none of that helped us much; with Home Secretaries sending minatory letters and Governors banning programmes and now the security services involved in vetting, the BBC's much-vaunted independence began to look distinctly tatty. Nor did it help that it was we who asked for the vetting – not they who insisted. The story rumbled on for some time and had one good outcome: it reminded us to check the numbers involved and reduce them drastically. Far fewer are now vetted than were previously.

But still we had not disposed of the *Real Lives* problem. The new National Governor for Northern Ireland, Jim Kincade, a Belfast headmaster, seemed to me to be the key figure. He had, in fact, been present at the original viewing of the film by the Governors though he had not, on that day, formally taken over from Lucy Faulkner; when he had been asked what he thought of the film, he had apparently spoken of resigning even before taking up office! But he stayed, and over a drink in my office towards the end of August, he spoke with urgency of 'healing wounds'. I said to him: 'You are a crucial element in getting this thing sorted out.' By early September, Rees-Mogg seemed to have had a change of heart because Stuart told me he had spoken to him and William was now agreeable to the film going out. I persuaded the Chairman to discuss the programme at a private supper meeting before the Governors' first formal autumn meeting and to be sure to call on Jim Kincade to speak first. The supper was on the evening of 4th September and I told Stuart I would wait at home and come back immediately if he needed me. I waited tensely till he rang about 11.00 p.m. He told me the Board had agreed after a long discussion that the programme should be transmitted but, he said, 'there is a price to be paid'.

'What is that?' I asked.

'The Board wants a meeting,' he said, 'five of them and five from Board of Management to discuss the management of the BBC.'

I said: 'Well, I don't mind that at all, but it'll be a very bloodstained meeting and I don't think it's very wise.'

The following morning, the Board was held at Television Centre. The Governors had their usual private meeting at 9.00 a.m. I was asked to join them at 9.30 a.m. Stuart was anxious to get agreement on a statement freeing the programme for transmission and that was finally agreed. But the Governors were in angry mood, furious about a *Listener* piece by Alan Protheroe where he had written: 'When the Home Secretary thanked the BBC Governors for banning *Real Lives: At the Edge of the Union*, it resembled nothing more than the White Star line congratulating the iceberg on sinking the *Titanic*. We could have anticipated such an eventuality; mercifully, unlike the *Titanic*, the BBC will limp into dry dock, critically damaged, but recoverable after a lengthy refit.' I thought it wry; they thought it insubordinate. They were incensed, too, that I had not, in their view, supported them in public. Rees-Mogg was pale with anger, Daphne Park almost spluttering with fury. Relations continued to be strained for some time thereafter; then a retired Governor was commissioned to review the situation and prepare a paper on the basis of which the two boards could attempt to resolve their differences. Each member of both boards was interviewed individually and in strict confidence. He wrote that:

There is a widespread feeling among the Governors that the obligations and responsibilities of their office are viewed less

148

ABOVE: A new Radio Centre – we decide to rebuild the Langham, December 1982, with George Howard, Norman Foster and Dick Francis.
BELOW LEFT: Alasdair Milne with Stuart Young, July 1985. Time for helicopter helmets – and smiles. BELOW RIGHT: Another new Chairman – 'Duke' Hussey arrives at Broadcasting House.

The winning programmes of the early eighties: Bob Peck in *Edge of Darkness;*

Albert Square – specially built at Elstree for *EastEnders;*

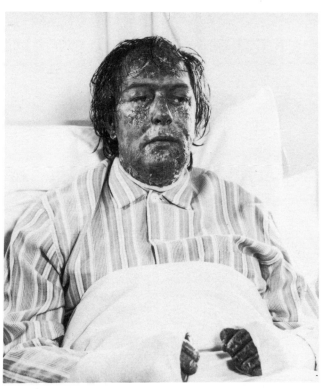

Michael Gambon as
The Singing Detective;

and the famous trio –
in *Yes, Prime Minister.*

BBC BOARD OF GOVERNORS AND
SENIOR MANAGEMENT, 1 JANUARY 1986

Stuart Young
Chairman

Sir William Rees-Mogg
Vice Chairman

Alwyn Roberts
*National Governor
for Wales*

Dr James Kincade
*National Governor
for Northern Ireland*

Watson Peat CBE
*National Governor
for Scotland*

Jocelyn Barrow OBE

Lord Harewood

Malcolm McAlpine

Daphne Park CMG OBE

Sir John Boyd CBE

Lady Parkes

Sir Curtis Keeble GCMG

Alasdair Milne
Director-General

Michael Checkland
Deputy Director-General

Alan Protheroe MBE TD
*Assistant
Director-General*

Richard Francis
*Managing Director
Radio*

Bill Cotton OBE
*Managing Director
Television*

Austen Kark
*Managing Director
External Broadcasting*

Patricia Hodgson
The Secretary

Margaret Douglas
*Chief Assistant to
the Director-General*

Brian Wenham
*Director of Programmes
Television*

Geraint Stanley Jones
Director Public Affairs

Bryce McCrirrick
Director of Engineering

Christopher Martin
Director of Personnel

Geoff Buck
Director of Finance

Board of Governors, 1982. BACK ROW LEFT TO RIGHT: Christopher Longuet-Higgins, Alwyn Roberts, Roger Young, Bea Serota, Alf Allen, Peter Moores, Lucy Faulkner, Jack Johnston, Stuart Young. FRONT ROW LEFT TO RIGHT: Jocelyn Barrow, William Rees-Mogg, Ian Trethowan, George Howard, Alasdair Milne, David Barlow (Secretary).

"Nobody actually understands it but it took 2000 years to set up the system!"

Brian Hanrahan on board HMS *Hermes* – trouble in the Falklands.

Kate Adie reporting from Tripoli – trouble from Conservative Central Office.

With the Prince of Wales and Asa Briggs at Milton Keynes.

Alasdair and Sheila Milne meet Mrs. Nancy Reagan at the US Embassy.

Alasdair Milne's
farewell: BBC Television
Centre, June 29th, 1987.
Bill Cotton presiding.

The pipers' farewell – a
coup de théâtre at
Television Centre.

seriously by senior management, sometimes to the point of implicit disregard or contempt, than either the Charter or their own understanding of their charge demands . . . The Governors feel themselves often to be inadequately informed and insufficiently forewarned. Too often the first knowledge they have of some development affecting the public position of the BBC is when they read about it in the press . . . They are uncertain how far or how faithfully opinions expressed by the Board arc transmitted onward within the BBC. The Governors find it difficult to believe that a crisper administrative style could not be developed which would put paid to charges of slack management.

For their part, the Board of Management are deeply unhappy about the adversarial relationship which seems to have developed between the two boards. The Governors seem to them chiefly interested in criticism, and they mourn what seems to them the loss of sense of partnership in a great enterprise, with the friendliness and mutual respect it engendered . . . The Board seems to them to be dismissive of their professional knowledge and experience and mistrustful of their capacity . . . Board proceedings seem to them permeated with suspicion.

His description of the management view was all too painfully accurate; I was, I confess, shocked at the depth of the Governors' antagonism and for that I must take the heavy share of blame. The retired Governor added in his covering letter to the Chairman that 'I found an equally strong desire to mend fences and make a fresh start.' All of us wanted to achieve that and he made a number of wise suggestions to help us on our road.

The way was now open for the programme to be transmitted. I looked at it again, changed two captions which seemed rather obscure, added some material of IRA bombing which I thought improved the programme and it was duly transmitted in October. Those who wrote about it were surprised at the drama that had, undeniably, rocked the BBC to its foundations.

I know that Stuart thought the Board had made a mistake and regretted that he had not shown his own hand more strongly at their first meeting. He wished he had led them more positively. For my part, I regret that the internal mechanisms had not alerted me to the programme's existence, though I have often wondered how the Board would have reacted if the Director General had been present at their first meeting and had argued against their seeing the film. I cannot forget that I was present at their second meeting and, in what seemed to me a remarkably cavalier way, they still overruled me. None of us emerges well from this incident, and certainly resentments

149

engendered at the time of *Real Lives* were harboured until the day I left the BBC.

Apart from damaged reputations, there was one significant casualty of the *Real Lives* affair. David Holmes, much respected as our Political Editor and then as Chief Assistant to the Director General, decided to retire from the pivotal job of Secretary of the BBC earlier than his time called for. He was certain he should go. His health had been shaky for some time. He now felt he could no longer stand the atmosphere without his health suffering further damage.

13 THE INTERNATIONAL BBC

The life of a Director General in modern times is relentless in pace but rich in variety. If you read Reith's diaries you can detect faint whiffs of boredom, days when he was not 'fully stretched'; there is no time for boredom for a contemporary DG.

For a start, there are meetings – lots of them. Any organisation the size of the BBC has to live off meetings simply to keep the flow of information and exchange going: Board of Management meetings every Monday morning to review the events and programmes of the past week, to try to resolve the immediate problems, to chart a way through the coming weeks. Regular meetings with the Chairman to exchange news and views, fortnightly meetings with the Governors and usually a Board Finance meeting the previous evening. Meetings, obviously, with senior colleagues on a whole range of broadcasting topics: can we achieve a fixed time-start for *Newsnight* without disrupting the earlier 'junction points' between BBC-1 and BBC-2 (a tale that has recurred recently); how shall we handle the tricky relationships between the new Joint Secretaries of our main union which has recently merged; how shall we open up the BBC to greater independent producer involvement (and is this a stand for Government to take anyway) without doing possibly great damage to the existing production process; how shall we maintain a television service to large parts of the North of England when one old transmitter, being dismantled, has become overweighted with a mass of ice and fallen through the roof of the transmitter building?

I tried, too, to attend the weekly retrospective programme reviews of the Television and Radio services – meetings where past programmes were vigorously dissected and which I knew well from chairing the Television one for nearly ten years; I went to them and to the weekly News and Current Affairs meeting as often as I could to hear at first hand reaction, opinion and, no less importantly, gossip. There were meetings, too, with people outside the BBC – MPs with special problems or anxieties, backbench committees at the House of Commons, regular quarterly meetings of the General Advisory Council (a body chosen from all walks of life and from all over the country), occasional meetings with the important Broadcasting Councils in Scotland, Wales and Northern Ireland. One had, too, to meet people with specific complaints against the BBC, High Commissioners from Commonwealth countries (BBC coverage of recent events in Sri Lanka brought strong reaction from their High Commissioner), visiting broadcasters from all over the world. There was, as you might expect, mountainous paperwork; however you try to cut it down, it generates its own momentum. Forward planning schedules, financial estimates, briefing papers, hundreds of letters daily (mercifully, the BBC enjoys a highly efficient Secretariat who handled most of this in terms of drafting replies), articles and periodicals to be digested, annual reports to be read and noted against possible future promotion. There was, too, much entertaining and being entertained up and down the country – perhaps three or four times a week. Too much, at times, for a sensible health pattern! Much travelling, too, to visit the national regions, the local radio stations all over England. I tried to make it a plan that every summer I would swing through a part of England for three or four days visiting a number of local radio stations every day just to be seen and to listen. When I spoke to the staff in Cardiff shortly after I became DG, Geraint Stanley Jones, who was then Controller in Wales, said in introducing me that he could not remember that any DG had even spoken to the staff of BBC Wales before! And there were the speeches. I remembered Hugh Greene saying that when he became DG, he accepted every invitation proffered and I determined to do the same. It meant some occasions which were not profitable to the BBC; but I spoke everywhere, sometimes two or three times a week, and I certainly got a better feel of countrywide response than I had before.

That is a slight sketch of the domestic side of the job: the DG is also the chief executive of a world-famous broadcasting organisation, in close and working contact with every major country in the world.

The stories underlining the faith of listeners overseas to the BBC's external broadcasting services are legion: quite recently, it was reported to us that Colonel Gaddafi, on the face of it an unlikely ally, had rebuked his Libyan broadcasters, reminding them that the BBC was the institution they should try to emulate. Gerry Mansell, who was for nine years Managing Director of the External Services, quotes in his history of Bush House, *Let Truth Be Told*, Malcolm Browne of the *New York Times* as saying about the External Services: 'They are to the free mind what Oxfam is to the hungry.' I doubt, in a troubled world, if our reputation overseas for telling the truth has ever stood as high as it does today.

But, of course, the BBC's relations with overseas broadcasters and producers is not limited to their receiving our broadcasts. There was, and is, a constant interchange of ideas and information throughout most of the broadcasting world. Apart from filming trips overseas for *Tonight*, my first real international assignment was being a member of the BBC delegation to the Commonwealth Broadcasting Association Conference held in Malta in 1974. This body, of which the BBC was a founder member, meets every two years, and has a membership of fifty organisations, ranging from big and relatively affluent bodies like the Canadian Broadcasting Corporation to Radio Turks and Caicos, or the Tonga Broadcasting Commission.

As with the Commonwealth itself, we share a language and we all share a profession. At my first meeting in Malta (it had originally been called for Cyprus but the Turkish invasion that year forced a change of venue at short notice) I was hard put to see what the BBC got out of the CBA. We contributed some twenty per cent of the budget, and we provided a home for the Secretariat in London. Moreover, we provided training opportunities in all kinds of broadcasting specialisms, and yet were accorded no special position, being treated just like any other delegation. Indeed, at the Malta conference, there was an unedifying scene when Charles Curran, the BBC's Director General of the day, was engaged with the Ugandan delegates in a noisy and bitter exchange about our treatment of Idi Amin. But at the Malta meeting and at the next one I attended in Singapore two years later, one learnt that these occasions were, for some overseas broadcasters, almost like the release of the psychiatrist's couch. For once, they were able to speak freely, and if the minutes the following day contained any potential embarrassment were they to be seen back home, the delegates could speedily call for their revision! I shall not forget hearing a most courageous speech from a delegate from Grenada who described, in Geary's time, how they were forced to tell lies over the air under that petty dictatorship. He, I gather, shortly afterwards went to prison.

These Commonwealth conferences were social occasions as well, with wives attending from many parts of the world. In 1984, I was the first Director General of the BBC to be elected President of the CBA, and we had, as the BBC had for thirty years, a few wives present at the meeting in Hong Kong. It was at that time 'open season' on the BBC, and some of our more lurid Fleet Street colleagues chose to make much of this further proof of gross BBC wastage. The fact that there were, for example, more Nigerian ladies present than British, did not interest them. But the Association is also a working organisation throughout the year, holding regional conferences all over the world, and the BBC's role in offering training posts to Commonwealth broadcasters in London and in sending experts out to train on the ground has been a crucial part in the development of broadcasting in the Commonwealth where resources are so severely strained. Almost my last duty as President of the Association was to make a visit to East Africa where in Dar-es-Salaam I saw a 1950s' radio valve, which the Science Museum would certainly have treasured, aglow and working on transmission. When I asked the Chief Engineer where he got his spares from, he said with an engaging grin that they overstocked thirty years previously!

Our relationships with the countries of the Eastern bloc were more complex. At engineering level, there were certain contacts to do with the handling of circuits or arrangements for the big set pieces like the 1980 Moscow Olympics. Editorial contacts, apart from sport, were rare. But with the Chinese we had, quite early on, a vigorous working relationship. Much of this was due to Aubrey Singer who was a devoted Sinologist and who beat at the doors of China until they fell before him. One result of his negotiations was that we found ourselves, in October 1976, on a diplomatic visit to China in order to sign a protocol of friendship. The delegation was led by Sir Charles Curran (Mr Sir Charles, the Chinese delighted in calling him), and had an almost nineteenth-century feel about it. We took train, as you might say, from Hong Kong, were invited to walk across the railway bridge into China and shown to a curtained rest room, where we were asked to wait while our luggage was cleared through customs. 'As honoured guests,' they said, 'there will be no customs examination for you.' In fact, as we found out later, the luggage had been thoroughly searched, but it gave us a comfortable feeling.

Then we were placed on the train to Canton, where smiling officials from the local broadcasting station urged us to sit down: 'You must be tired. Have a cup of tea,' and then moved us to the airport. There the first sign of the iron inside the velvet glove appeared. The air fares to Peking, they said, cost £1,500. Would we please pay now in foreign currency? But, because of a disagreement between American Express and the Chinese authorities over relationships with Taiwan, we had only been allowed to change $100 each at the border. We had no cash. Charles offered them an air credit card. 'We do not recognise this card,' they said. 'Very well,' we said, 'we are going to sit in the restaurant until you sort it out.' And there we sat for two hours drinking whisky until they finally reappeared and face was saved. We agreed to refund the Embassy in Peking for our flight money, the Embassy covered the fares and my passport carries that information to this day.

We arrived in Peking at an eerie time: two days before the Gang of Four were arrested. Correspondents in the town knew something was afoot. The *Daily Telegraph* correspondent was the first to break the story and I vividly remember Charles Curran and Aubrey Singer competing against each other with aerials hung out of the windows of the Peking Hotel, like fishing rods, to see who could first pick up the World Service reports of the upheaval. It was upheaval for our hosts too. I had struck up a cheerfully bantering acquaintance with the Deputy Director General (the Director General himself appeared only once at our farewell banquet, looking disconsolate, and was never heard of again) and on the Friday morning, the day after the arrests were made public, he explained to me why we could not visit the university which was the first stop on our schedule for that day. 'The students,' he said, 'have gone to the fields.' In fact, as we discovered later, the university was surrounded by tanks so the students had not gone anywhere. We went for a healthy trot up the Great Wall instead. Two years later, when back in Peking again, I asked after the Deputy Director General. They said they had never heard of anyone of that name.

Our times in China were often marked by strange incident. In 1978, we lodged a request to see somebody of importance in the Government. Quite early one morning, Philip Short, our Peking correspondent (the first, established as a direct result of the Curran visit two years earlier) rang to say that we were urgently summoned to the Great Hall of the People to meet one Ulan Fu, a member of the Politburo and the only 'ethnic' (Mongolian) member. Philip had at great speed prepared subtle questions about the 'windy faction' and the 'slippery faction' – groups which were being much talked about as the political situation changed after the downfall of the Gang of Four. Ulan Fu, who was a highly accomplished spitter, seldom missing the spittoon placed some yards from him, found these tricky questions hugely entertaining, while the diligent Chinese scribes solemnly wrote down every word of our exchange.

We had a similar surprise in 1980 when Ian Trethowan and Aubrey and I went to Peking to put further signatures to the protocol which Charles Curran had signed four years earlier. With our Chinese broadcasting friends from Peking, who set out on the journey almost like men going to Mars, Aubrey and I had travelled to the far Taklamakan Desert, on China's north-west frontiers, to visit the famous painted caves of Dun Huang on the Great Silk Road. Dun Huang had somehow escaped the onslaught of the Cultural Revolution which some Chinese experts estimate destroyed three-quarters of the country's cultural artifacts. In Dun Huang they had not set eyes on a foreigner for years, probably not since the last appearance of Western archaeologists in the 1930s. We were a new species. A short walk from the fairly primitive lodgings we inhabited to the shops in this remote Chinese oasis was the nearest thing I have known to being a new inhabitant of an old zoo. The locals were particularly fascinated by Philip Short, our Peking correspondent, who is tall and sports a fine head of wavy hair. He was the Pied Piper of Hamelin, to a turn. They followed him in a horde (Aubrey and I were lesser oddities but still of passing interest) and when we went into a shop they crowded in behind us. We were fenced in by muttering, admiring human beings. When we turned to leave, they shrank from us as if we were truly 'foreign devils'.

When we returned to Peking travel-stained and weary, even our Chinese guides were astounded to be told that instead of being assigned to some hotel or other, we were staying at the serene surroundings of Chou en Lai's old summer house by the Kunming Lake. The next morning we were spruce and properly suited for the ceremonial signing at 9.00 a.m. But nothing happened. There was much coughing and smoking and whispering. It transpired that the man whose duty it was to open the ceremonial champagne bottles was late, and nobody could take his place. In the end, it was all well done.

Although our contacts with the Soviet Union were rare (they were, after all, until quite recently jamming the output of the Russian Service and spending millions of pounds doing so, and when the Solidarity Movement began in Poland, they started jamming the Polish Service too, from transmitters that we easily identified as being within the borders of the Soviet Union). I thought, in 1979, it might be a good time to pay a visit to our Soviet counterparts in advance of the Moscow Olympic Games the following year. I was encouraged to do so by the Head of Soviet Radio, Yuri Orlov (no connection with the celebrated dissident) who, though wary of all our doings, had been a witty Vice-Chairman of the Golden Rose of Montreux Light Entertainment jury with me the year before. So, with Noble Wilson, the BBC's Controller of International Relations, I set out on my first visit to the Sovet Union.

Our Russian hosts were extremely hospitable, though the physical arrangements had a flavour all their own. When we checked in at the Sovietzkaya Hotel, our guide from Gostelradio (the Soviet broadcasting system) courteously asked what we would like for breakfast the next morning. I said I would be glad of coffee, and was there juice? In the morning, a terrific battering on the door of my immense suite, with a corridor dozens of yards long, announced the arrival of breakfast. Coffee, certainly, but no juice. 'No juice?' I asked tentatively. 'No juice,' the huge lady shouted at me. When I told our guide, he remonstrated with the mamushka at the floor desk. But it was the same pattern until our last morning when a huge, stinking can of tomato juice arrived. 'Juice,' she bellowed at me. But there was no coffee. The eating arrangements were also oddly eccentric. The night we arrived our correspondent, Kevin Ruane, had reserved a table for

156

us at the Nazional Hotel, overlooking Red Square. It was a Sunday night, there would be no crowd, he said. And, indeed, the place was empty. He ordered a vodka for us and a meal, and then had to leave for a prior engagement. Three other people came in. It was still three hours before the food arrived. It always seemed to be three hours before you could eat.

The man then in charge of Soviet broadcasting, Mr Lapin, had held his post for many years, some said since Stalin's time. He was a member of the Politburo and a powerful figure. He also had the reputation of being a hard and brutal character. When I called on Mr Lapin, he clearly intended to give me a rough time. I thought it polite to ask him how the Russians intended to handle the huge job of televising the Olympics the following year. He obviously thought such questions a piece of gross impertinence. How many cameras did they plan to field? I asked. However many they thought necessary, he replied. What was their budget for this vast operation? I asked. Whatever they needed, the Soviet Union would find, he said. He unquestionably got the best of the exchange. The age of 'glasnost' had not arrived in 1979.

For all the beauties of the Kremlin churches and the powerful effects of a Sunday morning spent in the great monastery of Zagorsk not far from the capital, I found Moscow a heavy, depressing place. By contrast, on our way home, we spent a couple of days in Hungary with Magyar Television. Meetings there always seemed to float by on an interesting combination of whisky and strawberries, and ended in laughter and many toasts. It was a liberating experience.

I had another strange confrontation as Director General. It was with the late Mrs Gandhi. Both Charles Curran and Ian Trethowan, my immediate predecessors, had been to India and met this formidable woman on her own territory. Mark Tully, our veteran Delhi correspondent, had been a witness of both these encounters and his stories of the first, Charles', were chilling. Charles had little small talk and Mrs Gandhi even less. Most of the fifteen minutes they spent together had been passed in silence. Ian had fared better. As he tells in his book, after bowling her a 'succession of long hops on such questions as Russia, China, Afghanistan and the UN', he tried a different tack. He told her he was a political writer by origin and asked her how she had won so convincing an election result. And then, seemingly, he was away. But the scars of the first meeting were still visible on Mark.

When we went for our meeting, he urged me not to be put off. We were kept waiting a long time in the outer office, then shown into the presence. The familiar hooded eyes and drawn face showed little interest. Did she have any complaint about the BBC? I asked. None that she could remember, she said. (Bearing in mind that under the earlier emergency, Mark had been thrown out of the country, and we had just had a bitter row with the Indian authorities over a documentary about a remote tribe and its sexual practices, it was as well to invite a spade to be called one.) I reminded her that the previous day I had seen her photographed visiting a game park and told her that Mark and I were soon going to see the famous tiger reserve in the Corbett National Park. She was a different woman. The subject of game conservation in India obviously absorbed her. For twenty minutes or so, she spoke about it with great excitement. Then, suddenly, she put her fingers together in an arch before her face, looked down at them and stopped talking. The meeting was over.

For the External Services, the early 1980s held the promise of a new financial structure but also brought difficulties with that promise. It seemed that the Conservative Government had adopted the policy that the domestic side of the BBC should continue to be funded by a licence fee set for a period of three years. Money for the External Services had, hitherto, depended on annual discussions with the Foreign Office, and through them the Treasury. The External Services are funded quite differently from the rest of the BBC through 'grant in aid' out of general taxation. The agreement is that the Foreign Office specifies the languages in which the External Services broadcast, and the amount of time involved. Thus, fifteen more minutes in Pushtu since the Russian invasion of Afghanistan, or more Spanish to Latin America since the Falklands conflict, or whatever. Bush House is then free to handle the editorial content on its own. But why shouldn't the External Services, we wondered, come into line with the rest of the BBC and be sure of its money three years ahead? After all, their capital problems in terms of replacing equipment or negotiations over staff wages and salaries were no different from the rest of the BBC. The main obstacle was the manner in which Government expenditure was organised by the Treasury – on an 'annualised' basis where every bid for finance was scrutinised on a yearly basis. We put this thought to the Foreign Office and they did not dismiss it. Clearly, though, such radical moves called for another committee, and the Perry Committee, chaired by a Foreign Office civil servant and including a BBC representative, was established to consider that proposition but also to study ways of achieving further economies in the running of the External Services.

It was a sensitive area. When the draft of the Perry Report came to the Board, it did indeed acquiesce in the argument about three-year funding; but it appeared to seek some sort of *quid pro quo* in asserting greater Foreign Office involvement in the operational control of

Bush House. Antony Acland, the Permanent Secretary at the FCO, and his people were adamant that it did not mean that. The prose seemed to suggest it did. We knew that the FCO was under pressure from the Treasury who did not think it kept Bush House under close enough financial supervision. At all events, the Governors rightly rose up in dismay about what they conceived as possible editorial intervention and letters were exchanged between Stuart Young and the Foreign Secretary to clarify the situation. When I left the BBC, the detail of the Perry Report was still a theme for controversy and discussion.

Bush House also nailed its flag to the mast of the new technology. In 1983, Douglas Muggeridge, the Managing Director of the External Services, showed me the draft of a speech he was due to deliver at some convention in San Francisco, in which he advocated a television version of the World Service, to be disseminated by satellite in the future. I was, frankly, rather dismissive. We had enough trouble at that time with DBS anyway. Who, I asked him, would pay for such an exercise when we were conducting an annual battle with the Foreign Office and the Treasury to get £80 million or so to keep the External Services going in radio terms? Although most people in and out of parliament agreed that Bush House was the best and cheapest advertisement for Britain and British values throughout the world, if they kept chipping away at this relatively small sum how did he think we would convince them to move into the much more expensive world of television?

Douglas delivered his speech in the States. Nothing was heard of the idea for a while, though the Voice of America became increasingly active in the making of television programmes for delivery to their embassies and other outlets throughout the world. Tragically, Douglas developed a brain tumour and died. He was succeeded at Bush House by his deputy, Austen Kark, and though his time was heavily taken up with the outcome of the Perry Report, echoes of the television possibility continued to reach my ears. And when Austen left and we appointed John Tusa, a 'Bushman' by background but someone who was better known to the public as the presenter for seven years of *Newsnight*, he picked up the torch and ran with it very strongly.

We put a case to the Government for a combined Bush House/ Television Service operation which would cost about £8 million a year. We knew, of course, that they would prefer any alternative to spending more public money; and ITN asserted loudly that they could do the job without spending a penny of public money. The Government has now rejected the BBC's arguments. I am convinced that the worldwide reputation of the BBC for telling the truth, established over many years during the war and after it, is the right basis for Britain to spend money of this order.

I think, too, that the BBC were good Europeans before the rest of us citizens were agreed to be so. We were founder members of the European Broadcasting Union, a powerful body, consisting of more than forty members including (oddly, one might think) several Arab countries situated around the Mediterranean coast, with a bureaucracy based in Geneva. Charles Curran was, for three successive terms, President of the EBU and spent much of his time on its business. Indeed, I am sure involvement in the affairs of the EBU was for him a genuine escape from the stress of being Director General. He was the key figure in establishing the authority of the Union in its daily free exchange of news items between its members (something the new entrepreneurs look upon hungrily), and of its crucial power in negotiating expensive sporting contracts, such as those for the Olympic Games or the World Cup, where its ability to deliver all European broadcasters, or withhold them all, has been a powerful card to play.

When Ian Trethowan succeeded Charles Curran at the BBC, he had no desire to emulate Charles' European interests though he took the EBU seriously enough, causing, in fact, a great furore at the General Assembly in Killarney by backing Albert Scharf, a gcnial, multi-lingual German broadcasting lawyer and Deputy Director General of Bavarian Broadcasting, against his French predecessor for the presidency by writing a letter claiming the Frenchman was too accommodating to the Arabs. When I became Director General, I myself doubted the value of the Union to the BBC and asked Noble Wilson for an early paper on it. We were, after all, spending more than £1 million on our EBU activities. Some of the meetings and matters under discussion seemed drear beyond relief, but gradually, as with the Commonwealth Broadcasting Association, I discovered that it was another forum where the small broadcaster's voice was no less important than the big one's, and that we all learnt from each other in a way we could not have otherwise easily achieved.

Cable and satellite were, of course, in my time the themes of constant and often quite bitter debate. Should Canal Plus, a French cable company, be allowed membership of the Union and access thereby to its benefits simply because it came under the skirts of the main French television channel? Should the Union prevent a Luxembourg broadcasting station from carrying sponsored sports programmes when football shirt advertising was prevalent throughout Europe? Could the Union, in fact, survive the proliferation of commercial channels such as Bernardo Berlusconi had successfully established in Italy? All of this debate Albert Scharf, as President, handled with good humour, considerable presence and fluency in three languages. The BBC's voice was very important in the EBU and Albert and I enjoyed a close friendship and, it must also be said, a taste for Glenmorangie!

So one travelled overseas frequently. On the familiar television circuit to Australia and California; to EBU meetings, usually in bitter December weather in Geneva but also in more congenial summer meetings in Stockholm or Naples; to Commonwealth Association meetings in Hong Kong, Toronto or Sydney. There were other ventures of a less orthodox nature. Early in 1983, three of us – Bryce McCrirrick, the Director of Engineering, Douglas Muggeridge, the Managing Director of External Services and I – took off for Antigua in the West Indies. We went there to inspect one of our relay stations for the Caribbean and South American area which we share with the German company, Deutsche Welle, but also because Antigua is the staging post for Ascension Island where the BBC also has important transmitting facilities.

We flew from Antigua in an American transport plane – canvas bucket seats, only one loo between forty-odd people, and ear plugs against the deafening noise – and, after a truly hellish night, spent a fascinating day meeting some forty BBC staff and their wives who live in, and seemed to love living in, the weird, barren moonscape of Ascension. The Falklands War was well over by that time, but Ascension was still the main stop-off point before the long haul, with mid-air refuelling, for RAF planes flying to the Falklands. The BBC not only runs the transmitters in Ascension; we also run the desalination plant, and since I was there, have by agreement with the Government taken over even more of the island's facilities. There was an administrator, who lived in a nice house high up in the clouds in the only green part of the island, with water ducts built by British sailors in the 1830s passing close by down to the shore. He kindly put me up. This was the occasion when Mrs Thatcher had just passed through on her way to the Falklands where, as I have related, Alan Protheroe had a flaming and rather public row with her Press Secretary, Bernard Ingham. As I waited on the open tarmac at Ascension to catch the RAF plane home, it dawned on me that I could well soon confront a Prime Minister who was, at that moment, even less well disposed to the BBC than usual. The Lord was kind. I took off about half an hour before Mrs Thatcher arrived from Port Stanley.

The international status of the BBC brought us many problems. None, I believe, more difficult than covering Lebanon and South Africa. For many months, Keith Graves for BBC Television News and Gerald Butt for BBC Radio and their crews risked their lives or

161

their freedom by kidnap, in covering the increasingly mad situation in Beirut. Time and again, we asked ourselves if the moment had come to pull them out and base them nearby, in Cyprus or elsewhere. Which, in the end, is what we did.

The physical dangers for Michael Buerk and Graham Leach in South Africa were probably not so immediate; but the political harassment was, and brought us into continuous dialogue with the South African authorities both in London and in Pretoria. Alan Protheroe had a particularly good working relationship with them and I encouraged him to make several visits to Pretoria when our correspondents' work permits seemed at hazard, or when some incident had occurred to imperil their ability to report properly. Again, we wondered often about whether it was better to withdraw the correspondents altogether, particularly when in the autumn of 1986 the South African Government introduced draconian press and broadcasting controls which compelled us to employ lawyers to stand over every word said. Years of imprisonment could have followed one false step by our people. Yet this was clearly one of the biggest stories of the last quarter of the century. Better to try and stay there and tell at least some part of what was happening rather than pack it in altogether. In the end, when the South African election was out of the way in the spring of 1987, the South Africans made up our minds for us by expelling both Michael Buerk and his ITV counterpart. Graham Leach was, however, spared.

Tim Sebastian, on the other hand, was not. Reporting from Eastern Europe has always been a difficult business and, at times, it has been essential to move correspondents on, as we moved Kevin Ruane from Moscow to Warsaw for radio. Tim had done a remarkable job reporting the development of Solidarity in Poland and seemed a natural to go to Moscow for television. But he was swept up in a 'tit-for-tat' response by the Russians to the expulsion of a number of Soviet Embassy people from Britain, and is now working in Washington.

The BBC stands, as it always has done, four square at the heart of international broadcasting. Towards the end of 1986, we received heartwarming proof of this fact in a series of occasions held in the United States to pay tribute to the BBC on the fiftieth anniversary of its beginning the first public television service in the world at Alexandra Palace in November 1936. I spoke at a dinner given by the Museum of Broadcasting in New York, hosted by the veteran CBS Chairman, William Paley, and addressed by Alistair Cooke, Walter Cronkite and other celebrated American broadcasters. After thanking them for their generosity, I said there were one or two footnotes to be added. One was that people in the United States generally

162

believed the BBC to be 'Government funded', if not 'Government controlled'. 'Any recent visitor to Britain who witnessed the governing party's attack on BBC standards will have been disabused of the notion that the BBC is, in any sense, a creature of Government.' (A reference to our recent exchange with Mr Tebbit over Libya.)

I went on:

The second footnote is about freedom for the creators of programmes. Over these fifty years, we invested heavily in talent and have trusted that talent. That trust involved knowing in advance where it might lead. You have to extend to producers the right to fail so that much more frequently they can succeed.

And thirdly, we have interpreted public taste in what you might call a leisurely fashion. If I am asked whether I like this or that, I can only draw on what I already know. If the range of my choice, however, is extended I might be induced to be interested in a subject about whose existence I previously entertained only the haziest notions. That philosophy has been at the heart of our activities over these past fifty years.

Our relationships embrace a worldwide network. Our reputation – for truth, for standards, for eagerness to impart skills and knowledge – is understood and acclaimed. I make no apology for seeming boastfulness. There are many reasons for believing the BBC has a strong and bright future. Its internationalism and its unequivocal support from all over the world is not the least of them.

14 PEACOCK AND THE PUBLIC INTEREST

The meeting at the Home Office with Leon Brittan on 26th March, 1985 had set the licence fee figure at £58, not the £65 for which we had argued. It had also established the existence of the Peacock Committee with terms of reference spelt out to us that afternoon and published the following day.

They were:

1) To assess the effects of the introduction of advertising or sponsorship on the BBC's Home Services, either as an alternative or a supplement to the income now received through the licence fee including:
   a) the financial and other consequences for the BBC, for independent television and independent local radio, for the prospective services of cable, independent national radio and direct broadcasting by satellite, for the press and the advertising industry and for the Exchequer;
   b) the impact on the range and quality of existing broadcasting services.

2) To identify a range of options for the introduction, in varying amounts and on different conditions of advertising or sponsorship on some or all of the BBC's Home Services, with an assessment of the advantages and disadvantages of each option.

3) To consider any proposal for securing income for the consumer other than through the licence fee.

These were clear terms. They encompassed, rightly, all those parts of the media where the BBC's possible incursion into the advertising field might have an effect, perhaps a very powerful effect. We knew the Prime Minister's views about advertising because she had told us over lunch. We believed the Home Secretary, Leon Brittan, was less immediately persuaded (his predecessor, Willie Whitelaw, most certainly had not been). Bernard Ingham had put it more succinctly when he came to lunch a few months earlier: 'Just take advertising on Radios 1 and 2 and don't argue!'

164

The issues were set out more discursively in Peacock's final report.

Why is it right to look at a system of financing the BBC which has been in operation for so long and which has been endorsed by every committee commissioned to review it? A system of this kind cannot be expected to last for ever. People's needs and desires change and so do the opportunities for meeting or satisfying them. Practices widely accepted during one decade may become quite inappropriate in the next, in which different social conditions may prevail and different technological considerations apply. No political decision as complex and detailed as that which determines the structure of broadcasting can be right for all time. It must be reviewed in the light of changing circumstances.

Or as Douglas Hurd, the Home Secretary who received the Peacock Report, said defiantly in the Commons debate on the report: 'We're not going to chunter on with the existing system for ever.' Cynics might, I suppose, read into that statement from Peacock a discreet laying of the ground for radical change, pleasing to a market-orientated Government. And there were many claiming that Peacock had simply been set up to do a hatchet job on the BBC.

But that is to run before our horse to market. We had to get to work to prepare for the Committee's investigations. First of all, I wanted someone in charge of drafting our papers who not only knew the workings of the BBC thoroughly, but who could also write with flair. I chose Brian Wenham, Director of Programmes for Television. The drafting group also included my Special Advisers, Stephen Hearst, once Head of Music and Arts in Television, then Controller of Radio 3 and, in Ian Trethowan's time, Controller of the Future Policy Group, a kind of 'Think Tank', and Dr Janet Morgan, formerly a member of the Downing Street 'Think Tank'. We also co-opted Professor Andrew Ehrenburg, of the London Business School, who was to produce sterling research work on the nature and value of the licence fee. By Midsummer's Day Brian's group's first paper came to the Board of Management for ratification. It was, in essence, an information paper for the Committee on how the BBC operated. We told the Committee that we would wish to offer further evidence in the autumn, embodying various research papers that we had commissioned.

The membership of the Committee was intriguing. Alan Peacock, the Chairman, a softly-spoken Scot, was a Professor at Heriot-Watt University in Edinburgh, who had moved from being an economic adviser to the Department of Trade and Industry to run the new, privately financed Buckingham University. He was a well-known free-market economist. As was Sam Brittan, the distinguished writer on economics for the *Financial Times*, and brother of the Home Secretary. Both of them were followers of the writings on broadcasting by Peter Jay, former Ambassador to Washington and one-time Chief Executive of TV-am. Then there was Alastair Hetherington, Editor of the *Guardian* for many years, later Controller of BBC Scotland, now Professor of Media Studies at Stirling University. And Judith Chalmers, who had worked in both radio and television for the BBC and ITV. We imagined that these two might take a more sceptical view of the market ideology as applied to broadcasting. Finally, there was Lord Quinton, philospher, broadcaster, until recently President of Trinity College, Oxford; Sir Peter Reynolds, Chairman of Rank Hovis McDougall; and Jeremy Hardie, a businessman with SDP leanings. They were certainly an interesting mix.

We first met the Committee on the morning of 24th September. It was only a couple of weeks since the row over *Real Lives* had been settled, and feelings were still running high inside the BBC. The programme itself had not yet been transmitted. But now we faced a different challenge and must do so from a position of unity. We had had a thorough rehearsal with our Peacock group the previous week to try to expose weaknesses in our argument. The meeting with Peacock was a peculiar occasion, I suppose because we did not quite know what to expect. Professor Peacock handled the niceties. Tony Quinton wondered whether we should trouble ourselves with doing 'commercial things' (entertainment, presumably, though it was not so openly defined); Alastair Hetherington was very keen that we should be precise and careful in our definition of 'public service broadcasting' and was clearly trying to be helpful and stem a hostile tide; Sam Brittan and Peacock himself both nagged on about the iniquities of 'regulation' and in their way were, I am sure, also trying to be helpful. They wanted, as they said, times without number later on, to 'liberate' broadcasting. We retired to Lockett's for lunch and to read the runes.

True to recent form, *The Times* had already had a word or two of advice to offer us and Professor Peacock. In May, when the members of the Committee met for the first time, they were warned by *The Times* that it 'had highlighted the shortcomings [of the BBC's case] before, its disregard of technological and political developments, its blithe assumption that Public Service Broadcasting (for which alone a universal licence fee can be justified) and the British Broadcasting Corporation are somehow eternally synonymous'. Sternly, it added: 'The BBC will talk a good deal about quality over the coming months. Quality, like Public Service Broadcasting [I assumed the capitals were intended to be derisory rather than helpful pointers] has grown to be defined by the standard of whatever the BBC happens to be producing at any given time.'

When we published our first submission, a leader headed 'POOR FARE FOR PEACOCK' told us what they thought of our work down in Wapping. 'Restatement is high on the BBC agenda: rethinking is not,' it thundered. 'An organisation which can claim – in contemptuous conflict with the facts – that it is not engaged in a ratings battle with its competitors clearly needs to be watched very carefully when it is dealing with the less clear-cut results of research.' It was quite like old times.

As the autumn wore on, intelligence came our way that there was deep dissension within the Committee, with Peacock himself and Sam Brittan leading the pack but finding the hounds reluctant. Sam himself has written, in the *Political Quarterly*, quite openly about what he calls their 'rough division into three groups'. He has stated that the Chairman played a dominant role, having been appointed in advance of the other members. His piece on the 'Dynamics of the Committee' sheds helpful light on the tactical positioning of a small group.

There were some unexpected cross-currents on the Committee. Peacock and I were both far too individualistic to form the solid phalanx that some members initially feared. Perhaps my greatest difference with Peacock was on how to win over Hetherington to a broadcasting market – and, by extension, on how to explain the case for the market and its application to broadcasting to a wider public. Hetherington seemed to be less antipathetic to a market-based approach if it was founded on the English liberal tradition of freedom of choice and opposition to censorship rather than on textbook reasoning, or econometric crystal-gazing. Whether or not this was wishful thinking, Hetherington and I did form an alliance at the end on the need for a clearly written and unambiguous final chapter, and in protest against the submission of numerous drafts in rapid succession which the Committee had had no chance to absorb . . . I was, indeed, disturbed (but not astonished) that liberal minded scholars and businessmen [e.g. Quinton and Hardie certainly, Reynolds too?] did not share my instinctive revulsion from 'regulation' in anything to do with news, opinion and artistic expression . . . Fortunately, a closer analysis showed that the more benign effects of regulation might eventually be achieved by the combination of a true consumer market in broadcasting and public finance for programmes of a clearly public service nature.

Meantime, we worked at the main evidence to be submitted before Christmas. It was sent to Peacock, after several redrafting sessions involving the Governors, on 20th December. It was, as Stuart said in his covering letter to Alan Peacock, 'bulky'. We had tried to address what we saw as the major issues: Broadcasting in the Public Interest; A Future for the Licence Fee; Advertising and the BBC; Income for the BBC; Other Options; Towards an Age of Plenty (in terms of communications) and Funding the BBC in the Future.

We also included three detailed papers. The first on the licence fee took a broad look at options that might be available within the existing system (extra licences on car radios, multiple television set ownership, VCRs). The second paper was about subscription television and the technical problems associated with it (Stuart himself had become excited about the possibilities of subscription as a future method of funding the BBC during the autumn, though many Governors and members of the Board of Management thought it a real hostage to fortune). The third, on the BBC's commercial opportunities, 'takes a considered look at future scope'. This was a theme close to many Governors' hearts. Despite great success by BBC Enterprises, our wholly-owned subsidiary which handled sales of programmes overseas, William Rees-Mogg, the Chairman and others remained stubbornly of the view that until we had an outsider running Enterprises, the BBC would never properly maximise its profit from sales. We now have an 'outsider' in charge, and he is committed to trying to double a turnover already of around £100 million. If he succeeds, which I am sure he will, it will make an important contribution to the BBC's revenue. But, after tax, still a marginal matter on the expenditure of £1 billion. With our second submission, we sent some important research papers, including those from Professor Andrew Ehrenburg, which underlined just how cheap British television was by comparison with other leisure activities.

Just before we finalised these documents and sent them off to Peacock, we had occasion to attend a strange meeting at Church Hall, Westminster. We had, earlier on, been given to understand that the Peacock Committee wanted to have a 'public meeting' or, as it later transpired, 'an invited public meeting'. That is to say we had messages from Mr Eagle, the Secretary of the Peacock Committee (an open invitation to poor jokes, that one) that they had decided that a small number of interested groups should be asked to speak. Others could attend but not intervene. This seemed a recipe for trouble. When we assembled at Church House on a bitterly cold morning, we found that Lord (Jo) Grimond had been recruited as Chairman. He did not seem entirely the right person because he began the proceedings by announcing with engaging candour that he was very deaf and that there was, therefore, absolutely no point in anybody trying to interrupt or create a stir because he would not hear them.

There followed a series of statements by the ITCA (the Independent Television Companies' Association. John Whitney was sitting there for the IBA but they had not been invited to speak and that made for bad blood straight off). Then ISBA for the advertisers, then, mercifully, coffee. There followed further orations from the newly formed Cable Association and from the Association of Independent Radio Stations. There was little excitement, except that during the morning those excluded from asking questions, including union representatives, became very noisy. Somehow, Jo Grimond heard them but remained good humoured.

After lunch, it was Peter Jay's turn; the only individual invited to speak for himself, the Peacock guru. Peter set forth, at his usual machine-gun rate of delivery, his picture of the new world of electronic publishing, where programmes would pour out of the fibre-optic cables in the same way that books had poured off the presses in the past. Sam Brittan smiled like a Cheshire cat. Then it was the turn of the Consumer Council – the consumer, after all, was king. Finally, the floor was mine. It had been a long wait but it *was* the BBC's finances they were all talking about, as well as their own.

I wanted to try to do three things: take Hetherington's advice about explaining the nature of public service broadcasting, nail advertising (though we believed the Committee had already shied away from it) and rebut the Peter Jay argument which we thought was illusory, although we also knew Peacock and Brittan were much taken with it.

The BBC [I said] was set up as a means of realising certain aspirations thought, in this century, to be in the collective interests of all of us. It was not conceived as a vehicle for expanding advertising airtime, or as a demonstration laboratory for the electronically interconnected society. It will be splendid if Professor Peacock and his Committee can suggest some financial device which will allow public service broadcasting to be provided at *improving, not declining*, quality and shared by us all at less overall cost.

That task is extremely difficult because the Committee have to have at the forefront of their minds the fact that they are working towards means, not ends. The end is not to help advertising agencies, by lowering their costs, nor it is 'to teach the BBC a lesson', as some people advocate. The end is broadcasting as a public service. Turning to advertising, we have learnt from our research that the advertising option is at best not proven as a means of financing the BBC. So far, those who advocate it have wholly failed to convince me that the new money – £1,000 million of it – is really there. I prefer to turn for insight to those who have to decide

169

whether to increase the amount they would spend on advertising. And here we find that only a small percentage of business executives would want to spend more on advertising. Even the most optimistic forecasts on potential advertising growth make total funding of the BBC by advertising exceedingly improbable. And partial funding with a little advertising, combined with a freezing of the existing licence fee level, has been shown to lead to a further deficit within a few years, and thus a need once again to raise the licence fee. What is equally important, there do not seem to be any segmented audiences in television to which particular advertising interests could address themselves. *Panorama*, it may be a surprise to some, is predominantly watched by a working-class audience. The full range of programmes would be at risk in competing for spot advertising . . . The present system produces a wide range of programmes at a low cost to the viewer. The new services in satellite broadcasting and in cable will increasingly affect existing available advertising revenue, so that the present advertising monopoly – if that is what it is – is gradually being broken already. These services have their own ambitions to pursue, and we wish them well; but it can't conceivably help them if we compete with them for small additional income.

Not unsurprisingly, some of this did not go down too well with some members of the Committee, though, as I recall, they were not fully represented anyway. Sam Brittan gave occasional evidence of profound dissent by pulling some grotesque faces. I had also to try to deal with the Peter Jay argument. Jay had argued for some time that talk of advertising on the BBC was an irrelevant distraction on the way to the fibre-optic society of the twenty-first century when every one of us would be wired up for vision, sound and the electronic expression of our wants. In his view, a broadcasting corporation as such was an absurdity and the proper business of the nation was to recognise its institutional redundancy.

This vision [I argued] is not only technologically very complicated and far away, but misses the essential point of broadcasting. Broadcasting is not a matter of one person sending a signal to another, or of one household sending one to another. Broadcasting is a process of scattering and thus sowing seed far and wide. Some will fall on stony ground and some on fertile ground. Broadcasting further means that the sower waits to see what grows. When it becomes clear where the fertile places are, you reap and come along with the next lot of seed. It would have taken a bold man only a few years ago to forecast that a programme like the *Antiques Roadshow*, which excites you to rummage in your attic for

170

potential artistic masterpieces, might command a bigger audience than edited football matches. Yet this is precisely what has happened. Public service broadcasting, however, goes further. It recognises that even stony ground requires patience. You never know what will come up. That is the point Peter Jay misses.

We broke up around teatime and went our several ways. It had been an odd experience. I have no idea what the Committee members made of it all.

The Committee had the Christmas holiday to mull over our second, substantial document and, presumably, the scores of others that came winging in their direction. Early in January 1986, we published our document and right at its beginning we tried once again to explain the concept of public service broadcasting that seemed to stick in the Committee's throat. Brian Wenham and I worked hard on the opening paragraphs which went through many redrafts.

The BBC wishes to re-assert its belief, in the face of argument to the contrary, that public service broadcasting in the United Kingdom is distinctive and that it is qualitatively different from what is commonly provided in other parts of the world. [Arrogant, you may say. True, I would retort.] It is based on a number of vital principles. We wish to record them here once more.

Universality of provision has been an essential objective from the start. Broadcasting services should be universally available, at the same price to everybody. Broadcasting in the public interest admits no new divisions between town and country, as cable and 'electronic publishing' most certainly will do. Alongside universality of provision, broadcasters have sought to make a wide choice of programmes constantly available. If you address yourself to the nation as a whole, you must appeal to the nation as a whole, in all its diversity. This appeal has never rested on giving people merely more of what they have experienced already. The drive has been to stimulate and satisfy latent interests in the viewer and listener. In this way, the choices offered to the public are true choices between programmes that are different and not simply other versions of the same.

And later on, because what surely matters is the material, 'the software', the programmes; not the 'hardware', the means of dissemination because they are simply arteries to carry the blood:

The major problem all broadcasting faces is the need to create a constant flow of new and high quality programmes. Because of the

171

scale of its operations, the BBC is able to attract and develop new talent. But good programmes – especially on television – are inherently expensive. This will remain so in any new broadcasting ecology. The consequent risks militate against the arrival of large numbers of new, low-cost producers. It is not, therefore, regulation but the shortage of attractive programmes from new sources that is everywhere stunting the growth of new methods of dissemination.

At the press conference, on publication, we were rightly cross-examined on ideas we had put forward for broadening the base of the licence fee, such as a car radio licence, a different licence scale for people owning several sets, and possibly for those owning VCRs. We were tentative about these thoughts; they would not be popular, would be very difficult to administer and would only, we calculated, bring in an additional £200 million. Marginal extra money, but if the Committee thought them feasible, welcome extra money. We were asked, too, about our thoughts on putting the collection of the licence fee out to tender. Traditionally, the Post Office did the collecting and handed us the bill. We had no voice in the managerial control and, since it was costing us some £55 million a year, we thought it was high time we did have control. Others might do the job more cheaply and better. The press was interested, too, in our fairly guarded remarks about indexation of the licence fee. We had said: 'We note that straight indexation rarely commends itself to a government, even when there is argument on the starting line on what the index should be.' This topic was to provide many hours of stimulating argument and correspondence, particularly between Sam Brittan and Geoff Buck, our Director of Finance.

We met the Committee in their spartan quarters at the Home Office a few days later, on the morning of 20th January. In the interim they had provided us with a set of questions, *viz*: number one: 'At our previous meeting, the DG said that one hundred per cent of the BBC's output was "public service broadcasting". Would he like to expand on that reply?' There were twenty-six questions, and we had duly furnished them with written replies. Some of the questions seemed to us to go far beyond their terms of reference. Were we running the place efficiently? Was local radio suffering from starvation of funds and so on? But that is the nature of committees. We had worked hard for this session, and Andrew Ehrenburg had the previous week given the Committee a brilliant presentation about the licence fee. On this occasion, Stuart did one of the best introductory speeches I heard him deliver. He was confident, he knew his stuff, finance was his game. He reminded the Committee that the one and a half hours we had been given (Alan Peacock had to leave at 11.30, I think, to go to Wales) was brief; spoke to them about the range of programming we provided as evidenced by the previous night's viewing, reminded them of the research we had commissioned into advertising on the BBC, and of the general conclusions of that research, and expressed mild surprise that none of their questions touched on this matter; pointed out to them that their last nine questions went beyond their terms of reference and wondered why; and ended by saying that although he had come to the BBC from the commercial world with a positive preference for funding the BBC commercially he had, in his time as Chairman, come to understand the destructive effects of any competition for scarce advertising revenue on the standards of public service broadcasting. It was quite a tour de force.

We then got down to amplifying our answers to the written questions they had sent us. We started, again, with 'public service broadcasting'. I argued that for sixty years the licence fee had been the engine force of a system designed 'to educate, inform and entertain'. The need to entertain, to offer enjoyment and delight, must not be disregarded. Without the security of the licence fee, I did not believe the BBC would have been able to achieve real quality and audience enjoyment in fields like comedy and popular drama. I cited *The Last of the Summer Wine*, a most unlikely concoction, on the face of it, of three Yorkshire pensioners ambling around their county engaged in inconsequential chat, which began as a risky venture but was by now the most highly viewed comedy series of all. The Committee showed interest; but clearly thought the same results could be achieved by a subscription system. We demurred. How could you support a subscription system if you didn't know what you were going to see e.g. *The Last of the Summer Wine*?

We moved on to a discussion about mixed licence fee and advertising economies, as in Germany (Alan Peacock appeared to have forgotten for a moment that there is no commercial broadcasting competition in Germany and the analogy therefore has no validity in terms of UK experience); to an examination of the possibilities of indexation of the licence fee and a ready agreement by all that Sam Brittan and Geoff Buck, the undisputed experts, should conduct a private war on that front; and to discussion of our proposals for opening the methods of collecting the licence fee to tender. We then had an exchange about the possibilities of subscription. Stuart pointed out to them that the only way of creating the kind of market which would persuade the manufacturers to make the sets in sufficient quantities would be to 'scramble' (i.e. make them impossible to receive without decoding devices) all four channels. This

173

provoked Sam Brittan to ask if we were really proposing that, under a subscription system, people who wished to watch ITV only should have to pay a BBC subscription before they could do so. Stuart replied that the Ehrenburg evidence showed that the numbers of people watching ITV only were negligible. Any talk of 'scrambling' the BBC services on their own involved reducing the choice of services currently available to the nation. They raised questions about our efficiency and about our structure, which we thought none of their business. In an hour and a half, we covered a lot of ground.

In February, we sent the Committee yet a further detailed written answer to the questions they had originally posed and which had been discussed orally on 20th January. Intelligence, the while, brought news of further oddities. There was, we were told, talk of 'privatising' Radios 1 and 2, whatever that might mean. We had a further meeting with the Committee at the Home Office in March, where Andrew Ehrenburg, as a fellow economist, having given them a vigorous defence of the licence fee with slides, had a sharp exchange with Professor Peacock. We were near the heart of the matter. Subscription was still a dominant theme, and there was more talk about the BBC trying to do too much.

In the midst of all this (and other events yet to be chronicled) Huw Wheldon died. I had seen him at the Royal Television Society meeting, of which he was President, in Cambridge the previous September. He was clearly mortally ill. I saw him again in November at a party given by Peter and Polly Dimmock and we talked of a game of golf when he was better. He always held a Christmas party at his house in Richmond. This year he didn't. I meant to ring and never did. On the morning of 14th March, 1986, Brian Wenham came to tell me he had just heard Huw was dead. I was stunned. He was, as I said then, 'a wonderful character, a great television performer and executive, and a true friend'. Sheila and I were at his funeral in Richmond, but, to my sorrow, we were abroad when his memory was celebrated in Westminster Abbey in the company of a great host of friends, at a ceremony I had helped the family to arrange, on what would have been his seventieth birthday.

In June, Grace Wyndham Goldie died. Much older, much more tired than Huw, but no less lamented. Writing about her in the *Guardian*, Stephen Hearst said: 'In a medium lavish with superlatives, she was one of the few figures who deserved them, but on whom they were rarely bestowed.' We buried Grace on a lovely June day in the churchyard at Frant beside her husband, Frank, whose death more than twenty years earlier had been such a devastating blow to her. I was able to say something of what I felt for her at a memorial service a few weeks later at All Souls, Langham Place. 'As I walked away from her grave, I remembered our last conversation. She was, she said, very worried about the future of the BBC as the clouds seemed to draw in about us. I hope, for her sake – and ours – that those fears were born out of temporary circumstances. Whatever our future holds, her work remains a massive achievement in the pioneering days of British television. She was a lion of a woman.'

The Peacock Committee reported to the new Home Secretary, Douglas Hurd, within their set timetable for July. The rumours now came thick and fast, and by early June Brian Wenham had been privy to a quick sight of their recommendations. All new television sets, not later than 1st January, 1988, to have a peritelevision socket (for 'descrambling'). BBC Television not to be obliged to take advertising for the time being. Licence fee to be indexed to the general rate of inflation. The licence fee collection to be put out to tender. A separate fee of not less than £10 to be charged for car radios. Pensioners on supplementary benefit to be wholly exempt from the licence fee. BBC should have the option to privatise Radios 1 and 2 and local radio – five members advocating the privatising *and* financing by advertising of Radios 1 and 2. Over a ten-year period both the BBC and ITV should be required to increase by not less than forty per cent the proportion of their programmes supplied by independent producers.

There were other important recommendations about Channel 4's advertising time, ITV and DBS franchises, pay-per-view and phasing out of censorship. We had a pretty good guide, at any rate. After that, there were leaks of every kind, most of them uncomplimentary about the report, from Government sources. It was thoroughly rubbished ('consigned to the long grass, old boy') before it was ever published. Sam Brittan, on a later occasion, set about the Home Office, with some justification I thought, for the way the report's advance publicity was handled. But the press conference called to reveal it to the world wasn't very edifying either. Two members – Hetherington and Chalmers – openly announced that the idea of privatising Radios 1 and 2 was a last minute floater and 'daft' to boot.

The general consensus seemed to be that we had been lucky that Peacock did not advocate the introduction of advertising to the BBC. The Prime Minister had wished it, after all. My understanding is that the Committee recognised very early on that it was not an option, some of them later claiming that they had made the BBC's case against advertising for it. Most of their time was then spent on teasing through the implications of subscriptions and the long-term future. Because it is such a complex subject, the Home Office later turned to Charles Jonscher, of Communications, Studies and Planning, a well-known consultancy, for enlightenment. Jonscher came up with the HMSO document *Subscription Television*, with answers that must have startled the commissioning department. He argued that 'scrambling' the BBC's services would not raise enough money to cover the production costs of the programmes, and that 'substantial losses in consumer welfare would result as a consequence of the exclusion of non-subscribers from the benefits of BBC television viewing'.

He went on to say that 'the UK television industry is clearly under-financed by comparison with its importance as a leisure activity . . . We reiterate that the financing of extra material on a pay basis is in economic terms a second-best solution. The optimal solution is to increase the licence fee to the extent necessary to allow the additional premium programming to be available to all consumers.'

Which is rather what we had said all along. The BBC was not, as *The Times* sourly declared, 'still fighting for their past'. We did say out loud, over and over again, that the licence fee was cheap, far cheaper than any subscription service would ever be, that it was, in essence, a kind of subscription fee paid by everybody because everybody watches television or listens to radio for rather more than three hours a day. By its very nature, the licence fee allows the broadcaster the freedom to attempt to satisfy all programme tastes without undue anxiety about what the ratings may show. It surely has a lot going for it.

Peacock, of course, posed problems for the BBC. The recommendation that within a given time forty per cent of the programmes produced should be made by independent producers is, in my judgement, a fantasy; though the Government, believing that independent producers' costs *must* be lower (there is no sound evidence for this belief) is pressing hard on the duopoly to introduce a lower percentage – twenty-five per cent – but even sooner, which I think will still prove immensely difficult to achieve. I tried to make the point at a Royal Television Society Symposium on Peacock at the Barbican in July.

A year ago I announced that we intended to move towards one hundred and fifty hours a year of independent production, and we are already discussing with independents how we might achieve that. Forty per cent of our output would be around four thousand hours. I think that is wholly unrealistic. In whole areas of outside broadcasts, this summer, to take only one example, I don't see how any group of independents could take on Wimbledon, the following week the Open Golf Championship, and the week after that the Royal Wedding and then ten days of the Commonwealth Games.

The biggest problem for the BBC is the recommendation, quickly accepted by Government, that the licence fee should be based on a £60 figure as at April 1986, and index-related to the Retail Price Index. At the same symposium, I spoke about indexation.

For all its superficial simplicity, it does seem rather odd to tie the BBC to an index which has decreased sharply this year with successive reductions in the mortgage rate. Does this mean that the building societies can dictate part of the BBC's income? In our evidence to the Peacock Committee, we pointed out that indexation would have to take some note of the rate of inflation within the television industry which Peat Marwick Mitchell and others have recognised is somewhere around seven to eight per cent. We have already exercised discipline – not least by terminating or curtailing many traditional activities during the last year and thus diverting more than £30 million into programme operations. Indexation, it seems to me, must be workable. You cannot ask people to pay more while being forced to offer them less. Had the licence fee been related to the RPI over the past ten years, I would now have £200 million – one fifth of our total budget – less to deploy than I currently do. As a result, there would certainly have been less original drama, less comprehensive news coverage and skimpier programming overall. It strikes me as odd that the Committee seeks to put additional financial pressure on the BBC, when the report clearly places the blame for overheating in the broadcasting economy on ITV.

For us, the year of Peacock was a year of intensely hard work which was in many ways highly productive. We were forced to challenge many of our own assumptions. The research we and others commissioned taught us many things about our audiences that we did not know before. A leader in the *Observer* seemed to me to get it about right: 'Peacock will have done a service if it succeeds in reminding people – from the Prime Minister downwards – that there are no glib, all-purpose solutions even to the problems of British broadcasting.'

15 'And Foul Contagion Spread'

Throughout the autumn of 1985 and the spring of 1986, writing for the Peacock Committee and meeting them for further discussion was our primary preoccupation. That work would, of course, continue until the planned publication of their report in the summer. Seminars and discussions were bound to follow publication. There would also be involvement in political manoeuvring before the Government expressed a view, presumably at the time of a Commons debate on the report itself.

We had many other preoccupations, however. The settlement of the licence fee, unsatisfactory from the BBC's point of view, and the setting up of Peacock had meant that everything we did would remain under a more than usually powerful microscope. Quite early in the autumn, the case of one programme in the series *Rough Justice* provided useful press fodder. This programme, which had been on the air for some time in occasional series form, was always extremely carefully researched because, by its nature, it set out to deal with apparent miscarriages of justice in the courts. This particular edition had highlighted the sentencing of a man called Mycock for an offence for which he had been sent to prison. The producer and reporter involved became convinced that he had been the victim of a miscarriage of justice. They travelled to California to interview the woman involved in the case, and she admitted on film that she had not told the truth in court.

Anthony Mycock was subsequently released. It later transpired that the methods used by our people to gain the woman's confession were, at least, open to question. These methods were subsequently lambasted by the Lord Chief Justice in the High Court towards the end of 1985. I asked Bill Cotton to conduct disciplinary interviews with the people concerned. He did so, and they were suspended for three months without pay. They had been instrumental in getting a man out of prison: yet, by their own admission, they had used methods the BBC could not countenance. The newspapers now had another case – a difficult one – on which to comment. *The Times*, reaching for the poisoned pen, wrote: 'It has been a difficult twelve months for the

178

BBC . . . Whatever the difficulties, there remains a clear case for the BBC to put its house in order.' (A familiar echo of a Prime Ministerial phrase spoken at the time of the Falklands War.)

I was genuinely troubled over the *Rough Justice* case. Our people had gone wrong, despite their long experience in these sort of cases, and I would have been more severe with them than Bill was. Yet a man had been released from prison. But for them, he would still have been in gaol. It was a genuine dilemma.

We had an even more intense internal problem looming, though. It concerned one of my senior colleagues, Dick Francis, the Managing Director of Radio. Dick never did anything by halves. In Lime Grove, in the late 1960s, he was the absolute king of the satellite and moonshot coverage, outstripping even the NASA spokesmen in his technological news-speak. In Northern Ireland, as Controller, he led the BBC in the Province through some of the worst events, including the Loyalist strike of 1974, and was uncompromising in his resistance to pressure and his commitment to telling the truth. Some of the papers he wrote then stand as classic definitions of the problems of broadcasting in Northern Ireland. When Bryan Cowgill, nominated by Ian Trethowan as his new Director of News and Current Affairs, suddenly upped and left and went to Thames Television, Dick was appointed to that office and really came into his own. He was immensely diligent, the file carried under his arm daily becoming fatter. He would rush anywhere, was for ever on the telephone, active on many national and international committees. He is an immensely resourceful but also a very stubborn man. A keen sailor of high expertise in his leisure moments, Dick would not easily haul down sails – or whatever expert sailors do! I speak as a humble fisherman.

But Dick and I appeared to have an increasing problem. He was a stout and proper defender of local radio. He had fought a hard, but most of us thought pointless, battle against the amalgamation of English local radio into the new structure of the English regions, which had been proposed by 'Black Spot', agreed by the Board of Governors and Board of Management in July 1985, and which he well knew I had wished to see carried through when I first became Director General. He continued throughout the autumn to defend the territory in a war that was long over. In September, Geraint Stanley Jones, hitherto Controller of BBC Wales, joined us on the Board of Management as Director of Public Affairs – a difficult job that embraced regional broadcasting, religion, education, and now, again, the BBC's publicity and information services.

Almost immediately, Geraint was caught up in Dick's fight against the details of the changes we had all accepted in July. Dick wanted new provisions written in and I would not have them. There were even unpleasant squabbles in front of the whole Board of Management. At our first meeting of the New Year, Dick announced he was 'considering his position'. Two days later, at a meeting with Geraint, we had cleared up the matter, but it was a relationship neither I nor his colleagues could easily accept for the future. Towards the end of January, I told Dick I did not want him to stay in Radio. Nor did I think it would be a good idea for him to move to the External Services to replace Douglas Muggeridge. I felt it was time he looked for work outside the BBC. What about the managing directorship of Visnews, the film agency in which the BBC still held an important share? It was vacant, and after all Charles Curran had done that job after he left the BBC.

But Dick didn't want that job. At the end of January, he had a meeting with Stuart which Stuart described as 'emotional'. The following week, Stuart was demanding a 'quick resolution' which I thought unlikely. These things need time and patience. Dick and I had several conversations and he wrote a number of memos. By the end of April, he had decided to exercise his right to address the Board of Governors. Unhappily, I had months earlier arranged a Greek cruise for a holiday but I had, of course, to come back, particularly after the experience of *Real Lives*. So I came home, from my first sight of Mycenae, to this sad meeting. In fact, it was odder and sadder than I expected. Immediately after the Board's private session, Stuart came to speak to me in my office. The Board was insisting, he said, that I attend for two minutes to speak about my reasons for wanting Dick to leave, with Dick present, and then sit while he delivered his address. It was William Rees-Mogg, he said, who was particularly insistent. I demurred strongly. The Board was fully aware of the situation, he (Stuart) had discussed the problem with other members of the Board of Management. Why should they force us to go through a sort of trial distasteful to both Dick and me? They would have it so, he said. So we met. I explained why I thought Dick should leave. He, in his turn and with great dignity and calm, explained why he thought he should stay. It was more than an hour and a half before I was invited back to hear a tired Chairman say they agreed Dick should leave, and he and Rees-Mogg immediately left to go to Stuart's office to give Dick the news.

When they returned, I proposed that Brian Wenham should succeed Dick as Managing Director of Radio. Immediately, William Rees-Mogg mounted a fierce attack on Brian. He was a cynic, he was a man of no conviction, he would regard it as a disastrous appointment. Daphne Park, as frequently, seconded William's argument. If they were to accept Wenham, they said, they wanted a proper man like David Hatch (the Controller of Radio 4) alongside him. That seemed to me an eminently sensible idea (though it put the present incumbent, Charles McClelland, swiftly out of a job) and I suggested I go and find Brian (who I knew was in the building) and ask him to come and talk to the Board and hear their views. He came and spoke. It was decided. It was then my job to tell Charles McClelland that they did not want him any more. New dispositions had been made.

It seemed the right moment to bring Michael Grade, Director of Programmes, Television, and David Hatch, Director of Programmes, Radio, on to the Board of Management. We could do with some younger blood. Both of them were in their early forties. Michael, with his big cigars, his red braces, his protruding contact lens gaze and his ready utterances had adopted (as he has since) a high press profile and the press loved it. He had inherited *EastEnders* and the move of Terry Wogan from radio to television when he took over BBC-1 from Alan Hart, but he made the very best of his luck. He wove his way adroitly through the flak that followed the suspension of *Dr Who* and the stopping of the *Play of the Month*, the long-standing commitment of BBC-1 to productions of classic plays, which had partly been overtaken by BBC-2's Shakespeare cycle but which Michael finally put paid to. Although Michael held strong views, he was always ready to concede a point; I thought his wish to abandon the single contemporary play on BBC-1 was not acceptable and he readily set about reinstating it.

David Hatch, a roly-poly figure, full of laughs, was a good counterpart to Michael. He is a genuine devotee of radio, and one who has been through the experience of making people laugh as well as sustaining their interest in 'sweet music' when he ran Radio 2, and later in the wide gamut of Radio 4. Michael has now gone from the BBC, though it beggars belief to abandon the leadership of the world's leading television service for the narrow pastures of Channel 4. What that highly competitive spirit and sharp scheduling brain will make of Jeremy Isaacs' legacy is a teasing prospect indeed. David Hatch, now the Managing Director of BBC Radio will, I am sure, do very well by it in the next few years.

It was not all trouble, though. We had recovered well in audience terms and were now easily holding forty-five per cent of the audience, even with Channel 4 well dug in. We were, too, enjoying rich success in public acclaim for our programmes. The previous year Troy Kennedy Martin's first work for us for many years, *Edge of Darkness*, had won a great response from the audience and the critics, and the BBC swept the awards at the British Film and Television Arts Awards occasion. We repeated that success in the spring of 1986 with Dennis Potter's *Singing Detective* and the *She Devil* heading a wide

181

range of BBC awards. After a slight stumble, the Television Service was back in its stride again. One of the warmest tributes to our success came from Sir Denis Forman in his 1987 Dimbleby Lecture. Touching on Government intervention in broadcasting, he said:

> This intervention in the business of the broadcasting authorities is not caused by poor programmes. In a secret place I keep a little black book in which each year I note the performance of my own company, and that of other companies, and the BBC. Despite all the rage and fury over the BBC, its all-round performance in the last three years has been as good as in any period since the early seventies. I need only mention *Yes, Minister, Edge of Darkness* and *Newsnight* to indicate the standards they reach in three different fields.

So much for *The Times* and other such owls with their songs of death.

We had, though, an even bigger time bomb ticking away. This time, I knew all about it. It was a programme called *Maggie's Militant Tendency*, an edition of *Panorama* concerned with investigating the activities of far-right members of the Conservative Party, and based on an unpublished report prepared for the Chairman of the Conservative Party by the Young Conservatives, to which *Panorama* had access. It was broadcast on 30th January, 1984. I knew about its background and it seemed to me a proper subject for investigation. When it was transmitted, I was away in India on a business visit, but Alan Protheroe was standing in for me, and Margaret Douglas, an immensely experienced current affairs producer whom I had asked to become Chief Assistant to the Director General when David Holmes moved on to be Secretary, was also involved. Margaret it was who, with our lawyers, sat through the programme before transmission and many changes – more than forty – were made at that stage. Margaret and the Editor, George Carey, were satisfied that the material they were screening could stand up to scrutiny.

I saw the video the evening that I got back from Delhi. It was provocative stuff, but at that time I obviously had no way of knowing whether it was wholly accurate or not. At Board of Management, I was warned that trouble was brewing and would break out at the General Advisory Council two days later. Conservative MPs raised the matter, but only in guarded terms because writs had already been issued by some of the people named. Exactly two weeks after transmission, Margaret Douglas and I met the Conservative Chief Whip, John Wakeham, and the Chairman of the Conservative Party, John Selwyn Gummer, at their request at Broadcasting House.

For two and a half hours we went over the transcript of the programme. They challenged us on no less than thirty-eight points of detail. I promised that all of them would be examined with the greatest care. They were in no doubt that we had got things wildly wrong. I worked through all the *Panorama* research, poring laboriously over page after page with Alan Protheroe and Margaret Douglas, and it seemed to us that it was, as we said in the BBC magazine *Ariel*, 'rock solid'.

The following day we had a further meeting with Wakeham and Gummer at 12 Downing Street. I told them we had been through all the research material and thought it stood up, though I could not show them the material while threats of libel writs hung over our heads. They detailed further alleged inaccuracies. There was a further meeting in my office at Broadcasting House and on this occasion Edward du Cann was added to the cast list, to underline the very serious view the Conservative backbench membership took of the programme. On 27th February, Margaret and I went to the Commons to see John Wakeham again. This time we decided she would wait in the Lobby and I would have a private word with him. I showed him some of the research material which we thought refuted John Selwyn Gummer's charges. What's to be done? he asked. I suggested he speak to Gummer again and come back to me.

At a further meeting early in March, John Wakeham produced two draft statements which he wanted us to consider issuing, but both implied that we had got the story thoroughly wrong and I did not think we had. Throughout all these goings-on, I kept Stuart fully briefed on progress, or rather the lack of it, but it did not look as if any accommodation could be reached. The Governors gave me full support at this juncture. Finally, we agreed to differ and Central Office fed the *Daily Mail* with a whole list of charges against us, suggesting the programme was a tissue of lies. We countered by pointing out again that it was based on the Young Conservatives' report, which said much the same thing. It looked as though the affair must be left to the due process of law.

In the course of the next two years, two of the writs were settled out of court on terms which we found reasonable. Those issued by Neil Hamilton and Gerald Howarth were not settled, and in the summer of 1986, the affair came home to roost. Alan Protheroe had several private meetings with Hamilton and Howarth on ground of their own choosing – the Institute of Directors; they parleyed. They seemed as keen to settle as we were but we could not agree terms. There were also certain details we apparently could not now prove – witnesses had fallen away and there were other difficulties. We wanted a settlement badly, but not on terms of humiliating disavowal. By the holiday season, we had reached a position of stand-off and the case proceeded towards the courts. Up till the summer, the Board had been fully aware of the progress of these cases as a result of the quarterly report by our Legal Adviser, insisted on by Rees-Mogg and others after the Dr Gee case. I had told them, however, of the secret meetings because these took place after the Board's last summer meeting.

We had, meantime, greater institutional and emotional problems to handle. Stuart Young had never fully recovered since his operation for lung cancer two and a half years earlier, though he had stretched himself to the limit on the BBC's behalf over the licence fee and the Peacock inquiry. Now, he had been on a visit to China and India and returned with a cough. Towards the end of July, he was no longer able to chair the Board meetings and William Rees-Mogg took over, even though he himself was due to demit office within weeks. For a while, they treated Stuart with radiation, and his breathing seemed to get better, though he was then troubled with phlebitis in his legs. It caused him great pain. I was due to go to Australia and New Zealand. Before Sheila and I left, I went to see Stuart. He was nervous, but full of talk about the future. As I left, he walked slowly with me to the lift. I was not to see him again.

When I got home a fortnight later, they told me he had had a bad weekend and was accepting no phone calls. I wrote him a letter of support. A couple of days afterwards, his doctor told me he had only a week or so left. There were too many complications. Early on the morning of 29th August, Patricia Hodgson, who had succeeded David Holmes as Secretary after the *Real Lives* incident, rang me to say Stuart had died soon after midnight. By 1.00 p.m., by a miracle of communication and organisation, the Chief Rabbi was leading the several hundred mourners at Stuart's funeral at the Jewish Cemetery in Bushey. It was a chill, grey day for August. I remember shivering with cold through the proceedings. We had plenty of warning of his end, but somehow it was still a deep shock. He and I had almost certainly reached the nadir of relationship between the Governors and the management of the BBC, yet I was very fond of him. His death upset me profoundly.

I had tried, some weeks earlier, in immediate expectation of his death, to write and explain to our own staff what qualities he had brought to the BBC.

He did not come to the BBC as an unqualified admirer. Originally, he believed that the Corporation should accept advertising. But the more he delved, the more he became convinced that the licence fee continued to be essential to maintain the BBC public service broadcasting organisation and was the key to maintaining broadcasting standards in Britain . . . Right to the end, he was intent on returning to complete the job he so manifestly loved.

Alwyn Roberts, the Welsh Governor, who shared few of Stuart's political leanings but whose support on any issue was very important to Stuart, said of him: 'In Stuart Young, the BBC expected a critic and found a champion. His advocacy of public service broadcasting sprang from a deep conviction of the BBC's role, not only as a broadcasting body but as a force of unity and tolerance in British life.'

Even while the Jewish pattern of obsequies continued, speculation about Stuart's successor was immediate. *The Times* weighed in with a typical piece:

Two different gear wheels are grinding within the programme making machine of the British Broadcasting Corporation. The first is vast, slow and inexorable. It is the wheel of technological change which one day will inevitably crush the BBC's cosy structures into a fragmented, freer pattern of electronic publishing. [*Sic!*] The second is smaller and faster. It is the wheel that actually drives the BBC . . . The man ultimately in charge of it is the Chairman of the BBC Governors. To appoint a man who has a businessman's reputation for knocking recalcitrant heads off would be a recipe for repeat disasters . . . It is, perhaps, early days to back horses in this race. But, exempli gratia, better Lord Barnett than Lord King.

As a matter of fact, we also thought Lord Barnett – earlier Joel Barnett, Chief Secretary to the Treasury in the last Labour Government – would be a good choice. For a start, it might redress the political balance somewhat, even though Joel joked that he was moving fast to the right, and his daughter, a member of the General Advisory Council, claimed he was even righter than that! Joel had a month earlier been appointed Vice-Chairman and would now have to act as Chairman until a replacement for Stuart was found. But other names were run and consistently run. Lord King, the Chairman of British Airways, was much put about and said to be keen, and also said to have Mrs Thatcher's backing. Some of our existing Governors – Jocelyn Barrow, Daphne Park, Sir Curtis Keeble – were spoken of. 'Who will be Maggie's man at the Beeb?' shouted the *Express*. Adding delphically, and with its syntax deserting it, 'Like the Roman Empire, the certainties are all vanished. Instead of one establishment, there are two or three scrabbling for supremacy. At different moments, David Owen, Norman Tebbit and Neil Kinnock rage at the screen, convinced that broadcasters are biased, and sometimes

185

rightly so.' Which, to be fair, was a bit hard on Neil Kinnock. And who were the *Express*'s candidates? Joel Barnett; or Robin Day or Alastair Burnet.

As the Board reassembled for the autumn meetings, this was the roll call of the membership. Vice-Chairman and Acting Chairman, Joel Barnett, a small, dapper, pugnacious man, brisk of chairmanship, with a taste for long stories and fine restaurants; Alwyn Roberts, Director of Extra Mural Studies at the University College of North Wales in Bangor, a man steeped in the activities of BBC Wales after four years on the Broadcasting Council and then seven years as its Chairman and National Governor, and one of the few liberal voices surviving on the Board; Jocelyn Barrow, a Trinidadian by birth, a statuesque lady of queenly demeanour, whose term has recently been extended for a further period; Sir John Boyd, former General Secretary of the Amalgamated Union of Engineering Workers, a Salvationist Scot with a taste for Cromwellian discipline in the name of the Board of Governors; Daphne Park, Principal of Somerville College, Oxford, a former diplomat in far flung places like Lusaka and Hanoi, whose strong resemblance to recent characterisations of Agatha Christie's Miss Marple concealed a tough and uncompromising view of life; Malcolm McAlpine, a quirky, charming businessman and director of the family firm, of conservative nature with strong business connections in North America and a good support to us in our property negotiations; Lady (Margaret) Parks, a JP and educationalist, formerly chairman of the Radio London Advisory Committee, wife of the Vice-Chancellor of Leeds University and a tireless visitor of far flung outposts of the BBC whose doughty champion she made herself; Watson Peat, the Scottish National Governor, an old acquaintance from my days as Controller in Scotland, a man deeply involved in the Scottish farming scene over many years, a radio ham and a man of unashamed right-wing views; the Earl of Harewood, a famous name in the world of music, recently resigned from being Managing Director of the English National Opera company – in fact, George was often away as he had taken on the job of running a festival in South Australia and as a consequence resigned from the Board the following January; Dr James Kincade, the new Northern Ireland Governor who arrived coincidentally with the *Real Lives* episode, Headmaster of the Royal School in Dungannon for thirteen years, and now for more than ten years Headmaster of the Methodist School, Belfast; and Sir Curtis Keeble, formerly our Ambassador in Moscow.

As the Governors reassembled, the name of the new Chairman became a recurring daily topic in broadcasting and political circles. On the first day of September, Giles Shaw, the number two to the

Home Secretary and the Minister immediately responsible for broadcasting, dropped in for a chat. He thought the press reports about Lord King were laughable. I drew across him the idea of Joel Barnett as Chairman with David Windlesham (a former ITV broadcasting executive and later Leader of the House of Lords) as Vice-Chairman. At their early autumn meetings, the Governors themselves speculated widely. I went to Willie Whitelaw to see what advice he might have. What about doing the job himself? No, he said, he was too old and, anyway, he would stay with the PM as long as she wanted him. Barnett, he thought, had no chance. We had wondered about Sir Robert Armstrong, the Secretary to the Cabinet, who was due to retire soon – though he was later asked to stay on. He dismissed that idea out of hand. Lord King, he thought, would be a poor outcome. He would do his best to fight that one off.

The next day, I went to see David Young, Stuart's brother, about the arrangements for a memorial occasion for Stuart which were proving complicated. He, too, was very exercised about who might succeed Stuart and was strongly opposed to the idea of Lord King. Throughout these weeks, names were freely bandied about. Sir Patrick Nairne, former Permanent Secretary at the Department of Health and Social Security, was often mentioned. There was even talk of William Rees-Mogg, though since he had turned down the offer of extension as Vice-Chairman and had already found himself in the odd position of being Chairman of the Arts Council and Vice-Chairman of the BBC, that seemed preposterous. The clamour continued till the eleventh hour. On 1st October, Ray Snoddy of the *Financial Times*, usually one of the best informed journalists in media circles, wrote that Sir Peter Carey, former Permanent Secretary at the Department of Industry, would be announced that very day. The same morning, Bill Cotton rang from the Conservative Party Conference in Blackpool to tell me that Christopher Chataway's name was on everybody's lips. He was a certainty. We knew from the Home Office that an announcement was to be made that morning. We also knew that we would get only short advance notice before the statement, embargoed for midday, was released.

I happened that morning to be chairing a conference arranged by the National Film Theatre on the development of relationships between television and film in Europe. Knowing that we could expect an announcement within minutes, I asked Brian Wenham, who was sitting near me, to ring Patricia Hodgson, then Secretary of the BBC, from time to time and check and let me know when the name emerged. Eventually, a piece of paper was passed up to me from Brian. His writing is marginally worse than mine and it took me some few seconds to decipher the name, 'Marmaduke Hussey'. And a few

187

more seconds to realise that this was 'Duke' Hussey, formerly Chief Executive and Managing Director of Times Newspapers Limited during the period of their long strike, and latterly involved with a commercial radio station in the West Country, but someone who had been out of immediate circulation for a while. I had met him and his wife, Susan, on a couple of occasions socially. As I read the note, Jeremy Isaacs, the Chief Executive of Channel 4, who was in full flood, stopped and said, 'You must now know who the new Chairman of the BBC is.'

'Yes,' I said.

'Are you going to tell us?'

'No,' I said. There were, after all, ten minutes to go to the embargo time. It seemed better to play according to the rules.

'What's your reaction?' he asked.

'I'm intrigued.' Which was the exact truth. I didn't quite know what to make of it.

Bernard Ingham happened to come to lunch at Broadcasting House that day. There had been rumours that William Rees-Mogg wanted the Chairman's job, though he himself denied it. Bernard was quick to confirm that Rees-Mogg had been consulted, but was not offered the job. Hussey had been the first choice. And, of course, Hussey and Rees-Mogg had worked together at *The Times*, were neighbours in Somerset and close friends. I had a quick chat with Hussey and then he went off to meet the press. The headlines the following morning pursued two different lines: *The Times* and *Financial Times* spoke of 'political storm over Hussey's BBC post' and 'row grows over appointment of BBC Chairman'. Others asked, 'Can the Duke bring the BBC to heel?' Gerald Kaufman, the Shadow Home Secretary, was injudicious enough to threaten that Labour would sack him when they returned to power, almost before the poor man had entered the front door. And William Rees-Mogg was extensively quoted, saying he was an absolutely brilliant choice, had the toughness to resist the 'BBC's blandishment and subversion' (*sic!*), and 'Hussey will be surrounded with molasses. They will try to coat him with sugar and flattery. Hussey will see through the BBC mandarins at a glance.' I never thought our former Vice-Chairman displayed much affection for the BBC, but he clearly was no friend. It was, in fact, another five weeks before Duke Hussey formally took office, because he had to wait for the Privy Council's agreement to his appointment. But he moved into the building, started getting to know people, had coffee and meals with the Governors but did not attend formal Board meetings.

In the meantime, a number of problems had reached an acute stage. Firstly, the Hamilton/Howarth case had gone badly wrong. We were having problems with some of the witnesses; counsel said we had a less than fifty per cent chance of winning the case. By the end of the first week in October, Alan advised me we must settle. When I spoke to counsel on the Friday evening of that week, he was still trying to negotiate a settlement but finding it difficult. On Monday, we would find ourselves in court.

Sheila and I had moved into a hotel in Edinburgh for the next ten days since I was presiding over my first full meeting of the Commonwealth Broadcasting Association since I had been elected President two years earlier in Hong Kong. I had asked Joel Barnett, as Acting Chairman, to come and speak at our formal dinner on the Wednesday evening. When he arrived, he was very disturbed about the Hamilton/Howarth case, now in court, and said he 'should have been consulted'. I reminded him that the Board had known about the case before he arrived; I had not brought it up at the Board a fortnight earlier because I was certain we would have a settlement by now. Wrongly, of course. Joel, Bill Cotton, the Scottish Governor, Watson Peat, and I caught the overnight sleeper back to London. At the Board, Joel became very excited and demanded that we settle immediately. I said that was exactly what we were trying to do. I then flew back to Edinburgh.

The next forty-eight hours were extremely tricky, with almost hourly reports from Alan in London about the progress of the case. On the Friday evening, he rang to say we had a settlement at last, but with heavy costs against us. Over the weekend, news that we had settled leaked out, even though the details of the settlement were not due to be announced in court until the Tuesday morning. The Monday morning papers were full of calls for my resignation, and statements that my position was 'precarious'. It was not the most cheerful atmosphere in which to chair the closing meetings of the Association's conference. I flew down to London, having asked Michael Checkland to call Board of Management together. One or two were very emotional about the settlement, feeling we should have pressed on with the case, others distinctly unhappy. I had a word with Hussey, who seemed fairly relaxed. I then flew back to Edinburgh to host the farewell dinner at Hopetoun House. The papers the following morning had a field day over the settlement: 'disaster, humiliating, Milne must go'. I did not quite understand why I should go because of a difficult libel action. Hamilton and Howarth were naturally gleeful, and heroes in the House. The press continued their campaign: one hundred Tory MPs signed a motion calling for my resignation and 'the restoration of proper standards at the BBC'. We had, undoubtedly, come out of it very badly through being unable to support some of the statements made in the film. But I was sure the

Board of Management was behind me. We must wait until the storm blew itself out.

But almost before it did, we had to hoist the storm cones again. Throughout the summer, there had been talk of the Conservative Central Office preparing a damning document to prove anti-Conservative bias in our television news. Norman Tebbit, the Party Chairman, had said as much at the Conservative Party Conference; all intelligence pointed to the coverage of the American bombing of Libya as being the event on which they would pick. On Thursday, 30th October, as we were discussing the Hamilton/Howarth débâcle with the Board, and beginning to hear the first mutterings from Governors about the *Secret Society* series, news came that the Tebbit document would be delivered to the BBC about 1.00 p.m. I had taken the precaution of asking to see the tape of the *Nine O'Clock News* on the night of the Libyan bombing some days earlier. The Deputy Editor of Television News, Robin Walsh, had at our instigation been at work for some time going through all edited and unedited material for that day with a fine toothcomb.

When the Conservative Central Office document arrived, it came under a covering letter from Tebbit.

> In the light of our evidence, [he said] you may feel that the BBC news reporting, in this instance at least, fell far short of the high standards which the Corporation espouses. Indeed, you may conclude that far from being balanced, fair and impartial, the coverage was a mixture of news, views, speculation, error and uncritical carriage of Libyan propaganda which does serious damage to the reputation of the BBC.
>
> From my many years of association with the BBC, I know that most of your staff are deeply proud of their association with the best known broadcasting operation in the world. I also know that many of them feel that the BBC has lost its way . . .

The analysis itself submitted that 'a comparison of the two bulletins for Tuesday evening, 15th April shows that *News at Ten* was able to preserve an impartial editorial stance, while the BBC took a number of editorial and journalistic decisions the effect of which was to enlist the sympathy of the audience for the Libyans and to antagonise them towards the Americans.' The hectoring tone of the covering letter and the careful insinuations of the accompanying analysis showed they meant business. I had a word about it with Bill Cotton and Alan Protheroe, showed it to Hussey and Barnett and then we issued a reasonably cool statement pointing out that there is 'a genuine worry that the complaint could suggest that the Conservative Party is

190

attempting to intimidate the BBC. I do not believe that it is in the public interest for the BBC to be in a protracted confrontation with any major political party and I hope we can resolve this difficulty as soon as possible.' The most important thing now was to get our detailed answer right.

Television News' careful rebuttal was delivered to me on Sunday, 2nd November, and we went through it line by line with the Editor, Ron Neil, at Board of Management the following day. One of the minor oddities of the CCO document was that, although they had named a number of our reporters, they had studiously avoided naming our chief reporter in Tripoli, Kate Adie. The BBC response said: 'Overall, we believe that a thorough analysis of the BBC and ITN bulletins reveals a fair, accurate and thoroughly professional approach by both the BBC and ITN. However, in the light of subsequent events, it was clearly wrong for the BBC to assume that the failed attempt to plant a bomb on an El Al jumbo jet was a response to the bombing of Libya – although many newspapers and an ITN reporter made the same wrong connections.' There was some discussion amongst us of holding a televised press conference to publish our reply, because a comparative use of the film could be important; some thought that too provocative an idea, and we decided against. Hussey and Barnett had together drafted a covering note to Tebbit to go with the rebuttal. I felt it was too anodyne, though it did contain the point that 'what you found biased was not so judged by an ex-editor of *The Times*, who was until recently a sometime critical Governor of the BBC' – Rees-Mogg. But they both said that it contained all they wanted to say.

It so happened that, weeks earlier, we had arranged for Norman Tebbit to come to lunch on Wednesday 5th, the very day we were about to publish our reply to him. I thought it politic to ask Margaret Douglas to check with his office that he still wanted to come. Yes, he did. So the Wednesday morning was fully occupied with television and radio interviews on our reply, which included the open admission that we had wrongly connected the Libyan operation with the Heathrow bomb attempt. Then we braced ourselves for lunch with Norman. He had been telephoned to see whether he would object to being interviewed on the threshold of BH and said he did not mind; so he faced a battery of cameras and recorders at the front door, apparently with geniality as we watched him live upstairs.

But when he arrived in the lunch room on the third floor next to my office, accompanied by Michael Dobbs, seconded from Saatchi and Saatchi to be his 'Chief of Staff', his brow was like thunder. Joel Barnett had invited himself for a drink before lunch, but when he saw Tebbit's entry, he quickly scurried out. These regular lunches I gave were always friendly and often very informative; not this one. Tebbit was sardonic and combative. I asked him about the Cabinet sub-committee on broadcasting. 'What makes you think,' said he, 'that I came here to discuss the Cabinet sub-committee on broadcasting? I would not consider doing such a thing.' Conversation did not flow easily. His own Chief of Staff seemed embarrassed. Even Brian Wenham, who is usually not short of a word or two, fell silent.

Tebbit now began to pick a bone or two with me. What about all these expensive libel actions the BBC was losing? he asked. I retorted that we only had, on average, about a dozen libel actions taken out against us in any given year, and most were settled reasonably. He took out a pad and began making notes. He wanted, he said, to know about the BBC's position about apartheid. Alan Protheroe had said on a radio programme that the BBC was against apartheid. He, Tebbit, was also against it. But surely the BBC had no editorial opinions. Did I confirm Alan's stance? No, I said, the BBC had no editorial opinion, though Hugh Greene had said twenty years earlier that the BBC was against racism, which was no more than saying we were against evil. Would I, therefore, he demanded, publicly correct Alan? No, I said, he spoke for himself. There was no need for public correction.

Ten days later, Tebbit returned to the attack. Writing to Hussey, he said:

> It would have been comforting to the great mass of the public who would wish to be reassured about the standards of BBC news had the BBC's claim that its reply was effective or even devastating proved to be well-founded. In my view that claim was wholly unsupported by your officials' paper which you sent me. To ensure that my reaction did not reflect a prejudiced view of my own case, I asked for an analysis on your defence from an independent non-political source. In fairness, I include the whole of that report which finds that significant points can be raised against my criticisms, but on balance it finds as an irresistible conclusion that the main thrust of my complaints is fully justified.

The 'independent non-political source', unidentified of course, did indeed concede that 'on points of fact, the BBC response scores several significant points against the CCO document' but pronounced: 'Overall the response fails. It is itself cheap and glib in many places. More important, it altogether fails to meet the substantial charge: that the ordering of themes, stories, paragraphs and sentences, and the colouring of the language, can and did turn a broadcast which makes no untrue statements into a slanted, confrontational and fundamentally political or "editorialising" *prise de position* or taking a line.' Clearly, we were not going to make much headway against Norman Tebbit's snideness or the polemical language of the original analysis and the independent non-political report. But Tebbit went further: he turned cheeky. 'While I am anxious,' he told Hussey, 'not to undermine the responsibility of the Board to uphold the Charter and the Licence, I have the confidence to put my case to a mutually agreed person, or persons, who would make an objective report to be used as the basis for a collective discussion by the Board. You may feel that might be a constructive way forward.' This time he got a curt reply from Hussey telling him that if, as Conservative Party Chairman, he was not willing to leave the matter in the hands of the Governors, who were the properly constituted authority, he should go and raise the matter with the Home Secretary. I am sure Douglas Hurd would have been deeply unhappy to have been dragged into this fracas. Rumour had it that Tebbit's Government colleagues had had enough of his squabbling with the BBC.

But Norman Tebbit still had the energy to write to me, challenging me yet again to make a public correction of what Alan Protheroe had said about apartheid. He was nothing if not persistent.

Other grim wolves seemed to emerge from the contagion during this difficult period. There was, for instance, the Falklands play. This piece, written by Ian Curteis, came about in an unusual way. He and I met late in October 1982 at a Writers' Luncheon Club at the Zoo where I had been asked to speak. It was a few months after the end of the Falklands War. I had greatly admired his plays, *Suez* and *Churchill and the Generals* and we fell to chatting about whether a similar exercise could be undertaken on the Falklands. He wasn't sure, it might be too soon, but he would think about it. Nearly four years later, the play landed on my desk with a nice letter from Ian saying that since I had, in a manner of speaking, commissioned it, perhaps I would like to read it. He had, he said, been discussing it with the Television Service in the normal way. I hadn't had the time to read much of it when he asked to come and see me on another matter.

We met in my office on 2nd June for an evening drink. He had, he said, written a play about Cecil Rhodes for the South African Broadcasting Corporation. Was there any chance of the BBC co-producing it with them? I said no. Apart from the politics of the matter, the Equity ban on actors performing there would make it impossible for a proper job to be done. If it was a good play, let us consider mounting it on our own. We then fell to talking about the Falklands play. I learnt for the first time that it was scheduled for production in the New Year and for transmission on the fifth anniversary of the war in May 1987. There was, incidentally, no reason why I should know about the production dates of every television play going through the system. I mused about the May transmission perhaps causing difficulties with the date of the forthcoming election, though on the whole I thought it might be all right because I doubted if Mrs Thatcher would go to the country before October 1987. I would write to him, I said, when I had finished reading it and tell him what I thought of it.

Which I duly did. I told Ian I thought it was a 'thumping good yarn' but I was doubtful about the casting of it. He replied that he and Cedric Messina (a veteran plays producer who, amongst many other credits, had initiated the Shakespeare project and produced the first twelve plays) had thought about this and had turned their backs on 'look-alike' casting. But in the next few weeks, various polls and political scribblings made me believe that Mrs Thatcher might well go to the country before the following October; there was certainly no point in spending around £1 million on a play (it ran nearly three hours) and then putting it on the shelf, perhaps for as long as nine months, or even longer. I wrote and told Ian we would not proceed with the production till after the election, and so instructed the Television Service. Quite independently of my thought processes, they had been going forward with production discussion, fuelled by the fact that Bill Cotton thought the play was 'one-dimensional' and Michael Grade did not think it was very good at all. Such professional disagreements are not that abnormal and are usually speedily resolved. To that end, the Head of Plays went to see Ian Curteis at his home in Gloucestershire to suggest changes, from which, in exchange of correspondence, he did not seem to demur. But soon afterwards, he declared to me that there was a monstrous left-wing plot afoot to dish a pro-Thatcher play and, despite increasingly sharp exchanges of correspondence, has continued ever since to proclaim to the world that he was being traduced for political reasons. I do not believe there is a word of truth in any of this. But Norman Tebbit certainly did because it was another topic he raised at our lunch. Even Hussey and Barnett began to smell rats where there were none. And Daphne Park, having received voluminous correspondence from Ian Curteis, was deeply suspicious at a Board meeting in early October.

There was also the fuss over the *Monocled Mutineer*. These plays, based on the story of a First World War deserter, were clearly plays. But in an attempt to get more of a fair hearing in the press we had recently hired an agency to take advertising space in the papers and they were promoted, foolishly (our fault, not the agency's) as being 'a real life story'. Which was certainly cutting corners. The press fell upon us for telling lies, and it added to their fury that most of the papers saw the plays as 'left-wing propaganda'. The fact that they were well-made drama counted for nothing. This was one of the crimes tabulated in *The Times*'s calendar when it wrote on Hussey's appointment. 'He should examine the character and the career of his Director General. He should read the internal reports of the *Real Lives* affairs. He should examine the making (and the marketing) of the *Monocled Mutineer*. He should ask himself what he has to do to protect an organisation that has been given a fresh opportunity to protect itself but seems to have so little will to do so.'

The most important and controversial matter of the autumn of 1986 was the series of documentaries called *Secret Society*. I do not think there remains much dispute about their genesis. They were offered to the Controller of BBC-2 by BBC Scotland as a result of conversations between a producer in Glasgow and the journalist Duncan Campbell, after another programme in which Campbell had taken part. Campbell, well-known as a thorough investigative journalist much of whose work was published in the *New Statesman*, wanted to try his hand at television. The offer, six thirty-minute investigative films by Duncan Campbell (i.e. researched and presented by him, but produced within normal BBC practice) 'each illuminating a hidden truth of major public concern', was accepted by Graeme McDonald, the Controller of BBC-2 on 12th June, 1985. Later, those who detected the cloven hoof in Campbell demanded to know why McDonald had not alerted others. He said, simply, he never recognised there might be a problem. And, anyway, the plan for the programmes' production was known to senior Television Service management.

Work began on the series. In April 1986 Alan Protheroe, acting on my behalf, was asked by BBC Scotland for permission to embark on programme one which involved the need to 'bug' a private detective who said he could access a Criminal Records Office computer. Permission for such covert filming or recording had to be obtained from the Director General or his nominee. After much legal discussion, permission was granted and the filming took place. Later, the police were informed that a potentially criminal act had taken place and the man was subsequently charged under Section 2 of the Official Secrets Act. This work was embodied in the programme later called *Data*. In June, the Head of Television BBC Scotland wrote to the Controller of BBC-2 filling in the details of the programmes as planned at that date.

1. The Secret Constitution. We're taught that Britain is a parliamentary democracy. But who really rules? Answer: small, secret Cabinet committees.

2. In Time of Crisis. Since 1982, governments in every other NATO country have been preparing for the eventuality of war. In Britain, these preparations are kept secret. So what will happen when the balloon goes up?

3. A Gap In Our Defences. Bungling defence manufacturers and incompetent military planners have botched every new radar system that Britain has installed since World War Two. Why? And can we stop it happening again?

4. We're All Data Now. The Data Protection Act is supposed to protect us from abuse, but it's already out of date and full of loopholes. So what kind of abuses should we worry about?

The fifth programme being discussed at the moment is about the Association of Chief Police Officers and how Government policy and actions are determined in the fields of law and order.

A sixth programme is at the early stages of discussion and is likely to be about communications with particular reference to satellites.

Alan had mentioned to me that work was proceeding on the Campbell series and that everyone in Scotland, from the Controller downwards, seemed to be on top of it. The programmes were still, of course, being made. But their shape was emerging, and at a press conference on 20th August to reveal the BBC-2 autumn plans, attended by Duncan Campbell, there was talk of the series 'which will disclose restricted information on Government emergency plans in case there is another war'. Reports of this press conference alerted the Secretary of the D-Notice Committee (the Defence Press and Broadcasting Committee: a means for the Ministry of Defence to communicate to the media matters whose publication might affect national security) who made remonstrating noises. It also alerted some Governors since the reports of the press conference were included in their regular press packs. They began to ask about the series. I promised to keep them informed as progress occurred.

Early in September, the Head of Television in Scotland, Jim Hunter, wrote to Alan to tell him that Joel Barnett had agreed to take part in one of the programmes (the one on satellites, named *Zircon*) in his former capacity as Chairman of the Public Accounts Committee. (Later Joel withdrew and his successor as Chairman of the PAC, Robert Sheldon, took his place.) On 10th October, Alan wrote to Pat Chalmers, the Controller of BBC Scotland, saying that we must have an urgent and full brief on the whole series as it then stood. A couple of days earlier, the interview with Bob Sheldon had been done and he complained to the BBC and Joel Barnett that he had been 'set up' by

196

Duncan Campbell and the production team. Things seemed to be getting very messy.

When Barnett came to Edinburgh to speak to the CBA dinner, he was not only tetchy about the Hamilton/Howarth case, he was very cross about the way he claimed Sheldon had been treated. Alan had briefed me over the phone and I had the transcript of the interview to hand in Edinburgh. I took Joel through it and satisfied myself (and I think at the time him) that Sheldon had come out of the experience perfectly well, even though for good reasons a question was sprung on him. But alarm bells were ringing all over the place. Daphne Park and other Governors were demanding to know why Campbell had ever been employed. He was 'a destroyer', he was not the sort of person the BBC should consort with. On 13th November, she and Curtis Keeble waxed very hot about the matter. Joel Barnett and Alwyn Roberts were the only voices counselling caution. Hussey, chairing his first Board meeting, made no bones about how deeply most Governors were getting to feel about this series.

Over the next few weeks, there was much bustle with Alan attending several viewings in Glasgow. In particular, the *Zircon* programme about an alleged British spy satellite, the cost of which the programme claimed had been concealed from the Public Accounts Committee in direct contravention of an agreement made when Joel Barnett was PAC Chairman, was causing anxiety. Campbell claimed, and has continued to claim, that his information was accurate. Alan's briefings, from a number of sources, changed his original view that the programme was fit for transmission. In a private letter sent to my house on 5th December, he made the positive recommendation to me that the BBC should not transmit the *Zircon* programme for reasons of national security. His memo was carefully, but strongly, worded.

Meantime, I had personally viewed all the programme rough cuts, as I assured the Board I would, and I invited other members of the Board of Management to see them with me. If we were working up to another confrontation, I wanted to be sure that the management, anyway, was of one mind. We concluded that *Zircon* apart (and some were doubtful of Alan's judgement on it) the other five programmes were transmittable. But all had flaws. Consequently, at a meeting in my office on 17th December, and again on 7th January, I told the Controller of BBC Scotland that I wished to clear an evening on BBC-2, cut the films down, and use them as evidence in a thorough programme discussion on 'freedom of information'. He was not happy, but I told him to go away and think about it. Over the Christmas holiday, I concluded that BBC Scotland would not easily encompass the new format and told Pat Chalmers to prepare the agreed five films for transmission. *Secret Society* was ready for the air, probably in March. I then informed the Board that five films would be transmitted but that one, *Zircon*, would not. We were giving further thought to a possible different programme format.

By now, Hussey and I had had a few working weeks together. A big, genial man, he seemed mainly concerned that I was being kept fully informed about who he was lunching with, but also went, ferret-like, back over all the papers on the Hamilton/Howarth case, writing me long memos full of fairly peremptory questions. He even sent for our counsel in the case and interviewed them at length. Later, there was a sticky meeting where he and Barnett sat in solemn judgement on the affair and Alan, Margaret and I were left in no doubt that they thought we had made a proper hash of the whole thing. Shortly after Hussey arrived, I gave him lunch at a restaurant we both enjoyed. There I learnt a lot about him, his terrible war wound at Anzio, his early life in newspapers, his troubled time at *The Times*. He was amiable and obviously a man of great courage. I touched then on my future, saying I would like to continue as DG (which was an option in my letter of appointment from George Howard) after my term of six years expired in July 1988. He said, I thought quite reasonably, that 'It's not the right time to talk about that.' I presume he already knew by then how he was going to act a few weeks later.

As he went around the BBC, we discussed amongst ourselves at Board of Management how the new team of Hussey and Barnett were getting on. Hussey seemed to go down very well with the staff, relaxed and friendly, as did Barnett also. It was inevitable that they would be dubbed 'Little and Large'. There were some who were anxious that Barnett had an office in the building and seemed a very active Vice-Chairman, and I passed this anxiety on to Hussey on one occasion. The increasing presence and activity of Chairmen in recent years was one thing; if you had an interventionist Vice-Chairman as well (and Joel was very involved in, for example, the White City development) there was a distinct danger of collision. Although Hussey was genial with the staff, one or two members of the senior management had received the rough edge of his tongue. To me, he could not have been nicer. The Board, on the other hand, showed all the signs of ragged nerves. At the last two meetings before Christmas, they grumbled about various appointments suggestions we put to them, hounded me unpleasantly over *Secret Society*, seemed thoroughly dyspeptic. Mike Checkland and I swapped notes after one meeting. 'They're throwing down the gauntlet,' was his comment. I was quite glad to see the back of them at Christmas.

There was one other incident towards the end of the year which perhaps had a hidden significance. We had all worked hard to arrange a celebration of Stuart Young's life in Guildhall, with many different interests to be accommodated. It turned out to be a splendid and moving occasion where a number of people, including the Prime Minister, gave readings and Bill Cotton, David Young and I spoke, David most touchingly. Afterwards, there was a reception, and I moved with Sheila to have a word with the PM who was talking to the Chief Rabbi. To my surprise, she effectively cut me dead. The very same evening, after a Board discussion on television, Alwyn Roberts dropped in to the office for a drink. Some Board members, he warned, wanted my 'head to roll' because of *Secret Society*. I had no need to ask who.

16 BLEAK MIDWINTER

The New Year dawned mild and very wet. Ten days later, the entire country was feet deep in snow and transport paralysed. The worst winter, they said, since 1962–3. The first Board meeting of the year was due to take place on 15th January; the General Advisory Council meeting the day before. It seemed only humane to cancel the GAC meeting since there were around sixty-five members coming from every corner of the country. And though we rang round the Governors and all were valiantly prepared to try and come to London for their Thursday meeting, when I met Duke Hussey in the lift on the Wednesday morning, we quickly agreed we should cancel the Board as well. Joel Barnett was still on holiday in Brazil and rumours in Broadcasting House had it that the wires between the Chairman's office and Rio de Janeiro were hot with usage. Had that meeting occurred, I suppose my execution would have taken place a fortnight earlier than it did.

We already had confirmation from the Home Office that in future the licence fee would be index-linked to the RPI. Over the next fortnight, too, the *Secret Society* affair gathered momentum. On the 18th, the *Observer* broke the story of my decision not to transmit the *Zircon* programme: 'BBC GAG ON £500M DEFENCE SECRET'.

The next day the press had heard that Duncan Campbell would be showing the film to MPs in the House of Commons on the Thursday. We thought it prudent to tell Pat Chalmers to remind our staff of their contractual limitations and to demand the return of the film. By the Wednesday, Treasury solicitors were busy taking injunctions out against Campbell. The Select Committee on Defence were insisting on seeing the film but the Permanent Secretary at the MoD, Sir Clive Whitmore, appeared to have refused them. On a couple of occasions, Hussey grumbled to me about why we ever came to make the film. It wasn't long before the Special Branch were running all over the BBC in Glasgow like mice, removing boxes of papers and impounding every foot of film they could find. It was a bizarre development to a long-running story.

On Wednesday, 28th January, the day before the first Board

200

meeting, there was a farewell dinner for Alwyn Roberts, the retiring Welsh National Governor. Alwyn had been around the BBC, first as a member of the Broadcasting Council for Wales and then seven years as National Governor, for a long time. He had been due to go the previous summer but his term had been extended for six months, just as he was about to have his first farewell dinner! These are big occasions, held in the Council Chamber, with seventy or so people present, including former Governors and former members of the Board of Management.

The tradition is that the Chairman speaks first, and the Director General follows, speaking for the executive. There is a presentation, and the guest of honour replies. When Hussey and I had done our bit Alwyn, speaking as he always did without a note and with the rhetorical skill of a trained preacher, spoke strongly and with candour. He warned the Governors and the management of the continuing dangers of confrontation. He was dismissive of those Governors who insisted on proclaiming that they and they alone were the BBC. What about the producers, the cameramen, the sound recordists, the film editors, the engineers, he asked; were they too not part of the BBC and the most important part?

Looking about me, I could see that this homily did not please some of the Governors present. There were frowning faces. A colleague of mine who was sitting next to Sir John Boyd told me later that John was muttering angrily: 'This is all nonsense. You wait until tomorrow.' As the party broke up for a farewell whisky, it seemed we had said a proper goodbye to Alwyn, which he fully deserved. He had also sounded a clear warning note.

At the Board the following morning, much of the business was routine. I fancied Hussey was in more of a muddle with his papers than usual, but thought nothing of it. Some Governors – Daphne Park, Watson Peat – were extremely sour about *Secret Society* again, but Alan Protheroe fought his corner well. As we walked down the stairs at Television Centre, I said to Mike Checkland, 'What did you make of that?' 'Awful,' he said. In breaks during the morning, we had been talking to our lawyers about the ghastly case of Michael Lush who had been killed rehearsing a stunt for the *Noel Edmonds' Show*. The case was being heard in the Coroner's Court that day, and I went into Bill Cotton's office, which adjoined mine, to speak to them again.

Then, as I walked down the corridor in the direction of lunch, Patricia Hodgson, the Secretary, asked me if I would go and see the Chairman. I thought it odd that she addressed me by my Christian name; everybody else did, but for some reason she had never done so before. When I walked into Hussey's office, Barnett and he were both there. I remember the blinds were drawn against the sun which was brilliant that morning. Hussey's lip trembled as he said: 'I am afraid this is going to be a very unpleasant interview. We want you to leave immediately. It's a unanimous decision of the Board.'

I was stunned. What was he talking about? Perhaps I should have seen the plot thickening, but I hadn't. 'We want to make changes,' said Barnett. 'We can't under the present circumstances.' I didn't speak. Hussey said again: 'It's a unanimous decision of the Board. You might prefer to resign – for personal reasons.' Barnett said, 'We are men of honour. If you resign, it won't affect your arrangements. You are going next year anyway.'

I had, in fact, eighteen months to go as DG. The Board which appointed me had also spoken of a mutual option of another two years. Hussey said: 'I've already spoken to Arnold Goodman.' What terrible people, I thought. I asked for a sheet of paper, couldn't remember the date: one of them said it was 29th January. I wrote out my resignation and handed it to Hussey. I walked back to my office and said to Ros, my personal assistant, 'I've been fired.' She said: 'Oh my God', and then I walked through to Bill Cotton's office, where Mike Checkland was too, and told them. Bill swore roundly; Mike looked totally disbelieving. I went downstairs and said to Eddie, my driver: 'Home, Eddie.' 'When shall I pick you up?' he asked. (We were due that evening at a party to launch Superchannel, where the Prime Minister was going to be present.) 'I'll be in touch,' I said when he dropped me at home.

At home, I was on my own. Sheila was out. As I prowled up and down the living room, the first impact was the humiliation of being discarded by such people without a word of explanation or discussion; one of them had been all of ten working weeks in the BBC, the other barely six months. I had imagined I still had eighteen months to serve as DG. Anguish was followed by despair.

Half an hour later, a letter from Hussey was delivered by a driver. The Board had, he said, accepted my resignation. They had asked him to 'express their gratitude for your many years of service with the Corporation'. Would I now put my lawyers in touch with theirs?

Within minutes of the BBC's announcement of my departure, the Fleet Street contingent was camping round my front door to chronicle the end of my BBC career. The horror of what had happened was softened in later days by the scores of letters from friends and colleagues all over the world. One of them, from a famous and distinguished British broadcaster, precisely echoed my own feelings. 'What has happened to you,' he said, 'is something that will stand high in the annals of broadcasting infamy.'

202

POSTSCRIPT

Do We Need The BBC?

As I come to the end of the story, it is now more than a year since I left the BBC. Time gives distance and greater objectivity. It is possible now to stand back a pace or two, look at the past and the future, and ask whether the BBC is necessary any more. The violence of the language used about the BBC in the press in the last few years and the unrelenting nature of the attacks have caused doubts to be raised in the minds of some about its future. Godfrey Hodgson, a well-known freelance journalist, wrote an article recently in the *Listener* on what he called 'Media McCarthyism':

> As all the expert manipulators of the twentieth century have understood, the bolder the misrepresentation, the harder it is to rebut. As Hitler said in *Mein Kampf*: 'The great masses of the people will more easily fall victims to a big lie than to a small one.' At the same time, much dripping wears away the stone; if you keep repeating that BBC executives are 'a Production Politburo' [this from the pen of Paul Johnson, a respected journalist and writer who worked with us a lot on *Tonight*], that the BBC is full of 'very left-wing producers' [this endlessly in the *News of the World* and to me in private correspondence from Woodrow Wyatt, former television reporter, former Labour MP, now ennobled], that 'the BBC not only lies, it lies for the Left. It not only rapes, it rapes for the Revolution' [Paul Johnson again] . . . then some alluvium of credibility is laid down.

Add to the frenetic chorus of disapproval the very real difficulties of trying to read a technological future fraught with uncertainties, and there should be no surprise that some people wondered if an organisation like the BBC had had its day. The Peter Jay notion of the future, based on a picture of fibre-optic cable with access to every home, might well render the present broadcasting structures otiose and out of date. Alan Peacock and his Committee were very precise about what they saw as the desirable way ahead. 'Our own conclusion is that British Broadcasting should move towards a sophisticated market system based on consumer sovereignty. That is a system which recognises interests which they can best satisfy if they have the option of purchasing the broadcasting services they require from as many alternative sources of supply as possible.' (The Committee chastised me in passing for my metaphor of the sower and the seed, saying such statements risk giving the impression that the viewer's main function is to react to a set of choices determined by the broadcasting institutions; to which I would retort, how else are the broadcasters to behave, at any rate until the arrival of the electronic millennium?) But Peacock also added: 'In practice we have no doubt that there will be a distinct and important role for the BBC as far ahead as anyone cares to look, not only in the supply of public service programmes in the narrow sense, *but in a wide field of entertainment, information and education* [my italics].'

In my own view, the Jay vision of the future is strictly for the birds, at any rate for twenty years or so ahead. If you analyse subscription television to date as Charles Jonscher of CSP International has done in his study on subscription television commissioned by the Home Office, you quickly find that subscription has done reasonably well in the United States. By the end of 1986, cable 'passed' seventy-five per cent of US homes and forty-three per cent of those homes were subscribers. There are two kinds of channel delivered by satellite to cable heads in America: 'basic' cable (news, women's programmes, weather, ethnic programmes) supported by advertising, and 'pay' services for which the viewer pays an extra fee. The latter are chiefly feature film services, with the signal 'scrambled' and therefore requiring a decoder. There is, additionally, the 'pay-per-view' system, much discussed at the time of Peacock. In the States, a small percentage (Jonscher says thirteen per cent or 2.7 million homes) subscribe to this system whereby you only pay a premium price for the programme viewed. These programmes are mainly big feature films or major boxing promotions or other leading sporting events.

The picture in Europe is very different. One of the significant advantages cable offers the American viewer, who normally suffers from poor direct television signals and relentless commercials, is a decent picture and, under some conditions, no commercials. But in Europe, television signals are usually much better than in the States and commercials are not omnipresent. Partly because of that, the growth of the new cable systems in Europe has been painfully slow. Even in highly cabled countries like Belgium and Holland, the uptake has not been large. In France and Britain, progress has been at a crawl. There is no cable in Italy.

The advertiser-supported services such as Murdoch's Sky Channel have been in operation for some time now, but have not yet made a profit. The ITV Superchannel, with the BBC acting as programme supplier, has run into trouble after barely nine months of operation and has had to cut back on investment. Europe appears to offer no bonanza to the new services for the immediate future.

Jonscher's study is also highly revealing about British viewers' reactions to their present television payments, confirming much of what Andrew Ehrenburg had written. Andrew's research had demonstrated to Peacock that it is a fallacy to believe that people watch nothing but very popular programmes with very high ratings. The evidence shows that we, the audience, watch only two or three out of the top ten programmes, spending an hour or two a week on them; the rest of our viewing time, some twenty-five hours a week, we spend on much more individual choices. He further pointed out that television does not 'segment', in the advertisers' jargon; the audience for *Dynasty*, for example, and *Panorama* are not in any way distinct. The *Panorama* viewer is very close to the *Dynasty* viewer in terms of the other programmes he watches. And Andrew's research was solid in answering the question: do we need the BBC? The market answer was: yes. The third of the audience who do the most viewing watches as much as three hours a day of non-ITV/Channel 4 programming. The rest of us – almost two-thirds of the population watching less than thirty hours a week – spend only about thirty-five per cent of our viewing time watching ITV. And when it came to affording the licence fee, Andrew reminded Peacock that we spend in Britain £1,700 per household per year on our leisure activities – £700 of that figure on drink in or out of the home. Hence, he argued, spending £60 for viewing television – much our biggest leisure activity – cannot be the intolerable burden we are often told it is.

Jonscher's research told much the same story. Ninety-six per cent of the population watch television almost every evening. Pensioners and the unemployed (twenty-one per cent of his sample) watch regularly during the day and at weekends. Almost all considered it good value for what they paid, most of the sample understanding that the licence fee goes to support the BBC and that commercial television is supported by advertising revenue.

The cable households emphasised that it is really cheap to receive four channels for just £1 per week [discounting, of course, what they pay at the supermarket for ITV] when compared with their pay-television channels at up to £6 a week. The cost of watching television related to the licence fee was *not an issue* [my italics]. Where respondents spontaneously mentioned the licence fee it was not in relation to its costs to them, but rather its injustices and anomalies, such as the burden it imposes on old-age pensioners and the difference in price between monochrome and colour licences.

207

Jonscher's report also records that while the average 'television only' household spends almost £11 a month on its equipment and licence fee, the television household which also has a VCR may spend up to three times as much.

The CSP Report, as I have mentioned, takes the view that 'we cannot recommend the replacement of any of the existing revenue sources (the licence fee and advertising) by subscription revenue.' They go on to point out that their study had identified consumer demand for extra television programming, backed up by willingness to pay for such material; and they argue the case for 'downloading' (using the night hours on BBC-2 and Channel 4, they suggest, for distributing extra material electronically to VCRs), perhaps replacing some part of the BBC-2 schedule by a subscription service, or for additional channels, by using parts of the existing UHF bands in selected areas of the country, or by reallocating to television the old VHF band which is currently intended to be transferred to mobile radio users.

So, another independent survey takes a very clear view of the BBC and its funding, different from Peacock, but in some respects complementary. Jonscher does not agree with Peacock that subscription is the long-term substitute for the licence fee: 'Access control technology,' ('scrambling') he says, 'would not provide a more economical method of collecting the licence fee than the present system. It would achieve some benefit in terms of reduction in the incidence of licence fee evasion, but these benefits would be more than offset by the higher costs borne by consumers and broadcasters.'

But even though our own research showed that eighty per cent of the population found no problem in paying the licence fee and Jonscher confirms that, all have identified concern for those who *do* find it difficult to pay. In our evidence to Peacock, we pointed out that there are, in Britain, some four million people receiving supplementary allowances or pensions, and a similar number receiving housing benefits. If all four million on supplementary benefit were to receive a free colour licence, the loss of revenue to the BBC would be £120 million and the colour licence would go up to £75. We noted that in Ireland, for example, pensioners and war veterans are given a free black and white licence. If they want colour, they make up the difference. A similar dispensation in Britain would cost £72 million and raise the colour licence fee to £64. We had no evidence that people would be happy to afford that extra sum. It really did seem to us a matter for the DHSS and the Government.

Recommendation six of the Peacock Committee was that: 'Pensioners drawing supplementary pension in households wholly dependent on a pension should be exempt from the licence fee.' They made it, they said, with some hesitation and on the strict understanding that the exception category was narrowly drawn and not extended to wide categories, such as all pensioners. There is still no resolution of this matter. I am convinced it must remain a decision for Government, though it undoubtedly helps to bring opprobrium on the licence fee.

All these studies and inquiries seem to have demonstrated that the licence fee is not as bad a system for paying for your broadcasting as some had stated. You pay for your broadcasting one way or another – either at the supermarket or through the licence fee. And you are going to pay multiples of the present sum to buy cable or satellite services. Again, if you could pay by instalment or if the existing direct debit or credit card possibilities had been properly marketed, the pain of annual payment could be further reduced. Already something like twenty per cent of licence fees are paid for by the purchase of stamps. I have not tumbled on a better way of paying for the BBC. Indexation, though it poses severe problems for the BBC, certainly reduces the amount of hassle with the Government when it comes to licence fee renewal.

So much for paying for the BBC. But I haven't answered my own question: do we need the BBC? Early in 1984, I gave a lecture at Southampton University. My theme that evening was 'Public Service Broadcasting and the Arts'. But much of what I said there springs from a deep belief that the principles that have guided the BBC over many years and that have shaped its practices will continue to drive it forward as the main programme power-house in Britain.

Every public service broadcaster worthy of that name seeks to extend public taste and the range of his operations. In this endeavour, he will differ totally from his commercial competitor. This is not because of any assertion of superior virtue on his part, but because the fundamental driving forces in the two systems are different. The commercial broadcaster must, sooner or later, make a profit for his shareholders or else go out of business. The best proven method of doing this is to invest in the well-tried and the familiar. In other words, you reinforce taste and depart from it only at your peril. That is the reason why so many American television series are kept going, by a sort of television equivalent of artificial respiration, long after their authors have run out of plot and ideas. The public service broadcaster, on the other hand, given that his income is assured and that he can count on a loyal and substantial audience, constantly departs from familiar ground and seeks to widen the base of his operations. Nothing has ever been more misleading than the seductively democratic slogan, 'Giving the people what they want'. That is the constantly reiterated leitmotiv of American programme executives and advertisers when you put a new idea in front of them. They at once point to the viewing figures of the night before and regard those figures as the indisputably democratic verdict of their audience. But how can an audience choose something it may like, but does not yet know because it hasn't tasted it?

If I were to tell an American executive that I had two promising writers under contract who wanted to describe the love/hate relationship of two London East End scrapdealers, do you for a moment think he would have invested in *Steptoe and Son?* Yet this unlikely couple at one time attracted the attention of virtually half the nation. And when the series was breaking viewing records, nobody forced the writers to write further episodes when they felt they had exhausted this particular vein. The series came to an end. Ironically, it was about then that the Americans bought the format, and Americanised it into a success of their own, *Sandford and Son.* If the cultural history of television in Britain comes to be written, I have little doubt that the degree of innovative thinking by the BBC and its producers and writers and designers will be found to be very remarkable indeed.

Paternalistic, some will say. Arrogant, others will surely cry. There he goes, attacking the Americans again, while he was responsible for putting on rubbish like *Dallas* and *Dynasty.* I admire much that the American networks screen, particularly in the news field, and we in Britain have always been happy to buy selectively from Hollywood, because they make drama differently from us and on a scale we often cannot afford. But we should certainly be careful what we buy. It does the BBC no good to screen a mini-series like the recent *Mussolini,* which was a travesty of historical truth.

As to paternalism, I do not cry pardon. Take two crucial activities in which the BBC is deeply involved – drama and music. In radio, music and drama provided the initial attractions for our parents and grandparents to invest in radio sets. But very soon people like Lance Sieveking found that radio was a wonderful medium for drama. The result of that discovery is that today there is barely a playwright in the country who does not owe his start or his first public success to radio drama. The significance of this support for the health of our theatre in general and for television drama in particular cannot be overestimated. Hundreds of radio drama scripts are now being written every year. Dozens of new writers are being discovered and many of these writers go on to write for television and the theatre.

Very little has been either written or said about this particular form of patronage by the BBC and yet it constitutes a conscious and immensely fertile cultural policy. As for music, the BBC involvement with it began with the days of the crystal set. Indeed, Admiral Carpendale, one of Reith's earliest associates, insisted that broadcasting was nothing other than electricity and music! Quite early on, performances were supplemented by explanations, a tradition pioneered by Walford Davies and then notably extended by Anthony Hopkins. Even when recording became technically easy, we continued, in sharp contrast to many of our continental colleagues (as, for instance, the Germans), to cherish live concerts so that today the BBC is probably the broadcasting body with the biggest number of live musical events to offer daily to its listeners. Relatively early in the BBC's history, important orchestras were created, not just to serve as broadcasting orchestras, but also to play to concert audiences at home and abroad. This function is of great importance outside London and fortifies musical life all over the United Kingdom.

We took over the planning and running of the Proms, some fifty-six or so concerts every year which, in their totality, amount to the greatest musical festival in the world. All these activities are taken virtually for granted and it is seldom pointed out that if it were not for the vast BBC investment in musical programmes, on both radio and television, musical life in this country would shrink dramatically. The Robert Mayer concerts for children, the St John's Smith Square lunchtime recitals and those in the town halls of Manchester and Glasgow are all firmly anchored in the weekly musical output of the Corporation. The process of commissioning composers is yet another token of the BBC's commitment not merely to music making, but to contemporary music. That this county, once known on the continent as 'the land without music' should today be one of the world's leading musical centres has a good deal to do with the amount of music broadcast by the BBC over sixty years, and the rigorous standards established in those broadcasts.

So it is with light entertainment, with comedy, with documentary programmes, with natural history programmes, with educational programmes. The range is very great. It is crucial to understand that broadcasters do not produce programmes they think are good for the rest of us, as the most often repeated sneer against public service broadcasting implies. They make the programmes they are keenest to make and believe in. It is then the public which ultimately decides whether it is interested in a particular idea, treatment or strand. Thus, over the years, programmes which started with tiny audiences have become national talking points. That is how archaeology, natural history, science programmes – or snooker which is the most dramatic example – gripped the attention of millions of people. Had they been asked *before* seeing any of these whether they were interested in Rameses the Second or the mating habits of frogs or black holes, they might have, ever so politely, sent you packing. That is why the Peter Jay proposal of an electronic provider of every cultural need by 1999 is no more than a splendidly theoretical solution of future broadcasting problems. Programmes are not produced the way he thinks they are. The decisive element of surprise and novelty essential to any public service network would be absent.

Brenda Maddox wrote an open letter to Professor Peacock in the *Listener*, saying: 'I wish the BBC dared to say as NHK in Japan does, "We are the sole public service broadcasting in this country. The rest is commercial television. That is why you pay the licence fee."' Unfashionable though it may be, I do say it and have said it often. The incantatory power of the phrase 'public service broadcasting' has brought all broadcasters in this country apparently to believe that they necessarily campaign under the same banner. I do not subscribe to that belief. Whatever fine programmes are made under other systems, the BBC is alone in this country in having one purpose only – the making of programmes as good as we can achieve. I do not claim that all BBC programmes are marvellous: they are not. What I do claim is that the BBC encompasses a critical mass of talent necessary to enable it to reach the highest level of production. Change that radically, and you run a terrible risk. Let the BBC continue to look to the critical mass. That is what gives it its standing, its vital importance in the broadcasting world. As some of us said at the time of the early cable debates and as is now, I think, generally recognised, the new technology does not of itself generate the making of more programmes: it simply disseminates in different form what it can buy or find. The 'software' shortage has been harshly underlined by the arrival of cable and satellite. The BBC is at the heart of the software business and I have no doubt that the nation needs the BBC now as much as it has ever done.

My story, beginning in terms of political controversy with Suez and ending with a calculated attack on the BBC by the Chairman of the Conservative Party, seems to me to chart the stages by which the BBC's roles in the national life began to diverge and then widen. Up to the time of the arrival of ITV and, shortly afterwards, Suez, the BBC had effectively been the voice of the Establishment; it had spoken for the nation during the war, and continued largely in the same vein until 1955. Then, increasingly, it became two things: first, a provider of radio and television programmes to the British people which (apart from the traumas of the late 1950s) it has continued to do with great success. The public as listeners and viewers have continued over the years to show a high and consistent level of satisfaction with the BBC's output. Second, it changed course to become an independent institution which has increasingly attracted the hostility of the consensus to which it once belonged.

The beginning of ITV started the process; the disillusion of the Conservative Party over the BBC's handling of the Suez crisis accelerated it. Again, *Tonight*'s disposition to identify with the viewers' interests and concerns, reinforced by Hugh Greene's general approach to politics and by *That Was The Week*'s licence openly to deride the attitudes of both major parties, sealed a new compact. The BBC was now firmly committed to the needs of the nation as an audience, not to the needs of the nation as represented by Government or Opposition. The Labour Party's disenchantment with the BBC, quick to follow their election to office in 1964, sprang from the shock of discovering that the BBC now behaved towards them exactly as it had towards the Conservative Party since the mid 1950s.

The Thatcher years have, it seems to me, added new spice to this brew. As perceived in No.10, the 'liberal élite of the media' have become anathema. The continuing troubles in Northern Ireland and the year of the miners' strike impelled both sides of the political spectrum to turn on the media and particularly the BBC. 'I that do bring the news made not the match' may be a favourite text for the broadcasters; it cuts little ice with politicians. Moreover, nine years of premiership brought about many gubernatorial retirements and their replacement by Thatcher appointees. The Governors found themselves growing further and further apart from what they saw as a liberal élite who dominated the news and, particularly, the current affairs output. This was not a prescription for harmony and understanding.

Can the Governors and the programme makers be brought closer together again without the BBC retreating to the negative and cautious role it espoused in the early 1950s? Will it remain loyal to the needs of the nation as an audience, as the BBC itself interprets those needs? Has it already been 'curbed' and 'brought to heel' as the Peregrine Worsthornes of this world gleefully proclaim?

One decision has been taken which I believe will have a healing effect of great significance – not immediately because time will be needed to allay suspicion and obliterate prejudice. I refer to the Commons decision to allow an experimental televising of the House. Many broadcasters have believed for years that, given editorial machinery that satisfied everyone concerned, the televising of the affairs of the House of Commons would remove much of the resentment politicians undoubtedly feel when the broadcasters are in the driving seat and they, the elected Members of Parliament, have to dance attendance on the broadcasters' invitations. Radio coverage

213

of the House was the first tentative step – though ten years of its presence has not commended it to some members, including the Prime Minister herself; the television transmissions of the House of Lords which we introduced in 1985, though manifestly of a different character from those that might emerge from the House of Commons, might have been expected to mollify some of the more extreme fears about what cameras and editors might get up to. Yet the Commons steadfastly voted the issue down till in February 1988, they turned table. Select Committees may find difficulties; the House may yet reject the proposition. I devoutly hope they do not. Televising the Commons would, I am sure, go far towards repairing the perceived breaches between programme makers and politicians and thus give every assurance for the future of a lively and independent BBC relieved of permanent political threat.

INDEX